Also by Amy Wilentz

Martyrs' Crossing: A Novel

The Rainy Season: Haiti Since Duvalier

I Feel More Often Happen

Simon & Schuster

Earthquakes Than They

COMING TO CALIFORNIA IN THE AGE OF SCHWARZENEGGER

Amy Wilentz

NEW YORK   LONDON   TORONTO   SYDNEY

SIMON & SCHUSTER
Rockefeller Center
1230 Avenue of the Americas
New York, NY 10020

For information about special discounts for bulk purchases,
please contact Simon & Schuster Special Sales at 1-800-456-6798
or business@simonandschuster.com.

DESIGNED BY PAUL DIPPOLITO

Manufactured in the United States of America

1   3   5   7   9   10   8   6   4   2

Library of Congress Cataloging-in-Publication Data
Wilentz, Amy.
I feel earthquakes more often than they happen : coming to California
in the age of Schwarzenegger / Amy Wilentz.
p.   cm.
Includes bibliographical references and index.
1. California—Description and travel. 2. Wilentz, Amy—Travel—
California. 3. Schwarzenegger, Arnold. 4. California—
Politics and government—1951–   5. Governors—California—
Biography. I. Title.
F866.2.W55   2006
917.9404'53—dc   2006045024

ISBN-13: 978-0-7432-6439-6
ISBN-10:   0-7432-6439-8

For Norma Hess,
with love and gratitude

Contents

First and last, accept no man's statement that he knows this Country of Lost Borders well. A great number having lost their lives in the process of proving where it is not safe to go, it is now possible to pass through much of the district by guide-posts and well-known water-holes, but the best part of it remains locked, inviolate, or best known only to some far-straying Indian, sheepherder, or pocket hunter, whose account of it does not get into the reports of the Geological Survey.

MARY AUSTIN, *THE LAND*, 1909

No migrant ever arrived in the region knowing less than I did.

CAREY MCWILLIAMS, *SOUTHERN CALIFORNIA:
AN ISLAND ON THE LAND*, 1946

California City

I WAS DRIVING TO THE END of the world, I was sure of it. Instead of flowing straight and flat, like a normal roadbed, this freeway was all up and down. The hills I was passing through bumped their way to the horizon, where there was nothing. The sun scorched the road. I'd left at nine in the morning, and it was past noon now. I'd made hardly any headway. It took longer than it should have to climb those heights, one after another, and then descend, steeply, on the other side. Already my car thermometer said 107. Far behind me were the comfortable fields and developments of Bakersfield and human camaraderie; now I was working my way east toward the Mojave Desert and Death Valley.

Desert was the right word for where I was. In these blank, dusty hills you could come upon a camel, no problem. You'd say howdy.

I was thirsty, and thinking about history: history always has something worse to offer than the situation you happen to be in. The gold prospectors of 1849, for example. I focused my mind on them, seeking their fortune in California. Poor things. They suffered terrible thirst and desperate hunger as they made their way (and didn't make their way) with their skinny oxen through hills very much like the ones I was passing through, very near the ones I was passing through.

Death Valley was only a jump of the imagination away from here, a few more miles on the odometer. The forty-niners had left home for this—this, and the gold beyond.

I was on my way to California City. I needed to see a city with a name like that in a place like this. I thought it would explain California to me; clearly California City's founders imagined that somehow their creation expressed the essence of the state—and maybe it would. You don't give a place a name like that for no good reason. And on the map, California City looked fantastical, a huge grid, dwarfing almost every city near or far. It was laid out in a broad, rational oval of ring roads around what seemed to be a town square. I conjured up a sort of Emerald City rising from the desert. I knew such a city could be built, if you had the right engineers and the right portion of pure ambition and ruthless dedication to profit. Look at Los Angeles.

Also I wanted to get to a place where I could feel safe (not that I wanted to plant myself for good out in the Mojave; probably a couple of hours would do). I just wanted to know that such a place existed. I'd been in New York on September 11, and I was still looking for a spot to live in that wasn't a reflexive, knee-jerk, obvious target. L.A. had not exactly served the purpose; it turned out that it wasn't removed enough from the national scene to qualify. But surely California City, so deep in the desert, so far from the 5 and the 99, those busy, flowing arteries, would be an enclave of peace, calm, and forgetfulness, a sort of modern-day, urban Xanadu, the kind of place so many people had been seeking for so long in California.

All along the 58, a lesser road, the desert rolled out around me like a faded rug, shaken for cleaning, twisted and contorted, its design, if it had one, indistinguishable. It was another planet out here: that's how it feels when the land takes over, when rock, mineral, and sheer topography are cold comrades and the world is bereft of the human touch, the human scale. You begin to go blank in these conditions, counting miles, zoning out, hoping the big rigs don't run out of control on the downhills and ram you off the road. I always watch for runaway truck lanes; that's what the sign says: Runaway Truck Lane, 1 mile. Then I wait to see the dead-end lane off the highway, a sandy embankment. It's a comfort to me—knowing that somewhere, someone has planned to avert disaster, no matter how infrequent.

There's someone out there.

Thirst and sun turn my mind to water, too: Is there any? Why did I forget to bring any? Can I get any?

As I pass a double rig, I suddenly remember a piece of ox liver. Kind, desperate, starving forty-niners on a Death Valley expedition gave this precious piece of liver to a Mrs. Brier, wife of the Reverend J. W. Brier, and to her three babies. That liver has been vivid in my mind since the day I read about its fate.

Mrs. Brier was busy doing something else at the moment the liver was presented to her—changing a diaper, kissing a bruised knee—and she put that liver on an upended bucket and she turned her back on that liver for one second. She was always ministering to someone in the caravan, not just her own. Meanwhile, some haggard fortune seeker, half-crazed with starvation, crept up to the overturned bucket in the evening's half-light and made off with Mrs. Brier's liver. Mrs. Brier and her babies—after several days without food—had to make do that night with bits of oxen offal, horrid things fit only for coyotes.

I didn't want to be in such a place, where the lucky people ended up eating oxen offal. Refugees, pilgrims, and pioneers—I'd always trusted that my era in history was going to spare me their fate, but like any reasonable former resident of the Upper West Side of Manhattan, a neighborhood filled with immigrant and refugee offspring, I worried. In the past I'd thought of people like Mrs. Brier as quaint artifacts of Americana, a breed almost unknown to me, and of which I certainly was no member. But September 11 made me realize that anyone at any time can join Mrs. Brier's ranks, and now out here on the 58, passing Caliente with not a soul in sight, I could imagine it all.

The splashes of black, watery mirage along the road as it bucks and plunges are dazzling and seductive. Can that be a lake, I ask myself, looking into the near distance where the hills meet a flat, blue-looking area. The forty-niners, ablaze with thirst, saw these phantasms too, huge lakes shining up at them as they gazed down from some peak dreadful to ascend, dreadful to descend. On closer inspection, they would find an arid lake bed, its surface dry for so long that it had hardened like rock and now reflected the sun like dark glass, or the surface of still water. When I drive off the highway to *my* lake, it turns out that it's nothing but smog or some other distortion of light, and so I head back to the freeway. I keep going.

The road winds on past Keene, Woodford, Golden Hills, and Tehachapi, past the Monolith cement factory (a huge, ancient-seeming piece of elaborate industrialization towering alone over the sands), and across the Los Angeles Aqueduct as its waters pour down from Inyo County.

My mouth felt dry. I never thought you could get dehydrated in a car traveling seventy miles per hour, with the air-conditioning on, but that's what was happening. I felt as if I might swoon and lose control, so I pulled over, not at a runaway truck exit, but on the plain old dusty shoulder. This was an unusual feeling; normally I am as sturdy as a farm animal. But now I'm in desert condition, like a Vermont calf stranded in a dry Middle Eastern wadi.

I got out of the car. It was about one in the afternoon. Of course, I had no hat. Stalwart, dependable Mrs. Brier would have had a hat, no doubt. Huge trucks passed by at barreling speeds. Otherwise there was nothing. A hill across the highway, another one behind me, the one I was on. Some greenish grayish low-lying bushes, a couple of rocks, and an ocean of dust and sand and sun lay before me.

I was not convinced this rest stop was helping my condition. Another rig passed by. I stood there, leaning against the hot car. Across the highway, in the distance, something moved. It did, I was sure. I squinted. I could have sworn that I saw something shift across a patch of sand, out from under one bit of brush and into the shadow of another. I waited, and it moved again—again from shade into shade. The thing that had moved looked like a rock, but even a New Yorker knows that rocks don't move. I watched it some more—what I could make out of it—but it didn't move again, and now it looked more like a shadow itself than anything else. Could I be hallucinating from the heat, or from thirst? I got back in the car. Mrs. Brier's companions hallucinated from thirst, but I didn't think I was that far gone. No, I thought. It must have been a desert tortoise, an ancient and endangered species that lurks out here amid the rocks. They like to forage for food and shade near noon. As far as I could tell from my experience so far, a desert tortoise was a fitter resident for this desert than any human, even one in an air-conditioned car.

About seventy miles east of Bakersfield, California City shuffles up from the desert, not like a jutting Emerald City, but instead as if it were made from the same materials as its surroundings, camouflaged in the sand like a desert rat, its lawns a wreckage of scrub brush, dirt, and jalopies, its houses flat tan-and-beige ranch prefabs or mobile homes or Section 8 housing. Tumbleweed and plastic bags blow down its undeveloped streets. A few trees have been planted here, but they don't seem to be making much of a difference. In the center of "town" there is a park. It's called Central Park, a weirdly green patch.

Cal City, as its residents call it, has no real topographical or geological reason to exist, and it barely does. It's purely a result of human imagination, engineering, hope, and greed. It is not a normal city, because it didn't grow up around anything. There was no water here to speak of, originally: when water *was* discovered at a miners' town called Cow Wells in the late 1800s, those wells had to be dug to fifteen hundred feet.

No river, no lake, no oil, no railroad station right nearby—the freeway, even now, more than ten miles away. No oasis—nothing. Nothingness, sheer emptiness, has always defined the area: it's a place through which huge aqueducts could pass without disturbing private property; a place for long runways that accommodate superfast, low-flying military aircraft; for experimental bombing runs complete with bombs; for the army's desert training; for automotive manufacturers' proving grounds, where cars are raced and crashed and swiveled and forced to somersault at high speeds, their performance rated; it's a place for open-ended dirt biking, paragliding, and wave soaring; it's a place to put prisons.

It surprised me, then, to discover that—after San Francisco and Los Angeles—California City, at 204 square miles, is the state's third-largest city, in terms of area (it is the eleventh-largest city in the United States). More reasonably, it was recently the state's 347th most populous city, with 11,422 residents. Because of its empty expanse, it feels sparse, almost dead, deserted—although more accurately, it has never quite been inhabited. Many of its streets still have nothing built on them, forty-nine years after groundbreaking began. It's hard to imagine what fueled the dream of California City for all these decades, right down to now. There are some jobs: at the borax mines several miles east, at Edwards Air Force Base seventeen miles to the south, at the new Cal City correctional facility just outside town, at Monolith Cement, at the Hyundai/Kia and Honda proving grounds. The housing is inexpensive. But for someone not from around here, this desolate place looks like nothing but a huge mistake, a grave miscalculation about human nature and human habitation.

It's hard to imagine why anyone imagined California City, much less began to build it. You could posit, for example, that only a dreamer or a fool would dare to build on so grandiose a scale, but also, of course, confidence men might try it, and rip-off artists and scammers too. And indeed, a few men of this kind were mixed into the real-estate brew from which the city was conjured.

In 1958, "visionary" developer Nathan K. Mendelsohn, a Czech-born sociology instructor at Columbia University who specialized in land use and demographics, decided to build a model desert city here, following the great successes of postwar planned suburban towns like California's own Lakewood and Long Island's Levittown. As a canvas for his vast project, Mendelsohn bought up some eighty thousand cheap Mojave acres. This was urban development in the wild, in a place where the biggest junction up till then had been some irrigation trails that connected with the Los Angeles Aqueduct, and the lonely, crisscrossing tracks of the desert tortoise, my endangered friend.

———

The occupied space nearest to California City, adjacent and overlapping, and also blocked out by dreamers, is the Desert Tortoise Natural Area, which, at 39.5 square miles, is less than a fifth the size of the neighboring human city and even more sparsely populated. This area is the spot to which the hard-shelled reptilian former denizens of California City are supposed to repair in *their* mobile homes—but do not, always. The desert tortoise can often be found outside the "natural" area; in fact, the area perimeter fence is built so that he can enter and leave on his own recognizance. That must be how mine got under his scrub brush by the road.

The desert tortoise is certainly better suited to this environment than I am, and better outfitted even than the obstinate trailer dwellers of California City. He can live where the ground temperature reaches above 140 degrees Fahrenheit. He spends more than 95 percent of his life, which can last as long as a hundred years, in underground burrows, which is what any sane creature would do when faced with the Mojave Desert. He can survive for more than a year without water, and can, in a moment of dehydration, even suck back urine that has collected in his bladder. This would have been a true plus for anyone living in the original California, before the advent of William Mulholland, the notorious supervisor of the Los Angeles Department of Water and Power. In the fall of 1904, Mulholland drove out of L.A., heading north on a two-horse buckboard, with a friend and some hard liquor, searching for water to feed the expanding city he worked for. After an arduous trip, they came upon the Owens River, and thus began the construction of the Los Angeles Aqueduct, which I'd just crossed over. The aqueduct runs for 250 miles between Owens Valley and Los Angeles, and it made both California City and modern-day Los Angeles possible. It also devastated the farms of the Owens Valley.

The desert tortoise survived the construction of the waterworks, incredibly. Hardy as the tortoise is, he is vulnerable to the extreme changes in his environment caused by humans. Those changes may not look extreme to the humans; to this human, for one, the Mojave, as represented by California City and its environs, still looks much like a desert, only worse, with roads and banks, slapdash houses, a couple of spots reserved for off-road vehicles, a mini-mall here or there, a gas station every once in a while, an aqueduct, a cement factory, everything low, flat, and cinder-blocked. But to the desert tortoise, everything has changed, changed utterly. Odd to think, too, that many of these beasts have lived long enough to have witnessed the change personally—if you can use the words "witness" and "personally" where a tortoise is concerned—unlike other creatures, who experience the phases of their own extinction only generationally. Imagine the eighty-five-year-old tortoise, now a resident of the Desert Tortoise Natural Area. Does he put air quotes around the word "natural"? With his flat front legs, designed for burrowing?

Here's what happened to the poor little turtle—not so little, really, at more than a foot long in many cases. The usual hunting grounds of the tortoise have been cut into and carved away by developments like California City, which bring in their wake huge numbers of ravens, eaters of offal, attracted by tasty human refuse. This artificial community of ravens, camp followers of desert development, then also preys on the slow and delectably meaty tortoise and is now responsible for more than half of the deaths of the young and tender of that species. The ravens use telephone and electric wires as perches from which to attack their prey.

Also encouraged by development, and the concomitant razing of native plants, inedible invasive species of grass and grain have pushed out the tortoise's normal fare. And off-roaders, who are attracted to both the basins and the hills of the desert, sometimes make a sport of flattening super-slo-mo tortoises that cross their path, in a sort of mad, topsy-turvy, fuel-injected version of the Tortoise and the Hare. Intense off-roading has also ruined the soil in prime parts of tortoise land and created a sterile zone in some former tortoise grazing areas.

So although no real-estate boom ever happened in California City, at least not on the scale that Mendelsohn had envisioned, the human population of the Mojave eventually doubled and doubled again, while the tortoise population was reduced by 90 percent, in spite of the animals' evolutionary ability to survive in this place of extremes. Humans are still slowly moving to California City, as all of Los Angeles County to the south becomes urbanized and people grow tired of megalopolitan life. The urban sprawl to the south is out of control. Palmdale, the closest big town on the other side of the Tehachapi range, already has a population of 131,153 and is growing rapidly. When Mulholland passed through Palmdale on his way to the Owens River, the population was 25.

When California City finally filled the artificial lake at the center of the town's Central Park (the name Mendelsohn gave it), the town gathered to celebrate. It was a big moment for Mendelsohn, and as the city's hundreds of residents laid out their picnics below, an airplane he'd hired overflew the park and dumped water that had been taken from the lake in New York's eponymous park into the new lake in the desert. But in spite of its founder's attempt to compare it to the country's greatest urban agglomerations, California City never attracted the kinds of universities, shopping malls, or corporate investment that Mendelsohn and his salesmen described when hawking parcels to newcomers.

Over the years since Mendelsohn invented it, the town has been the subject of real-estate speculation, lawsuits, and interventions by federal and state government. No skyscrapers went up here; today, the tallest buildings are the abandoned movie theater and a couple of apartment buildings constructed with Section 8 funds. One of the many suits filed against the developers alleged that there was insufficient water for the California City project. Nor did the value of the land appreciate rapidly, as Mendelsohn had predicted. One poor fellow who bought his parcel in 1959 for $3,490 had it assessed by Kern County at $3,755.64 thirty years later, according to a 1990 *L.A. Times* report. By then, Mendelsohn was long gone, but not before he and his company settled lawsuits with various purchasers to the tune of more than $3 million. He left behind a largely empty city and went on to found a resort community in Brackettville, Texas, before his death on the golf course there in 1984.

Yet California City persists, like a good desert denizen, and over the years has spread out slightly, in a halting, sporadic way. This odd collection of houses, shacks, and trailers even has a City Hall, and I've come upon it by chance. It's a cinder-blocker, another California building with no history. Inside, I find Helen Dennis, California City town clerk. I wonder if perhaps she might know where I can get some water. Dennis has soft, powder-puff skin, what used to be called an ample bosom, a plump physique, and a no-nonsense attitude. She's all business. Only the desert tortoise is more perfectly formed than Dennis for life in the California City area. To me, she looks nice and friendly but, above all, hydrated.

Somehow, though, it seems rude to go directly to water, so I start out slowly. Dennis tells me she came up here from a trailer home in Los Angeles, when California City was barely a scrape in the ground. "My parents were rock hounds," she says, meaning they collected and traded interesting rock samples. "They spent a lot of time in the desert, picking up rocks, so I went along with them. I was used to the desert." Dennis looks at me funny when I say that I come from New York. I tell her that I guess I just don't get California City: what makes a city like this one appealing?

"Well, we don't get *New York!*" Dennis laughs. "California City was a beautiful city, back then," she says. "There was a movie theater, a hotel, the park. At the beginning, Mr. Mendelsohn built forty-one ranch-flat homes, all with the same floor plan. There were fifty-five thousand subdivided lots. It was a land rush." In fact, it was rank land speculation. By 1965, Mendelsohn had sold about forty-nine thousand of his lots, but in fact, only twelve hundred or so optimists turned up who actually wanted to live in California City. Mendelsohn had paved and graded many of his roads without any houses on them, and no houses scheduled to be built. Many of those roads—with developers' imaginative names slapped on them, names like Harvard, Princeton, Bennington, Dartmouth, Cornell, Amherst, and Georgetown; or Melville, Fenimore, and Cooper; or Bentham, Arnold, Keynes, and Hume; or Orchard, Sylvan, Verdant, Eucalyptus, Dogwood, and Catalpa—have hardly a house on them.

After Dennis's family moved the mobile home up to California City, she married a navy aviator, so proximity to the Edwards base was useful. Later, she got her broker's license and went into real estate, first for Mendelsohn, then for a man she calls "Mr. Billionaire Billy White" of Billy White Enterprises, and then, as the business became more corporate, for Great Western United Corp., which bought out Mendelsohn in 1969 for over $27 million in stock.

As I talk to Dennis, I'm thinking mostly about how to get out of here and where to find water. I feel faint, as if I might fall out of my metal chair onto the linoleum at any moment. My mind is confused. And I have a right to be confused. First, a lot has happened in California City today: that is, there's been a visitor (me), and also, there's been a car crash not far from City Hall, with many injuries, some serious. The mayor, Larry Adams, comes in from the scene of the accident, bearing the bad news. He looks shaken. A woman no one recognized hit a van filled with elderly California City residents being ferried on their daily rounds. People at City Hall are making phone calls to daughters and daughters-in-law of the victims. People are coming in and out during my chat with Dennis.

And second, I can't really understand Dennis's flat, all-American accent. So my conversation with the town clerk is jarringly interspersed with give-and-take like this:

Me, finally: "Can you tell me where I can buy a bottle of water for the road?"

Dennis: "Cassidy Market. How's the woman?"

Mayor: "Well, when they're not moving, they're usually hurt pretty bad."

I'm not a person who enjoys dwelling on car crashes, especially when I have a lot of driving ahead of me. My head aches; my heart is still beating a little too fast. Now I'm thinking about motionless bodies in the road.

I ask where Cassidy Market is.

"Cal City," says Dennis. "Cal City Market. On Cal City Boulevard." Then, thoughtfully, to the mayor: "She must have been going pretty fast."

Mayor: "Yup. I think she was looking down. Looking away, anyhow. Poor kid. Helicopter took her."

Never look away. That was Mrs. Brier's mistake, with the liver, and I don't want it to be mine. I promise myself not to fiddle with CDs while I'm on the 58 back to Bakersfield, and from there, on the 5 to Los Angeles. I promise myself not *ever* to look backward while driving forward. And I will drink enough water if I *ever* find the Cassidy Market. I promise, in other words, never to take my eyes off the liver.

People are feeling shaky everywhere today, not just me. It's the day after the London transit bombings, with so many bodies in the road and the tunnels. You could argue that the British were looking away. Having been in New York on September 11, I've thought a lot about being prepared and not being prepared, and whether preparation makes any difference. For people so far away, so utterly removed, from London, the officials of California City are deeply touched by the events. This bothers me, because I had imagined I was entering the American zone of safety, but something about Dennis's and Adams's deep empathy with the London victims tells me I'm not there yet, at least not psychologically. Talk of the London bombs even manages to divert their attention from their own immediate car crash.

"When something like London happens, I say we should bomb Mecca," Mayor Adams says. "In return."

I look at him in a friendly, open sort of way, as if it's possible I might agree.

"And if the French start whining," he adds, "bomb them too."

I must make some doubting face, because he says, "No, I mean it."

Outside the office we're sitting in, in the lobby of City Hall, is a bunting hung with red hearts, each one representing a child of California City who is fighting in Iraq; I count around twenty hearts and

Dennis assures me that these are not the only residents in service there.

"Oh, I have something to show you," she says to me. "Since you're from New York." My imagination begins to race along with my heartbeat . . . what will it be? I hope illogically that it will be water, but I know it won't be . . . I feel panic. I don't want to be held responsible for New York; I can't take on that kind of burden. Not out here, with no one to rush to my defense.

She guides me out the front door of City Hall, the one that gives onto a patch of lawn instead of the parking lot. The heat smacks us as we exit. It's afternoon now, but the sun has a few more hours until it begins to set. Half sun-blind, I follow her down a short path, where she gestures, open-handed, to a piece of sculpture in front of the building.

And there it is, sparkling at me: a replica of the World Trade Center in brushed steel, and just my height. It all comes back to me in a sort of dizzying rush, the cloud that settled on the city that day and then those eerily bright September days afterward, not long enough ago. Now the structure shimmers at me like a mirage, as if it were made of water. I am tottering a bit, from disorientation, so I take hold of one tower, the north tower (at least here it is the north tower). I can wrap my arm around it, like an old school chum, and I do, to steady myself, leaning a bit to peer at the plaque between the towers, which begins, God Bless America.

I think: this is where it all begins, it all began, at the Twin Towers. In a way, it's how I ended up here in California, in California City, it's why I ever agreed to be in such a place. Here's the World Trade Center on a lawn in the middle of the Mojave Desert, weirdly rebuilt: the people of New York couldn't, but the people of California City *could* put it together again. Yes, it's smaller, it's been reduced, downsized, it's useless and hollow. But it's *here*, nonetheless. It must mean something.

Oh, now I know what it is. It's a symbol; I get it. But a symbol of what? To the town clerk of California City, a symbol of what? That we are not defeated? That we remain strong? That we are one nation . . . etc., etc.?

"The world has changed, hasn't it?" Dennis says, looking for my reaction as I droop over the tower. I give her a friendly if defeated look.

"But we can't let them win." That means something to her, and to Mayor Adams too, with his sorties over Mecca and Paris.

And to me, a symbol of what? I feel suddenly too large, and in comparison to these towers, ridiculous. The scale is all wrong. I'm holding on to the north tower chatting with Dennis, another giant: why, at *this* size, we could have saved them all. We could have cupped our hands and broken their fall; could have doused the fire with a pail of water, could have stood between the buildings and the planes, and stopped it all, and felt nothing.

Dennis escorts me to the parking lot, giving me careful directions once more to the Cal City Market; she obviously feels I am not ever going to get there, even though all I have to do is turn right after I get out of the lot. Perhaps she's hoping to avoid a second car wreck today in California City. I shake her dry, soft hand and pile myself into my car, sticking to the upholstery through my clothes. The paper in my notebook is curling from the heat. The car thermometer says 107 again.

Dennis has gone back inside to deal with more wreckage, the rest of the survivors and their relations. I turn right on California City Boulevard toward the 58, like an obedient girl, just as Dennis told me to, keeping an eye out for the Cal City Market on the left. And there it is at a light, my personal oasis, in the corner of a mini-mall, the Cal City Mini Mall. There's not much in the Cal City Market in the Cal City Mini Mall on Cal City Boulevard: some sad old frozen meat, a shelf of frozen fish, pork rinds galore, bulk bread, cigarettes, paper goods, many different kinds of Cheetos.

And cold water. I buy myself two big liters. At the cash register, my head is spinning as I count the bills and begin to make my way out of the store. And then I drink one full bottle right off, sitting there in the driver's seat in the mini-mall parking lot with my head back and the door open and my feet kicking at the side of my car. I take a couple of deep breaths and toss the empty into a bin, sit back down, and shut my door. I turn the air-conditioning on full blast, switch on the radio, and just idle there for a few minutes, with a hand resting lightly on the other water bottle beside me.

Whatever, I say to myself. I'm back in my car, my pod, my tortoise shell. I pull out.

PART ONE

Focus Puller

CHAPTER ONE

The Dead Point

I T'S A BEAUTIFUL DAY in Los Angeles, two years earlier, in the flatlands at the foot of the Hollywood Hills. It's fall, but you might not know it. I'm in my garden—my own backyard. I can hear a neighbor's lawn mower going, can see his gardener's straw hat moving back and forth among the leaves of the high bushes between our yards. My neighbor's dog is swimming in the pool. He's calling to the dog: "Bella, Bella! Come." Flies buzz through the sunlight; they lend a drugged charm to the scene. The sprinklers have just finished going and there's an uncharacteristic moisture in the air that lets you inhale deeply—not like desert air, not scratchy, not physically demanding. In the backyard, the Chinese elm is swaying beneficently in a cool breeze. The grass and ficus and boxwood and lemon trees are green with a kind of sparkling purity that seems to promise honesty and freshness and present pleasure. The house is white with green shutters. Its windows reflect the fluttering, descending leaves and light. It's a dream, birds are singing, a mourning dove gurgles in the lattice of the rose arbor. This is where I live, in a dream.

On a shelf inside the white garage is a blue bucket, and in that bucket is a boat. It's an inflatable boat, and it is all curled up tightly in a stuff bag in the bucket. The boat seats five. The garage in all other visible respects is a normal garage: a Ping-Pong table, a few bikes of different sizes leaning against the walls and hanging from hooks, cobwebs draping the roof corners, a blade of light coming down from a dim window, a bunch of old backpacks hanging from a rusty nail, two skateboards tucked under a ledge, two broken scooters nearby, a cast-off pair of Rollerblades pushed under a shelf, a red bicycle pump in a corner, and next to the door, a basket of baseball bats, mitts, gloves, caps, and balls. There are no cars in there, though. In L.A., you keep your car or cars outside, because the garage is often not a garage, it's an office or a playroom or a pool house, or a studio, or a guest room. Anyway, there is no weather here, no snow or sleet, and very little rain to destroy your car—except for the automatic showers of the garden sprinklers. At least, that's what I thought when I was living in my dream: I was no meteorologist.

On another shelf in the garage is a pump to inflate my boat. It's a battery-run pump. You could also blow my boat up by mouth, but it would take a long, long time and might cause hyperventilation. The hard seats and floor of my boat are up on a plank just beneath the garage ceiling, along with two old wooden doors from the house, and screens from the side doors; some miscellaneous rods and rope for the boat are in the basement of the house.

I look at my boat and its accessories with some embarrassment these days. After all. Even if there happened to be no traffic (which has never happened in Los Angeles), I still live a half an hour away from any useful ocean, and anyway, this kind of boat is not a seagoing vessel. This kind of boat is usually employed as a dinghy for a big sailboat. It's a harbor boat, not a Pacific boat, although it does have a place to attach a small outboard motor. I bought the motor too, but it was too heavy for my purposes, so I returned it. I had never realized how heavy a motor is. I was glad to be rid of it.

I bought my inflatable boat when I still lived in New York City, on the twelfth floor of a prewar co-op apartment building on Riverside Drive, a few hundred yards from the Hudson River. It was July of 2002; I was in the country on a summer vacation, sitting in front of a computer late at night, contemplating the return to Manhattan and ordinary life. Outside in the night, skunks and groundhogs and raccoons snuffled and prowled over the dark meadow. I was trying to conjure up my life back in New York—it seemed to me, thinking of Manhattan from a black, cricket-filled night in the country, that it was too tense, too anxiety-provoking; that I didn't want to be there anymore—and then I remembered inflatable boats. A friend of mine, a sailor from the age of six, had one. An inflatable boat would allay my anxiety, I thought. Why didn't everyone in New York City have one? Manhattan was an island, I wanted to remind them.

So I went online and bought one. I put it in my shopping cart, just like that—a boat in your shopping cart. Rescue was on the way. In my late-night mind, a little rowboat seemed like a perfect conveyance to carry my family and me across the Hudson River to New Jersey, which is my original home state and where I should end up, anyway. In case of catastrophe. I had a friend I'd once considered sane, a newspaper reporter who had covered wars and remained unmoved. But after reporting on the World Trade Center's disintegration on September 11, this well-balanced, rock-solid, *grounded* person ("grounded" is a word I've learned to use since coming to California to mean something other than keeping safe from electrical currents), this grounded person put together a safe room in his apartment with a huge barrel of drinking water, gas and germ masks, food supplies that included vast quantities of powdered milk, antibiotics, a hand-cranked radio, and duct tape. That was a little extreme, I thought. It was in the children's bedroom, crowding things—and what must the children be thinking?

Arnold Schwarzenegger, the Austrian bodybuilder who was soon to run for governor of California, and who is a man who knows a lot about survival, told *Oui* magazine in 1977 that an athlete—one who wants to put his fist in the air when the competition is over, and all others have been eliminated—must "go through that pain barrier, that dead point" in order to survive. Why was this muscleman so wise? My friend was clearly confronting his pain barrier, and so was I. Would we ever get past the dead point?

To cope with that monolithic pain barrier after the events of September 11, it seemed more reasonable to lay out six hundred dollars for a boat than to construct a safe room among the bunk beds. Six hundred was, it seemed to me, a small price to pay for a means of escape. No one can argue that I was thinking rationally. I am only sporadically logical when beset by emotions—especially fear. A little boat, a chubby boat, friendly as a tub or a beach ball. I had an image of me at the prow (wind in my hair) and my husband rowing like crazy and the children having a grand time, as Manhattan, in flames, slowly disappeared behind us. I thought I would feel more secure with that boat under my bed in apartment 12B.

When the boat arrived, though, I scrambled to hide it. It was shameful, of course, and pathetic, and possibly weird. I didn't want anyone else to know about it: it was like a drug problem or alcoholism, a dirty secret. Except for the rods and ropes and seats, the boat in its stuff bag did fit quite tidily under the bed. In the flesh, though, I realized my dinghy was quite an unwieldy thing that would be hard to get to the river's shore on a calm and sunny Sunday in May, much less to inflate and put together and drag down to the riverbank and pilot to Hoboken or Fort Lee in the midst of major chaos—with the city in flames, nuclear detritus floating above, and millions of terrified people pushing through Riverside Park down to the Hudson, trying to get away. Me there too, with three children and a sixty-pound boat tucked under my arm . . . the dog . . . After all this planning, I felt, my boat wasn't really going to save us. I was not convinced it would get me past the dead point.

So when the opportunity arose, I agreed to move to California.

As if that would help.

Of course, I didn't want to go there. (When I say "go there," I mean "travel to a destination," as opposed to what my friends in California mean when they say "go there"—"to discuss or refer to an off-limits subject.") California had never appealed to me in any way. It was too far away, and it was on the wrong side of the country. It faced Asia, not Europe. The sun set over the ocean there, instead of rising over it. When you said "west" in California, you could mean the Far East; when you said "east," you could mean Nevada. I didn't want to be in a place where there was no real theater district and no Lower East Side. (When I say "be in a place," by the way, I mean "dwell in an actual location," not, as my friends in California might mean, "take a certain emotional or psychological stance.") I didn't want to be in a place where—according to the tropes, clichés, and stereotypes that I'd absorbed as a proper New Yorker—everyone was blond, tan, cute, strong-jawed, empty-headed, and athletic, and possibly spiritually inclined. I was dark, bespectacled, bookish, and both physically and mentally not tan. I did not belong in L.A.

But my husband had been offered a job as an editor at the *Los Angeles Times,* and so I had to consider the place more carefully. California's strong suit for me—at the moment when a chance to move there arose—was precisely that it wasn't New York. I looked around New York and the whole place reeked of the aftermath of September 11; there were checkpoints at the subway stops, armed guards at entrances to bridges, and something called "police actions" that occasionally stopped all traffic in both directions. I knew the city had psychological problems when the articles I ended up writing about it—even for women's fashion magazines—centered on post-traumatic stress disorder and whether it was now possible to compare New York to Jerusalem during the Intifada.

I thought I could do with a break from the stress.

After some time living in Los Angeles, however, I realized that stress and fear will follow you. In the blank, unsignifying land of the West, as yet unscarred by terrorists' craters, I was not immune to the fears of the age. And naturally there were some new, place-specific worries I could delve into out here. As my friends in California would say: It's not about where you live. It's about who you want to be. You need to get to a place where you're secure. You have to work on it. You've got to go there, over and over again, and then you must rise above.

Whereas I was more of a catastrophist, an inflatable boater. I believed that planning an escape—however elaborate—was the only rational tool for confronting our times. Everyone, I thought, should have a personal exit strategy.

Mine, however, was clearly flawed, because from the beginning, it was obvious that California would not rescue me.

———

First of all, the state was not in a condition to rescue anyone, I discovered to my surprise. I had always thought of California as the jumping-off point for all that was shiny and bright and full of promise, or at the very least, for all that was new. California was not really a state but a country. A country whose decisions on matters of policy could direct legislation for decades in the rest of the nation. It was a state whose property tax revolution had utterly changed the way the rest of the country thought of and legislated on such taxes. A place whose smog controls and organic standards had become the standard for the nation, and where every ruling on cars and gasoline immediately had an impact on Detroit and in Japan. A state whose economy was, by most estimates, the world's fifth largest. It was the land of silicon chips and wine and macrobiotics, of smog checks and solar power and windmills. Whenever I thought of California, I thought of that lyric of Steely Dan's Donald Fagen: "We'll be clean when their work is done/We'll be eternally free, yes, and eternally young."

Perhaps I'd been thinking more of Northern California, not L.A.

But instead I landed in L.A. and entered a world that, like New York and New Jersey, felt a lot like the Third World. California was $28 billion in debt. It was just recovering from an energy crisis—much of it artificially induced, it later became clear—during which the lights had gone out in parts of the state. The California I arrived in wasn't clean or perfect; it was a deeply flawed place with bad public education and poor health care—a gas-guzzling consumathon with hundreds of thousands of miles of asphalt but barely any public transportation. There wasn't even a shared language for its people, though in the areas around my neighborhood, if you had to guess which was the official language, you would have said either Korean or Spanish. Often, indeed, it seemed that hundreds of thousands of the state's residents had no rights at all, because they were here illegally. And yet this was the place we all had grown up thinking of as America's best offering, the place everyone used to want to move to, the state to which hundreds of thousands of people continued to migrate each year (though many more were leaving), a state where new housing developments were coming on line every week.

So it was no utopia. That was fine with me. I was used to dystopian living; as I said, I grew up in New Jersey. But California was also in the middle of a political crisis. Governor Gray Davis, a Democrat who had been reelected little more than a year before I arrived, was facing a recall vote—almost entirely because the state was in such bad fiscal shape, and because the Republicans sensed a weakness; not for any particular malfeasance on Davis's part. A recall election for governor—such a thing had never been done before in California; indeed, the only other time a governor had been recalled in U.S. history was in 1921, in North Dakota.

When I finally came up for air after arriving in Los Angeles—with three children, moving is never easy—I began to hear rumors about this recall election: that it was not an empty threat; that it really was going to happen; that provisions for recalls were really included in the California constitution; that enough signatures were going to be gathered to force a recall vote; and that Schwarzenegger or even Warren Beatty might be among the candidates. That the governor now sitting might lose. Coming from New York, where George Pataki was in his third boring term, it seemed amazing, and even a little ridiculous, that I might soon be living under a Governor Schwarzenegger—or Beatty. I was beginning to learn about the eccentric charms of my new state. It really was a different country out here, all right—the early pioneers and the adventurers of the Gold Rush had been right about that—and soon I would learn more.

At my sons' new elementary school in a church in Hollywood, I was encouraged to supply what are called "comfort bags" for them. I was given a flyer that told me what to include in the bags marked with their names: a favorite stuffed animal or security object, a book, games, a change of clothes, a toothbrush, and perhaps a photograph of the family (which sounded ominous). This was in case of earthquake.

The school itself, at the parents' expense, also had a stock of earth-quake supplies—powdered milk, bottled water (replaced every year), canned foods, blankets, etc. The school itself, I later found out, is located on a major fault line.

I learned, too, from a small green photocopied notice tacked up discreetly near the door of my fourth-grader's classroom, that there was an emergency command chain at the school, as well as a medical team, an evacuation team, and a damage assessment team that would follow "the sweep route" after an earthquake to check for damage and to report "critically injured to the medical team." There was a plan for triage. A heading entitled "The First Hour" advised teachers that "if children are in a bathroom, they need to crouch against a wall." It went on to inform the responsible adults at the school that "most injuries occur while trying to evacuate during the shaking." It pointed out that the school's hallways "are safer if you are not under the sky-lights." The notice went well beyond what I felt was acceptable to envision.

I had arrived in L.A. hoping to avoid catastrophe, only to find that I was living in its capital. My new friends advised me: Cash and water in your car (Tampax too). Full tank, always. Slippers or flip-flops next to each bed (for walking on the inevitable broken glass). Flashlights everywhere, especially in night tables; make sure the batteries are live. Emergency lights. Hand-cranked radio. This all was beginning to sound too familiar. And don't forget: The safest spot is still in a door frame or under a sturdy table; outside is dangerous until the shaking has stopped; door frames without doors are better because doors can swing and knock you out. Bolt all your bookcases to the walls.

Well, I was no stranger to destruction, so I decided that the wisest plan was to shrug, to shrug it off. I was a former foreign correspon-dent, after all. That sounds brave. I had faced the Israeli Army from the Palestinian side and, cowering in a corner, had survived. I'd lived in Jerusalem during a period of bus bombs, and I'd gotten used to it. I had lived in Haiti for years and covered violent demonstrations there—which happened with the regularity of holidays elsewhere. I had felt safe in Port-au-Prince, the capital, even when I was dodging gunfire, since most of the people with guns couldn't shoot straight and weren't aiming for me, in any case. I'd hung out with torturers, dictators, and terrorists, and I'm none the worse for it. And I had walked across Manhattan on September 11 with my children and emerged with only an inflatable boat as a sign of my anxiety syndrome.

I could *do* earthquakes, too, I knew it.

In my travels, I'd already been in a few small ones and they seemed innocent enough, little reminders that the earth is not really solid ground beneath your feet. But in California the reminders are not so friendly, I knew. From the earliest recorded California quake in 1700 through the year 2000, there had been seventy-six major earthquakes here (over 6 on the Richter scale), which killed a total of 3,451 people, injured tens of thousands, and caused billions of dollars' worth of damage. The earth plays a major role here. I tried to cast out of my mind my friends' descriptions of the Northridge earthquake of 1994, the last big earthquake to strike Southern California. The jumping armoires, the hallways of broken glass, a baby a friend of mine "forgot" and had to run back in for, the bouncing freeway, the word "pancake" used as a verb for the first time in my memory.

Right away, upon moving here, I became something of an earthquake connoisseur, a specialty catastrophist. In Jerusalem, I'd studied sonic booms versus bus bombs, like the rest of the population, and discovered that if you could hear the roar of a jet right after the bang, the bang was probably not a bomb. Sometimes after a bang, the whole crowd in the street wherever you were would stand suddenly quiet, at virtual attention, listening for either the telltale jet or for sirens beginning their wail. When the sound of the passing plane made itself heard, the return to relaxation was palpable, the murmur of the crowd starting up again, breath being taken, the pedestrian to-and-fro commencing once more. Knowledge does play a part in controlling fear, although too much knowledge can exacerbate tension. It's best not to know how many moving parts are involved in lowering the landing gear, for example.

I was pleased to note that, according to the inspector's report, my new house in L.A. was not on a "known fault line." *That* was all to the good. Except for the earthquakes (and the plane that took off from a small airport and crashed into a low apartment building in Holly-wood, and the old man who ran over dozens of people, killing ten, in the Santa Monica Farmers' Market, and the wildfire season, which was *now*), every day in California was like every other day, sunny and warm, at least to the unschooled, and I was unschooled. I came here thinking that, beyond earthquakes, there were no problems in L.A. anymore—race riots having ended.

Something else I have in my garage: medium-weight jackets for the whole family, a wrench to turn off the gas, two two-gallon containers of water, that eternal powdered milk, a flashlight, batteries, half a bot-tle of Scotch. I've now become like my friend who was so deranged after September 11 that he became a virtual survivalist. But the major difference between me and him is this: most of my friends in Califor-nia have similar supplies. This is a state of the disaster-ready. Now that I too am prepared, I await my earthquake with something like interested, even eager, anticipation. In fact, I feel earthquakes more often than they happen.

Carey McWilliams, the great Southern California observer, might have diagnosed me as having earthquake syndrome: "How deeply the experience of living in an earthquake country," he writes, in *Southern California: An Island on the Land*,

> has impressed the residents of the region is clearly shown in the novels about Southern California. In many of these novels, one will find that the climax of the tale invariably is reached at precisely the moment when the dishes begin to rattle, the stove to bounce, and the chairs to dance. According to the novelist Lawrence Rising, there is a stillness and expectancy in Califor-nia "found only in earthquake countries."

I have been known to visit a site on the web that is called quake.usgs. gov in order to check on whether an earthquake has just occurred. "Last week, last day, last hour" are the categories; of course, you can also check by the whereabouts of the epicenter. (In my excitement at finding one near me, my hand must tremble, because a message will occasionally come up from the site: "Sorry, your mouse click did not fall inside an earthquake.")

You'd be surprised at how many quakes there are in the vicinity. Sometimes the little tremor I thought I felt *was* an earthquake. Then I consider myself very geo-sensitive and feel quite smug. But sometimes, more times, there was no little tremor, except in my head. One night at about two in the morning, there was what I considered a biggish quake: it woke me out of sleep with a bang, and I could feel the house moving. My family slept through it, and so did the dog. So much for the theory that animals give you a warning: there he was, snoring on the floor at the foot of our bed. I lay there thinking: Was that an earthquake? Or a dream? In the morning, there was evidence. The bathroom mirror had fallen. And a neighbor called to me from across the street: "How'd you like your first baby?" Well, I liked it fine. But I wanted the next one to be a little higher on the Richter scale. But not too high. I wanted the dog at least to awaken. I didn't tell my neighbor that, though.

I was having dinner a few days later with new friends in Silver Lake, an L.A. neighborhood on a hill near downtown. Natacha was going on about L.A. and how surprising it was that she had remained here. She's Swiss, but everyone here who is an expat talks like this, as if the place they left more than a decade earlier, or two decades earlier—especially if it was New York City, but even if it was some spot on the western border of Ohio—is still home. People here talk as if they are on extended leave or on assignment or on sabbatical from real life. They're all doing fieldwork.

"I must have been so in love with him that I didn't care how bad L.A. was," Natacha said. She was talking about Bob, the man who became her husband, who was in the other room.

"One night I came home. Bob was away, and it was raining and the lights had gone out and I couldn't find my flashlight. There was a mudslide down the hill and the kitchen was flooded, and when I finally found the flashlight, I saw that there were snakes just, you know, *slizzering* around on the kitchen floor, and I thought, My God! I've got to get out of this crazy place! There were dozens of small earthquakes at that time, and thunderstorms, even. But over time, you forget."

Natacha was clearly afflicted by a not very well-known but endemic local condition. It's called sclerophylly, and it's a botanical term. It's what happens to vegetation (over eons) in climates like L.A.'s, or around the Mediterranean. According to Mike Davis, a California writer and urban critic who likes to flirt, passionately, with catastrophe, botanical sclerophylly is "the development of small, tough, evergreen leaves . . . as a defense against drought." More technically, the *New Phytologist* of October 2003 defines some of the traits shown in a study of sclerophylly: "Of the structural properties, strength, toughness and flexural stiffness each made substantial independent contributions to the variation in sclerophylly indices, but the best individual explanators were flexural stiffness and strength."

Flexural stiffness—the ability to remain stiff yet yielding. Davis doesn't say so, but the humans who live here appear to share plant responses to certain kinds of privation, exposure, and suffering (flexural stiffness is also required by building codes in regions prone to earthquake). Sclerophylly turns you into a hardened survivor, like a Sicilian or a Marseillais—or an Angeleno or longtime L.A. transplant. You become a kind of resilient hybrid (or you go home). I think of all the sclerophyllic transplants in my personal garden: Bob, Natacha, Jake, Susie, Martine, Chuck, Marisa, Ken, Margie, Marla, Wesley, Michael, Jamie . . . and maybe someday, after long exposure, me. I haven't lived in this semiarid place long enough, yet. I remain a deciduous species, and when the seasons change, the leaves fall down.

Knowing all I now know, I still sometimes feel comforted here in the sun, under the palms. First of all, it's not the bleak New Jersey town where I was raised, an industrial backwater near the Jersey Turnpike, that dark, clotted artery of the East Coast. Even though California warns me at every turn about carcinogens and methane releases and earthquake bolting, at least the place doesn't look—as my town did back then—like detritus and debris in the gully of an abandoned railroad track. My town sometimes smelled bad; it smelled like sharp chemical releases (because it was under the plumes of many smokestacks), and there were weird sempiternal creaks, grindings, and groans that issued from the nearby factories. The bay near my house was brackish. Water rats lived there under the decaying docks, scuttling through oily foam and old beer bottles. Carcasses of horseshoe crabs slain by local boys lined the dirty bit of beach. You have to look hard to find this kind of thing in California.

The fogs were strange too. It was a Dickensian setting. In the old days, as you came into my town from the north on the Jersey railroad line, you passed over the city dump, a heaving mess of garbage and compacted wrecks, above which an unusually honest municipal official had erected a billboard that read "Welcome to Perth Amboy."

Second, the omens and signs here in L.A. have been propitious so far, and I pay some attention to omens and signs, having lived in Haiti in close contact with people who take such things pretty seriously. If the omens are good, the gods are feeling friendly. These have been among the positive signals: a rainbow over the Hollywood freeway during rush hour, timed to be viewed by millions, including me; a speckled kitten sneaking in my front door; my first name in the scramble of letters and numbers on a license plate ahead of me on the Pacific Coast Highway; and not least, lovely, cheering, recognizable Muzak playing over the sound system at the Grove, a nearby outdoor shopping mall: "We'll Meet Again," "Oh, Happy Day," "All You Need Is Love"—all wafting up mysteriously from the trees and planters, fountains and benches, and refuse bins. The way life should be.

I was trying to be optimistic, and my optimism was justified because there was a large measure of comfort in knowing that, no matter what, I would never have to get my boat out of its bucket.

There's a pale light in Los Angeles in the fall that takes over the sky in the evening, as if the city had been carefully lit by a professional who wanted to disguise its true face. You wouldn't expect that this hard city was capable of anything so subtle, so ethereal. After some time here you begin to value very dearly each thing that is sweet, every word that is kind, each gesture that is heartfelt. That tender light, almost lavender, floats like gossamer over the place, part smog, part atmosphere. It means the weather is changing, and you say, thank God. Not so many bloody sunny days. The cold is coming in. The seasonal change stuns the city into a kind of beauty at the end of the day: the light is benign and cosmetic, like candlelight; it smooths things over, like Botox. It blankets the place. On Sepulveda, on La Cienega, on La Brea, on Olympic, drivers open the window to feel the change. It's a little silky, a little chilly.

This is late October. My neighborhood, just south of Hollywood, is festooned with skeletons. In front of each house, harvests of pumpkins trail over stoops and pergolas, and down front paths flanked by red, badge-shaped security-firm signs that read Armed Response. (It can take the LAPD up to an hour to respond to an alarm or a call, so my neighbors rely now on a security firm that provides its own armed patrols.) I have a contract with the security firm, too, but since my house has more than seventeen first-floor doors, I can't afford to have everything secured. Those shields in the bushes, with their chin-quavering braggadocio, are my greatest protection against random attack. I can imagine how they would make hardened criminals roll their eyes.

And it's Halloween. Spiders the size of men, and bigger, keep watch over the neighborhood, too, their thick black webs cascading down over gleaming, well-kept eaves. A life-sized dummy with a chainsaw haunts one front yard; one roof is garlanded with infrared bulbs. I have stationed a plastic rat the size of a chimp at my front door in an enthusiastic if foolish attempt to get into the spirit. Movie people live in my neighborhood, and they like special effects.

When the temperature sinks below sixty-five, which sometimes it will do around Halloween, the occasional ancient, malodorous scent of the tar pits we're living over disappears.

I left New Jersey years ago, long before I came to California, and though its darkness still resonates in my heart, I'm from New York now—which of course is a long-standing joke in Los Angeles. I'm a recent New York transplant: in L.A., that's a stereotype. Most of the people I know here are from somewhere else (most of the people here are in general from somewhere else). The ones I know are mostly from New York. Like most transplanted species, they want a lot of care and attention to survive, even those who've developed sclerophylly. Other transplants ask me, "How do you like it?"

If I say I do, which I do say on good days, they are horrified, or shocked. They want everyone to acknowledge how hard the soil is here for their delicate sensibilities. They have the usual list of complaints, well known from the days when the pale, skinny, shrimpy, clever, bespectacled New Yorker Woody Allen came to L.A. and recoiled, almost electromagnetically repelled by all the halter-topped perfection and Frank Lloyd Wrightism (at best) around him. The pools are too blue. Larry David, another New York comic who came to L.A. (and who lives here now, which gives him a more intimate anthropological understanding of the place), has taken the Allen syndrome to new levels of sophistication and despair.

Here are some of the things New Yorkers famously love to despise about L.A.: cars, blondes, lawns and pools, cosmetic surgery, fashion, vapidity, cultural emptiness, sunshine. What they like: each other, money, "the industry." Also, they like cars, blondes, pools, and sunshine, it turns out. They also love what's considered "noir" here. They seek it out, and they say they can live here only because of this noir aspect; it's the guilt-ridden New York mind's natural reaction to sunshine. New Yorkers here search for what's dark: the insects clicking, scratching, and reproducing in among the grass of carefully tended lawns; the sordid acts taking place (one can only hope) behind spotless suburban façades; cockroaches going for a sidewalk stroll after nightfall, snails oozing across the driveway; witchy middle-aged and even elderly women morphed into blonde babes, disguising their true selves with waxy masks of grafts, tucks, and suctionings; and more generally, the corruption that grows everywhere here, and the stench of money, its octopuslike reach into every corner of the culture.

Expats like everything that tells them that all is not well behind the blank, pale sweetheart stare of Southern California. All of Nathanael West's L.A. work is suffused with this noir; he was from New York. Raymond Chandler virtually created L.A. noir; he was from Chicago. Favorite piece of L.A. noir: that the darkest Beach Boy, Dennis Wilson, knew Charlie Manson and bought one of his songs (with a wad of cash, not a check, not credit), which the band recorded on its *20/20* album. Manson's song was called—no great surprise here—"Cease to Exist." The Beach Boys kept many of the lyrics but renamed the song "Never Learn Not to Love." Manson, a true artist, it seems, never forgave them for not crediting him and for changing some of the words of the song. But even in the final whispery Beach Boy cut, the lyrics are creepy: "Cease to resist, come on say you love me / Give up your world, come on and be with me." When Dennis Wilson drowned while diving under a yacht at Marina del Rey in 1983, Charlie Manson was quoted as saying, with some satisfaction, "Dennis Wilson was killed by my shadow because he took my music and changed the words from my soul."

This is the kind of thing New Yorkers like to discover about L.A., along with the widely shared belief that Manson's real target was not the ingenue Sharon Tate but the record producer Terry Melcher (the only child of Doris Day). With his then girlfriend Candice Bergen, Melcher had been renting a house up on Cielo Drive in Benedict Canyon but was subletting it at the time to Tate, who was pregnant, and her husband, the director Roman Polanski.

Melcher met Manson through the Beach Boys and, after encouraging him, in the end rebuffed Manson's attempts to get a record contract. Since the murders, the Cielo Drive house has been demolished, rebuilt, and given a new street number. In L.A., Manson's 1969 murders—which cultural commentators like to say marked the end of the

1960s' "free love" era—are taken, probably more accurately, for the extreme act of a deranged entertainment-industry loser.

Manson is now seventy-one years old.

I remember very clearly a morning in late August 1965. It was summer vacation, and I was walking around the block on the Jersey shore. The sky was very blue and there was a light wind. I'd decided to go down toward the ocean, just to get out of the house so that I could listen to my transistor radio with the volume on as high as I wanted it. We were staying at my grandparents' house for the summer, and upstairs in her air-conditioned bedroom, my grandmother was playing Brahms on the violin. At the time, Brahms was not the toppermost of my poppermost. I was wearing shorts, a T-shirt, white anklets, and red PF Flyers. On Surf Lane, the broad leaves on the trees had begun to turn, a subtle browning and crisping at the edges. It was hot out; worms trying to make it across a span of sidewalk around the corner had been surprised by the morning sun and shriveled up midway in their tracks. I skipped to avoid them. Big cars with fins sped by on Ocean Avenue toward Asbury Park, where there hadn't been any riots yet, and which was not yet famous for providing a venue for Bruce Springsteen's band. Martin Luther King was still alive.

"California Girls" came on my radio.

It was number three on the WABC playlist, and was the first Beach Boys song I'd ever listened to with any attention. It was sprightly and cheerful, full of sunshine. More important, it seemed to be addressed to *me*, to girls. But its message was mysterious; like all men, the Beach Boys seemed to me to be talking in code. I was such a kid. Did they want all those girls to be *in* California? I wondered. The "Midwest farmer's daughters," the hip East Coast girls (the Beach Boys really dug the clothes they wore: could they mean shorts, a T-shirt, PF Flyers?), "the northern girls, with the way they kiss," the southern ones, "with the way they talk"? Or did they simply want those girls to be *like* California girls: tan, French-bikini-wearing, on the beach in Hawaii, "by a palm tree in the sand"? It seemed to me that I would never be like any of the girls in these categories, and yet I was—though plainly unhip, and absolutely unfashionable—obviously an East Coast girl . . .

I'd never thought about California before: this song was my introduction. But soon I would begin to notice things. Surfboards. Surfboards were a frequent spring and summer prop in fashion photographs in my *Seventeen* magazine, while fall and winter were represented by photographs of prep-school-style models in kneesocks and kilts fastened with big gold pins. There was volleyball on the beach, also—an unheard-of thing. I noticed too the big white teeth of Californians; for some reason big white teeth and California are forever associated in my mind. The Beach Boys' Wilson brothers, with their floppy hair and bland faces, were a part of this. An entire fashion gestalt came from California, I thought. Tans, and Breck shampoo—and thick, thick blond hair that could be tossed over a bronzed insouciant shoulder. The word "Hollywood" was another California thing that came under my consideration. To me it seemed to conjure up a forest, and Christmas, reds and deep greens, something festive yet full of shadows.

Before "California Girls," I'd been the type of serious young lady who dreamed of velvet party dresses, satin sashes, houses covered with moss, and saturnine, glowering heroes. I read English novels, and imagined being in love with dark characters like Mr. Rochester and Heathcliff. At age ten, I wore tortoiseshell glasses and had a headband. I was as far as a girl could get from being a Californian. I was more like a Londoner, but not one from the Swinging Sixties—no Rocker, certainly, and not even a Mod. I was a Victorian. I was from the Old World entirely.

But now, on this corner of Ocean Avenue and Deal Esplanade, my red-sneakered foot was tapping away and my head was filling up with Beach Boys. I loved them, even if the Beach Boys (although my compatriots) did seem more alien than the Beatles; I knew more about where the Beatles came from, but the geography and vernacular of the Beach Boys were new. They sounded clean and happy, a western version of the Beatles. I loved this song; I knew now that I wanted to be above all other things a California girl.

On that morning so long ago—bopping along Ocean Avenue with my silver Sony transistor—I could never have imagined that anything could tarnish the Beach Boys' shine. Drugs, death by drowning—any coloration other than the bright, the glistening, and the glowing had nothing to do with the Beach Boys or with California, that warm and happy wonderland. And how could I guess—indeed, how could the Beach Boys guess?—that in virtually no time at all wild girls from the Manson Family would be going home to Dennis's house on Sunset for some fun? The Manson girls were (by Beach Boy definition) California girls. That odd, unhappy assortment of *chicks* with their dissonant names—Linda Kasabian, Leslie Van Houten, Squeaky Fromme, Patricia Krenwinkel, among others—were not only living *in* California, but many of them were, indeed, *from* California, even if none was tanned or particularly bikini-wearing.

And finally I have achieved my dream. now I too am a California girl, loosely defined. Because now, against all odds, I've ended up in Los Angeles and I consider myself to be as much a California girl as any of the millions of other Californian women who were not born in the state. I am as Californian as Liz Taylor, elder stateswoman of Hollywood (born in London); or as Barbra Streisand, queen of the movie industry (born in Brooklyn); or as Nancy Reagan, former first lady of the United States and California, and chief dowager of Beverly Hills society (born in New York City); or as Maria Shriver, current first lady of California (born in Chicago).

If they can be California girls, why not me?

As mass murderer and king of noir (there's nothing darker in L.A. than killing a pregnant starlet), Manson was not particularly original or early in the annals of California. Edmund Wilson, the critic and man of letters, came to visit Los Angeles in the 1920s and, as he traveled in his train compartment, wrote that

a somewhat morbid state of mind had already been induced by
my following . . . the story of some gruesome murders which
had taken place in California: a homosexual boy had been prey-
ing on other boys who, one by one, had come to work for him
and his mother; when they were done with a boy, they mur-
dered him in order to prevent him from talking. They buried
him on their ranch.

Noir came early and naturally to this sunny place, even before West's
The Day of the Locust and the 1940s. Wilson himself mentions the
grisly murders just after writing about the loveliness of the state, or
"this country," as he calls California: "A silver-filamented stream—the
metallic dark green orange-orbed orange groves—the dry fragrance
from the warm eternal noon . . ."

It's brazen, and admirable, in a God-tormented sort of way, that a
place should have all that good healthy light ("the West Coast has the
sunshine . . .") and all those waving palm trees, deep green canyons, all
those blondes, that promise of Paradise, orange and lemon groves,
bumblebees, hummingbirds, high chaparral, horses, cypress, bougainvillea tumbling over walls and down the hillsides, and be, at the same
time, and nonchalantly, a geological cauldron, a cultural vacuum, and a
pit of sin, pollution, and deadly avarice. Not bad. All places where
humans live are pits of sin, of course, but not all of them look—or at
least, looked—like Eden.

Now noir is just another cliché about L.A. And yet almost seventy
years after *The Day of the Locust* was published, the dark heart is still
passionate and seductive.

If you visit Los Angeles, or even if you live here, the La Brea Tar Pits,
the real dark heart of Los Angeles, seem like a mere tourist attraction,
an entertaining stop along the way. Yet the whole history of the city
lies buried here, from the late Pleistocene era on. The tar pits are noir,
figuratively and literally. They are a wide, gaping, black graveyard, in
some places hidden and paved over, in others visible, and sticky. The

tar pits contain L.A.'s earliest resource, pitch (as in "pitch black"), which is really solidified petroleum, also called asphaltum, a thick layer of goo between the surface and L.A.'s later, deeper resource, oil.

I have a fascination with the tar pits because I live on top of them. That's what my dream house is: a clapboard construction built over a tarry ooze.

Surprisingly, the open pits—which are part of a larger geological phenomenon that is now almost entirely covered up and developed— are prominently located on Wilshire Boulevard next to the Los Angeles County Museum. You drive past Ralph's, Rite Aid, a Wells Fargo bank, Smart & Final, the IHOP, *Variety*'s offices, EMI, Baja Fresh, and Koo Koo Roo to get there. You drive beyond the Miracle Mile. You drive almost all the way to Flynt Publications, a large, dark, ovoid building that is the headquarters of Larry Flynt's pornography kingdom.

A few months after I came to California, I drove over to the tar pits. The pits on Wilshire are not far from my house—not far by Los Angeles standards, a ten- or fifteen-minute drive. My neighborhood and the tar pits were once all part of Rancho La Brea, a land parcel of 4,450 square acres right in the middle of what is now L.A. Until the late 1920s, most of the rancho was still undeveloped. Gaspar de Portolá, the Spanish governor of Baja California, crossed the Los Angeles River in 1769 and—according to information posted in the museum—"proceeded west along what is now Wilshire Boulevard" (that is, he was heading toward my neighborhood, on horseback), and came upon the pits.

"In the afternoon," wrote Juan Crespi, a priest who accompanied the expedition,

> we felt new earthquakes, the continuation of which astonishes us. We judge that in the mountains that run to the west in front of us there are some volcanoes, for there are many signs on the road. . . . The explorers saw some large marshes of a certain substance like pitch, they were boiling and bubbling . . . and there is such an abundance of it that it would serve to caulk many ships.

The Indians who lived in the area used the tar as an adhesive and for waterproofing.

A Portuguese sailor turned businessman, Antonio José Rocha, became Rancho La Brea's first owner, and in 1855, by which time California had been taken from Mexico by the United States, Rocha sold the ranch house to the county to be used as a courthouse, jail, and municipal office. By 1883, comporting nicely with Los Angeles's cultural history, the ranch house had become a realtor's office, with a moneylender conveniently on the premises and a booth where you could buy discount railway tickets if you needed to get out of town fast.

Female bones excavated from the bubbling asphalt in 1915 used to be mounted in the museum, alongside a life-sized dummy purporting to resemble the woman to whom the bones had once belonged. The exhibit was called La Brea Woman. La Brea means "the tar" in Spanish. La Brea Woman died about nine thousand years ago, probably from injuries inflicted with a blunt instrument: a piece of bone is missing from the top of her skull. (This flaw has been patched over, the poor old skull having been unearthed in the land of cosmetic enhancement.) La Brea Woman died with her dog by her side, scientists believe, pointing to canine bones found near her remains. La Brea Woman, another California girl, is nine thousand years old and has a hole in her head and a broken jaw, and I feel connected to her. That's how I feel at dinner parties on the west side of L.A., among the blond second wives and pontificating producers.

It was the 2003 fire season in Southern California. The weather was searingly hot, witheringly dry. It happens every year, and every half decade or so, the fires, fueled by heat wave, high winds, and dried-out foliage, come licking at the city's edges from all sides, as if L.A. were a final redoubt at the farthest reaches of an inferno. That fall, which was the fall of the recall vote, the Cedar Fire was rampaging through the San Diego area, and the Old Fire came hammering up the side of the San Bernardino Mountains, threatening a last line of defense on a road called Rim of the World. The Cedar Fire alone would eventually consume 273,246 acres, destroy 2,232 houses and 588 other buildings, and kill fourteen people. The Piru and Val Verde fires were hurtling into the Simi Valley. It felt as if the city were about to be consumed. Certainly we were under siege. Although it seemed to me like a holocaust descending, I noticed that the citizens of L.A. went on about their business utterly unperturbed. They were resistant.

At lunchtime I drank my soda and watched firefighters protecting another development. This town was called Crestline.

Already, scores of houses had been destroyed, and the fire was now lapping at the back of one of those pseudo-classic, portholewindowed, arched-doorwayed, cathedral-ceilinged, gable-roofed pink stucco homes that line the lushly treed cul-de-sacs in such highprice developments. The fire was lurking behind the swimming pool, peering through what remained of the landscaped foliage—now here, now there—like a curious, uninvited neighbor.

I'd been up to several threatened developments like this one in the past few days, firehunting. Up near Rancho Cucamonga (a "master-planned residential project," in the words of its developers), smoke came pouring out over the beautiful mountains where the highway turned, pouring out and down over the whole plain below, which was blanketed with well-heeled developments. The smoke seemed to follow in the path of the power lines that marched down the ridge to service all the new housing. It was otherworldly up there, near the fires. Huge fires were burning behind another development called Falcon Pointe at Hunter's Ridge, which advertised "spacious homes" up to 2,450 square feet, from the low $300,000s.

The streets at Falcon Pointe (what is there to say about that final, fanciful e?) have names like Manor Lane and Brunswick and Regina, as if we're suddenly inside some private joke about Britain; these are soap opera names, developers' marketing names. The logo for the Falcon Pointe development is a purplish mountain range in shadowy silhouette in front of a sunset sky, like a label on a California wine bottle, but what I saw up there behind the ridge was a fire cloud. On the way up toward Barstow, there were weird patches of blue clarity amid the tangle of orange and gray above the fires. Fifty-foot flames were crossing Laverne Avenue. There was a fire on Cherry.

"There was fire everywhere, even *under* my car," a woman from the Rancho Cucamonga development told me. She'd sent her husband out on one of their children's scooters—off through the flames—trying to get help.

I wondered if the pool would save the house in Crestline. You heard a lot in those weeks about families jumping into the pool as the fire rushed over their heads to devour the house. (You had to put your head under the water too.) The firefighters were pouring flame retardants on the giant walls of fire behind the Crestline house. They were standing next to the pool in their yellow outfits. Helicopters flew right through towering curtains of flame to dump chemicals from within the huge plumes of smoke and fire. Television reporters wore masks and ran back and forth, dodging the temperamental fires, leaping over walls and crouching behind cars as if this were a war. The sky in Crestline was an unlikely verdigris color, when it was not filled with orange flames or black soot, ash, and debris. An hour or two later, I looked at the television news to see if the house in Crestline had been saved. It had; at least, I think it had. There was a house that looked like it, and firefighters standing in front of it, saying the danger was past. But then, every house in Crestline looked like that house.

When I drove out to the Simi Valley, it was like landing on another planet. Ash and charred, denuded trees lined the highway. In the gated Portofino community at the top of the Porter Ranch development, the fire had been stopped only fifty feet before it would have consumed the houses.

"And these are million-dollar houses," a security guard outside the Portofino gate said, sweeping his arm indignantly at the street behind him, as if the fire had done it on purpose. Across from the gatehouse and the guard's rickety chair, the hill was scorched. Everything was carbonized. The hills near the highway I drove away on were blackened, and a lowering cloud appeared to be parked in the sky just a few thousand feet down the road, and getting bigger by the minute. Beyond this, the highway was closed, and that was okay. I had no desire to explore the farthest reaches. The sky was getting too dark. Fire trucks filed past the ordinary traffic in a caravan. I turned my car around.

There was no delicate autumnal light over here, only a murky sweat of ash and smoke and the carcinogenic airborne contaminants created when the materials used to build subdevelopments and other modern buildings are incinerated. I know about such contaminants because the state of California likes to draw its residents' attention to them and the harm they can cause. California doesn't necessarily want to *do* anything about those contaminants—it's not that kind of state— but it does want you to be *aware,* so that if *you'd* like to do something to protect yourself, you can.

In California, when you enter a garage (or what Californians more grandly call a "parking structure"), or a hotel, a museum, a movie theater, or even a restaurant, there is often a plaque, prominently displayed near the entrance. Because I come from the East—where such plaques can be relied upon to say things like "Upon this site formerly stood the Brennan Mansion in which resided from March 1844 to August 1845 Edgar Allan Poe and here during such residence he produced and gave to American literature and to immortality The Raven . . ."—I am always caught by surprise when, in California, the plaques say, "This area contains chemicals known to the state of California to cause cancer and birth defects or other reproductive harm." Thanks for the heads-up, state of California. You are warned but not protected: it's a libertarian, individualist approach to the citizen and his responsibilities.

The fires were progressing, carrying the choking fumes with them. Even in my neighborhood, which is at the center of the megalopolis and nowhere near the freeways that ran through the fire lands, the sweet violet light was turning green. It didn't feel hard to breathe, but a cough came over you after three or four inhales.

———

Then suddenly, the fires went out—with plenty of help from human intervention in the form of chemical drops and water from air tankers, and line after line of courageous firefighters. If you'd been watching the fires on a daily basis, and running after them, it did seem as if, because of some change in the weather or the atmosphere or the time of year, they'd simply come to an end, burned out. They had seemed to begin that way as well, but perhaps there was a reason for their suddenness: the authorities speculated that at least four of the most damaging ones had been "human-caused," as it is called in the firefighting vernacular. This means either accident or arson. But they were over now; the air was clearing, though a thin layer of ash remained over everything. You noticed it when you got into your car: it took a swipe or two of the windshield wipers to clear the view. A season had passed.

And another was upon us. In a spasm of inclement weather, six inches of unexpected and ephemeral hail fell down out of a tremendous black thundercloud onto parts of the city, including Watts—the site of some of the country's most violent race riots in 1965. With what must have been a janitorial broom or a snow shovel (though, on reflection, who would have a snow shovel in Southern California?), someone wrote "WATTS" in huge fat letters in the white ice, right across the macadam of a parking lot: an airplane passenger could read it, written in neat capital print bigger than a man. Did that mean there was pride in proclaiming it? My neighborhood near the tar pits is also not far from the inner city, if you can call the sunny sprawl of South Central an inner city, with the term's ghetto connotations—at least for those of us from the East Coast—of project high-rises and dark, narrow streets. In 1992, during a week of rioting there, my neighbors, standing on their lawns or looking out of their children's bedroom windows, could see the fires burning in South Central. Some fled at the sight; others bought guns. Dozens of houses in my neighborhood came on the market cheap.

This was when the security business began to boom; it was the era of armed response. Almost a decade after the riots, around a million residents of the state were living in gated communities, some behind barriers you could open with a click of a remote, some behind gates that were closed only at night, others in neighborhoods guarded by a manned gatehouse, where you needed a card or other identification to enter. California leads the nation in the creation of gated communities. One of my favorite examples is Irvine, a spread-out city south of L.A. that is filled with upscale developments and enormous public schools with rolling playing fields the size of stud farms. When I visited Irvine for one of my sons' baseball tournaments, I noticed that almost all the "communities" that together made up Irvine were gated—leading one to speculate about exactly whom they imagined they were excluding. Were they keeping out people from the other gated communities? Or was it just visitors to their ball fields whom they considered suspect? Were there criminals roaming the streets in cars, ready to prey on the ungated? In any case, all of Irvine's "Ranches" and "Crests" and "Ridges" and "Villages" seemed to face the quiet, broad suburban streets with unremitting walls.

The places touched by wildfires are also often gated or walled communities built at a physical remove intended to ensure security, but that actually places them at the mercy of seasonal fires. Yet rarely is this consideration a stumbling block for developers of hillside and canyon townlets, nor is it the subject of more than passing debate as firefighters mass each fall to protect those new-luxe houses.

"... Politicians and the media," writes Mike Davis,

> have allowed the essential land use issue—the rampant, uncontrolled proliferation of firebelt suburbs—to be camouflaged in a neutral discourse about natural hazards and public safety. But "safety" for ... luxury enclaves and gated hilltop suburbs is becoming one of the state's major social expenditures, although—unlike welfare or immigration—it is almost never debated in terms of trade-offs or alternatives. The $100 million cost of mobilizing 15,000 firefighters during Halloween week in 1993 may [become] an increasingly common entry in the public ledger. Needless to say, there is no comparable investment in the fire, toxic, or earthquake safety of inner-city communities.

———————

I'm on the 101, now, a few days after the hailstorm in Watts. The other name for the 101 is the Hollywood Freeway, until it crosses into the San Fernando Valley and becomes the Ventura Freeway. I'm always driving, a condition New Yorkers find alienating, while the rest of America just does it. I have only two reliable subjects of conversation in L.A.: weather and traffic. Traffic conversation includes both conditions (accidents, volume, rush hour, etc.) and directions: How did you get here? What freeway did you take? What exit? Are the "surface" roads faster than the 101?

On the 101 near Universal Studios, there's a billboard. I passed it almost every day once my children started going to school in North Hollywood. A giant man in sunglasses with scratches and blood on his face looks out impassively over the traffic, like the optometrist Dr. T. J. Eckleburg presiding over the wasteland of ashes in *The Great Gatsby*. It's just his three-story face; his sunglasses alone must be four feet high. In the background beside his chin, you can see a few robots and skulls as you inch by, but they are comparatively tiny and obscured by actual treetops.

The sign says "Buy *T3.*" This great big fellow on an enormous black background was to end up being our new governor. At the time, it seemed as if Arnold Schwarzenegger's candidacy in the recall vote was all part of a *Terminator* promotion package. Was this, you asked yourself, a campaign billboard? Schwarzenegger's DVD was about to be released when the billboard went up in the fall of 2003. If elected, he was to be sworn in six days post-release. In Baghdad, pictures of Saddam hung in every public place; in Thailand, the king's portrait appeared everywhere. In Haiti in the old days, hillsides and intersections were decorated with signs and billboards depicting the dour, bespectacled dictator, Dr. François Duvalier, and later, his wideheaded son and successor. But this was different, supposedly. It's an *ad*, stupid.

There was a long story behind the billboard and how it got there, and why it remained for so long (in the end, for more than two years, as the foliage grew up and around it, obscuring the jutting chin and making Schwarzenegger look somewhat rabbinical); it was a story that I would come upon later. For now, all I knew was that the candidate's face had replaced the *Jurassic Park* tyrannosaurus, which used to consider commuters as possible forage as it looked down with big teeth over our travails.

I had that feeling of being watched over by the Terminator too—though not as a prospective dinner. Being watched over, monitored—I think that was supposed to make us feel good. I was already beginning to like Schwarzenegger as a candidate, of course. I enjoyed him. He said "and all that kind of stuff" or "and all that kind of thing" when he meant "et cetera" (a perfectly good translation from the Latin) and he used the expression freely. He'd finish sentences about the biggest policy issues, for example, funding for needy children, or education, or immigration, with "and all that kind of stuff." All that kind of stuff—it's Hollywood big-picture talk: "Gimme the poster, gimme the trailer," they supposedly say to writers who are proposing movies. Detail subsumed to overview. That was Schwarzenegger—not a policy wonk.

"I care," he once said, "about families, about children, and all that kind of stuff." And he meant it.

Maybe he cared about me, too. I am *that kind of stuff.* I hoped so, anyhow, because I *needed* him. A man like that fed my rescue fantasies. Like the superheroes he played, he seemed above the fray (no fire dared to lick at the back of his house in Brentwood) but at the center of it too. He liked to present himself as shoving aside all ideology and storming through controversy as if it couldn't get its tiny, weak hand around his great big biceps. "I don't have any weak points," he said in *Pumping Iron*, the documentary that helped propel his ascent to superfame.

In moviemaking, there is a job called focus puller. The focus puller—or assistant director of photography—sees to all of the camera equipment and makes sure the shot is in focus for each scene or set of frames. He or she is an optics technician with an aesthetic edge. Commonly, the actor must remain within a constricted, laid-out space for each take, in order to keep the focus.

In the story of his life, Schwarzenegger was used to being in the focus puller's crosshairs. He also was, metaphorically, the focus puller himself—the committed professional who decided how to frame his narrative and where the star (himself) would figure in the picture. That's how Schwarzenegger organized things. He did not fade out of the picture; he did not bleed to the edge of the film. He wouldn't move outside the boundaries that kept his image clear. Politics was like bodybuilding and acting. The spotlight had to be on *you*. Even if he happened to be thousands of miles away, Schwarzenegger intended to be in the middle of the frame.

Schwarzenegger would be reliably present, not the kind of leader to disappear in a crisis; even if he really was not right there physically, you knew you'd be hearing from him immediately. He was not an executive who would be found trundling about on his bicycle in a park in D.C. while the Capitol building was being evacuated. He would not be reading a book about goats while the World Trade Center was under attack, because it wouldn't be good drama. Schwarzenegger was not a man to waste a scene that was set for him. On the television one evening during the worst of the fire season, I saw Schwarzenegger on a dais. He was in Washington, D.C., meeting with the vice president, and he looked perfect and shiny. "I am cutting short my trip to Washington," he said at the press conference, as if he were a dictator and a coup were under way at home. He was returning to save us.

Crisis was his element, he believed, because crisis demands not just a hero or a star but a focus puller to frame the narrative for the viewer, to let the viewer know what is the important element (Schwarzenegger), and which are the lesser elements (everything and everyone else). In Schwarzenegger's world, the way he had structured it for decades, he would always be the focus. That's why he left Washington for the fires, even though he was only the governor-elect and ended up touring the damage with Governor Davis; the fires exerted the pull of the focus. They were in the blocked-out spot where the cameras were watching. That's why the state of California voted for Schwarzenegger. He could be counted on . . . for something, although what it was was not immediately evident. To be there, where we could see him—that was one thing.

Could he save us? Did he want to? Did we want him to? That was another thing.

CHAPTER TWO

Stardom in Its Purest Form

I HAVE TO GET HOME SOON from my hike because a location scout is coming to my house. It's his second visit; his name is Ken or Scott—I can never remember the scouts' names. Ken or Scott works for a company that collects images of houses and other sites for film and commercial productions and posts them online. The one he's scouting for now is Bank One. An insurance company also liked the look of the house. They told Ken or Scott that the carved banister in one of the photos online was "evocative" for a robbery scene they were staging. "Yes, shoot it from there," says one guy working for the insurance commercial, who came to check out the banister in person.

He was standing in the pantry on discarded sheets of my children's homework, surrounded by his colleagues. "The doorway frames the stairs," he continued, "and you can see them creeping up toward the bedrooms . . ." His colleagues all look up, envisioning the scene, talking, theorizing, imagining: the robbers' ascent, what the robbers are wearing (maybe all black, and should there be balaclavas?), how the robbers come back down my front stairs, the white banister gleaming in the night shoot, what the robbers are carrying away.

I feel a surge of hope; this sounds possible, even likely. But the insurance company does not bite, and the talkers, theorizers, and imaginers never return. I've also had Toys "R" Us look around. They decided not to use us. I had some bug spray company. Also, they were not interested. The biggest client I didn't land was the movie *Cheaper by the Dozen*; they used a much bigger house a few blocks away. My neighborhood is popular with commercials and movies because it has inauthentic suburban houses of all kinds: colonials, Spanish, craftsman, Tudor, brick Edwardian, Victorian, and German country chalet among them.

All the architecture here is relatively inauthentic, in part because the area was settled by people from so many different places, each eager to abandon his past, and each alive with a sometimes peculiar fantasy of what California might turn him into. My house, for instance, is a classic American white clapboard, with green shutters and vines climbing up the front. (Unlike a house seven blocks away, which is white brick and has nineteen white reproductions of Michelangelo's *David* standing in the front garden behind a tall, white-painted, cast-iron fence.)

My house has interior moldings that another location scout is now telling me are too "upscale" for the house in *Elizabethtown*. The scouts say blunt things that wouldn't be considered acceptable in other settings, as if they were buyers visiting an empty house with a real-estate broker. The bookshelves we built in the dining room are a real minus: no one in America has bookshelves, and if they do, we've been told, they are certainly not in the dining room! And the palm tree out front—considered a plus by me—is the wrong kind of tree to have in front of a colonial classic. ("It reads wrong.") Better for stucco or mission.

One scout sent out a notice the other day; the first line read, "I need a bathroom!" They called later to ask if we had a bathroom "that wasn't white-tiled." The key, the notice said, "is that the showerhead is not mounted on a white wall, white tile or marble. . . . We've found a bathroom that we *love* [italics original] a few blocks away and are very interested in staying close by for the other bathrooms." The working title for the commercial was "Scrubbing Bubbles."

They pay you for using your house. Every year, payment for up to fourteen days of filming is tax free to any specific location; a neighbor of mine made $50,000 tax free when her house was used to film a television pilot. She and her family had to go live in a hotel, but that too was paid for by the production. If the shoot extends beyond four-teen days, the government may then tax you for the entire amount, not excluding the first fourteen days. I've learned, now, that you must therefore be careful not to let people use the house for too many low-paying, one-day shoots or real-estate company ads, or exteriors, because if someone should then come along who wants to do a long stint for a lot of money, it might turn out that you've wasted your tax-free days on chump change.

Now that I know more about locations and scouts, I always think I recognize people's houses in the movies. Watching *School of Rock*, I thought I saw my son's orthodontist's office, which looks out sweep-ingly over the Hollywood Hills. It breaks your willing suspension of disbelief to see something in the movies that looks as if it could be the orthodontist's and to know that it just might be.

The scouts also say odd things. One was "You won't mind if we're using ants. They will be in a controlled space in your kitchen and we will have a professional insect handler there at all times." Another was "This will be the farmhouse." Another: "We will have a three-year-old, coloring on the wall." Another: "He could just kick in the win-dow . . ." Sometimes they and their colleagues are wearing earrings and noserings, spiked hair and black boots, and visible brassieres; sometimes they look like anyone else in the neighborhood.

But all they need to do is say "I'm scouting locations for Fox," and you let them into your house to take pictures of your interiors and shoot the backyard and look at your alarm system and make friends with your Rottweiler or your Doberman or, in my case, your rather unassuming spaniel, in spite of all the stories about burglars pretend-ing to be gardeners. You should know better.

One reason you should: Schwarzenegger himself takes scamming very lightly, almost seeing it as a point of honor. By his own account, admittedly with an obvious touch of bravado and exaggeration, he claimed he once went from customer to customer in L.A. in the wake of an earthquake, doing questionable repairs on brick chimneys. On the *Tonight* show in the early 1980s, Schwarzenegger boasted that his partner would "[climb] up on the roof to check the chimney, and he is a very strong guy . . . [and] he pushed all the chimneys over so they fell down." According to Laurence Leamer's Schwarzenegger biography, *Fantastic,* Schwarzenegger told the story in his usual cheery, shameless way, pleased with the idea that he'd put one over.

"You go and push chimneys down," Johnny Carson, then the host of the *Tonight* show, said, "and then rebuild them . . ." And then he and Schwarzenegger laughed. The implication is always that a sucker is born every minute and Schwarzenegger is not one, although *you* may be, Carson may be. Schwarzenegger was good at providing something no one had needed until he arrived on the scene and made people need it (the mark of a true salesman). Now with the world seeming to fall apart quite well all on its own, his insouciant destructiveness seemed a little worrisome. Was this really the guy you wanted as your contractor? Sometimes it seemed as if he might be running for governor on a lark.

I'm returning from a hike in the Hollywood canyons. We walked up and down a dirt path that meanders through patches of wild mustard past electrical power towers, water tanks, and cellular phone transmitters that are almost hidden amid pines and sagebrush. Here and there along the way, the city appears below, through a space between ridges, far in the distance. Far below, on Highland Avenue south of Santa Monica, is the gigantic iPod billboard, the only advertising inflicted on hikers at this height, its content interpretable even from this distance. My neighborhood is down there too, a noticeable square of green grass and foliage in a sea of gray strip malls and macadam that is flanked by distant, Lego-like skyscrapers.

Since the fires, I haven't been able to look at chaparral and forests the way I used to. Once you've watched them burn, they no longer look like a refuge from civilization. Instead, they look like kindling. A sylvan retreat is next year's fiery blaze; forget the lake region with its pines or the lonesome appeal of brushy chaparral. I've finally understood why Southern California developments are virtually tree free; it's not, as I had assumed, because these people don't like trees obscuring their views of the neighboring houses, or of the nice cars parked along the winding development streets. It's not because they want to be able to show off their houses to their neighbors and the odd passerby. It's not even simply to allow the bulldozers and earthmovers and trucks easy access to construction sites. It's for protection. Since the Simi Valley and Rim of the World fires, Southern Californians have been ordered to clear all vegetation thirty to fifty feet back from their houses, and low brush two hundred feet back. Insurance might not cover you if your land is not cleared. By the fall of 2005, such clearings would save hundreds of homes from a similar conflagration.

I hope one day to be able to feel the seduction of the forest again; California has a tormented relationship with nature, and now I'm suffering from the syndrome. The woods are the soul of the state; the woods, the mountains, and the desert. In Mill Valley, in Marin County up north, I know a dog that takes its walk every day in a deep, dark redwood grove in the middle of town, as if it were a normal thing to do. The woods and the chaparral are symbolic of the state, and the seasonal burn-off is California's capricious personality at play. There is, the fires remind you, a danger in nature that no amount of human intervention can control. Nature will reassert itself, a reality that no amount of artificiality can mask. Tile-roofed, porticoed, couple-million-buck houses burn for the same reasons that dyed, enhanced, Botoxed, and siliconed actors do still eventually die. It's nature's course, and in the beginning, before the South Asian tsunami and the hurricane in New Orleans widened my frame of reference, I thought that nature was never so vigorously combated as it is here in Southern California, and rarely so ironically, inevitably, and utterly triumphant, nonetheless.

My hike takes an hour and a half, not including the drive to get to the hike. Along the way there is a special water fountain for dogs. Hikers with dogs are confronted by issues of leash control. It's early morning, after school drop-off for the carpooling parents. Women walk in groups of twos, threes, and fours, ponytails bouncing. Men come by at a run, listening to music. The mountain bikers are polite, and few. Those who walk alone are on the cell phone. Everyone is in good condition, very good-looking, put together. They are—many of them—of actor or actress caliber, although it must be admitted that La Brea Woman is breathing hard. You start out cold and end up hot.

I get home in time for my scout, who is bringing another round of people from the production over to look at my house. This is further than I've ever gotten into a project: a second visit. The commercial's designer is a man; the director and assistant are women. The assistant has rings through every angle of her nose, and more through her ears, but I've grown used to the look. She is wearing black garments and the kind of thick boots that this style demands. She's goth. She and her two friends seem unenthralled by the house. One goes outside to talk on his cell phone. Of course, that means nothing: one always goes outside to talk on his cell phone. They look the house up and down as if it were a potential but not too attractive conquest. On a second visit, I would like to see a little more enthusiasm. I want to tell them that I'm from New York and don't normally open up my house to strangers of any kind, no matter what they claim to be. They might at least be appreciative, complimentary, positive, even. They do act as if they like my dog, but that's because—although he looks inoffensive enough—they think, judging by the noise he makes, that he might otherwise eat them.

They never call back.

The first time I saw Warren Beatty in person was in Cambridge, Massachusetts. I was a junior in college. He was the guest of honor at the Hasty Pudding Show—an annual Harvard tradition—and I was sitting behind him in the audience. He was with Michelle Phillips, a member of the Mamas and the Papas, a San Francisco-sound band of the late 1960s. It was now the mid-1970s. What I remember best about Beatty is that while all the people in the room were craning their necks to get a look at him, he too was craning his neck in order to examine the people in the audience. He was about thirty-five years old then.

For a time after we moved to L.A., Beatty was a fixture in my life.

No matter where we went, he was there. He seemed like the unofficial mayor of Hollywood (though there are many who vie for that title), and a grand old man, except that he doesn't seem old, exactly. As I've gotten older, he's gotten younger. I think that we would have seemed to be around the same age when he was fifty and I was thirty-five. That's where we crossed each other on the aging ladder, and for every year I've ascended, he's descended one, so that now it's as if I'm fifty, and he's more or less thirty-five. He still has his boyish charm.

For the grand old men of Hollywood, politics seems to have replaced sex and work as a preoccupation; important, since it can be terrible to remain sex-obsessed here for too long, a path carved out by figures like O.J. Simpson, the actor Robert Blake (acquitted of murdering his wife), the record producer Phil Spector (accused of killing an aspiring actress). Work for the aging actor is likely to be more difficult to find than sex, though perhaps not as fraught with dangerous emotion.

Beatty was always talking about politics in his friendly, chatty way. (Joan Didion calls Hollywood political interest and involvement that "peculiar vacant fervor.") He liked to discuss the possibilities inherent in Schwarzenegger and the recall election. He enjoyed speculating about George Bush and who could beat him. Beatty had hosted this Democratic presidential candidate last weekend, he would tell you, and then he'd go on to talk about it at length. There was, as is common with movie stars, little concern about whether you were interested in what he was saying. Of *course* you were interested. He was *Warren Beatty*. Beatty would go on: He had spoken on the phone yesterday with that presidential candidate; right now, he said, he preferred this new guy. And how, he would like to know, did that other guy even think he could win one single state? The nationally syndicated newspaper columnist and political commentator Arianna Huffington, who is also an L.A. hostess, said that Schwarzenegger was living Beatty's dream: to run for high elective office—the *Bulworth* dream. (*Bulworth* was Beatty's 1998 movie about a liberal politician who makes a point of telling the truth in unconventional ways. It was written and directed by Beatty and starred him in the title role.)

Schwarzenegger was also living Rob Reiner's dream, which is the same as Beatty's dream. I once listened to Reiner, an actor and movie director and producer, gab about Medicare legislation, in enormous, overwhelming detail. Perhaps such policy wonkism—if not the office that such mastery of policy might lead to—is the fate of all Hollywood men no longer in their prime. It would be amusing, too, if while aging actors were in the process of becoming politicians, former politicians and political losers could equally easily turn their hands to acting. Clinton, say, could be cast as a leading man in a romantic comedy, perhaps in a role Steve Martin turns down; George McGovern could play a grandpa in an American heartland saga; Gary Hart would take a part playing an affable country doctor. Poor John Kerry would not be able to escape politics: he would be cast only as a statesman, because his patrician accent, sweeping jaw, and wavy, lustrous, grizzled hair are the stereotypes of the profession: he'd be a senator, a diplomat—perhaps a president. George W. Bush could get walk-ons as, say, an aging college jock or a junior exec or an eternal legal associate who plays bass guitar in the firm's band.

Schwarzenegger, though, is different from Beatty and Reiner in many ways. They think about politics within certain norms: they want to redirect the public discourse, or rethink education in California, or bring government more into line with a liberal agenda. None of this was on Schwarzenegger's mind when he decided to run for governor, not even a conservative version thereof. He was not traditional in any way. He wasn't interested in wonkism; the issues attract his intelligence, and he considers them as they arise, but he wasn't drawn to politics because he really wants to help people or change funding formulae. Schwarzenegger was drawn to politics as another stage on which he could perform and be watched, loved, worshipped. He's a pure narcissist—contentless, and in this way highly appropriate to his times. An uncontrollable element of egotism is characteristic of all who present themselves for very visible office, of course, but pure love of their own image is not usually the only element that propels them.

A narcissist is often someone who does not feel himself to exist unless others can be made palpably to experience his existence, and to express their experience and appreciation of that existence. This is why narcissists are so often drawn to performance. Could there be a better expression of people's experience and appreciation of Schwarzenegger's existence than success at the box office? Only success at the ballot box. The box office and ballot box are like a mirror held up to the mouth to watch for breath. The breath registers, and a cloud is seen for a moment on the clear glass before evanescing: he's alive. That moment of proof is the performer's raison d'être, and Schwarzenegger has always been a performer, even before he became a movie star.

Another thing that gives a narcissist a sense of his own importance is action. In action and movement of all kinds, he feels his own blood surge; he can see himself as he makes his way through time and space, affecting others. To remain at rest is frustrating and pointless.

Schwarzenegger is not a thinking person's politician, not naturally, in any case. A thinking person has to stretch a lot to support Schwarzenegger. Nor is he particularly appealing to the East Coast mind-set. Even though he is from the very Old World, the world east of Manhattan, Schwarzenegger is very much a California creation. A Californian I knew early in life once explained the difference between Californians and New Yorkers to me: "You people talk too much because the weather forces you to be inside all the time. You argue. Californians don't talk, we don't argue. We go running. We play volleyball. It's too nice out to sit around inside." She was laughing, but she was right.

"California has given me absolutely everything," Schwarzenegger said repeatedly during the recall. He had that intuitive understanding: California was the right state; he was the right candidate, no matter that he was a Republican and the state Democratic. Although it was a manipulative campaign mantra, it was true.

At the end of the recall campaign, after attending party after party populated by Schwarzenegger detractors, Stewart Resnick, a billionaire businessman who owned the Franklin Mint and huge tracts of California farmland, and who was a close friend of Huffington's, began to say—half jokingly, half not (and partly in irritation with the politically correct blah-blah-blahers around him)—that he was going to vote for Schwarzenegger. In Resnick's circle of complacent Hollywood liberals, it was a mini-*scandale.* No one knew if it was true. But if it was, everyone could understand. After all, when the recall vote was over, Resnick, with his agricultural interests in the Central Valley, would still be doing business with the state—and whoever was running it.

Nothing could be more ridiculous than Schwarzenegger as governor, I thought at the time: actually larger than life—or anyway broader and more bulked-up—Austrian, a bodybuilder, with an uproarious foreign accent and a body of work behind him as an alien and robot that doesn't seem, at least at first glance, particularly gubernatorial. He was fifty-six at the time he announced his candidacy, and aging out of the box office, but he still had something special. You will not find a Mario Cuomo or George Pataki soundboard on the Internet where you can hear those New York governors say "Fuck you," with various intonations. Nor will you find a Google image of them naked, whether flexing their muscles or not, as you can of Schwarzenegger, who has the distinction of being the first U.S. governor in history whose penis can be seen not just by an intimate, select few, but by anyone who has an Internet hookup.

On the other hand, Schwarzenegger reconsidered and reinterpreted might work. As I said, the thinking man has to stretch to support Schwarzenegger. The stretch: not so much a "bodybuilder" as someone who, like so many Californians, cares deeply about the physical self and works with commitment to improve it; a man perhaps not so much "narcissistic" as bent on self-improvement, a California tradition (narcissism and self-improvement often being purposely confused in Hollywood, sometimes in order to give moral standing to what would otherwise be labeled vanity); not "Austrian" but rather an immigrant, like approximately 25 percent of the state's residents; and not "an action hero" but a movie star, like three other major California politicians before him, Ronald Reagan and George Murphy (a Republican U.S. senator first elected in 1964) and Clint Eastwood, former mayor of Carmel, to say nothing of lesser lights like the late singer-songwriter Sonny Bono, once a U.S. congressman and also a mayor of Palm Springs. And of course, Schwarzenegger was a Republican but also a Kennedy in-law, which could soften him in the voter's eye. Finally, and most important, he was a self-invented figure, like so many Californians, both illustrious and previously unknown. He was outside history and beyond his own past.

As I watched Schwarzenegger laconically announce that he was running, on the Jay Leno show, I imagined what it would be like to have a movie star as governor, like Ronald Reagan, but only sort of like Reagan. Reagan's long but not very distinguished career as an actor was far behind him when he became governor, and he was never as amusing a personality, as original, or as much of an icon as Schwarzenegger. You could say, for example, that Schwarzenegger is genial, which is what people said about Reagan, but you could never say that that is his dominant characteristic.

Schwarzenegger was a celebrity candidate. Just as a performer no longer has to be any good at singing to be a successful singer or good at acting to be an actor, so a political figure no longer has to be good at politics, or really have any idea what he's doing, to become a politician. For celebrities, values are inverted. As California Assemblyman Lloyd Levine, a Democrat who represents the San Fernando Valley, says, "You never say to a person, 'Okay, *skip* medical school, oh, and here's your scalpel. Get to work!'"

As the recall campaign progressed, the political moment became more and more confused, politics and celebrity melding with fluid ease. During his campaign for governor, the focus puller would emerge from his black SUV in his crisp white button-down shirt, open at the neck, and the crowd—the very large crowd—would scream and shout as if he were the Beatles; they'd try to hustle past Schwarzenegger's bodyguards to get his autograph. It was a weird upending. In the days before there were such international celebrities, crowds came out to cheer the king, the queen, the tsar, the president, the prime minister, the reichschancellor, or the führer. The ruler was the celebrity who caused emotion among the people: his picture kissed, his children beloved, etc. Now people wait like that, cheer like that, for film stars, athletes, rock stars. All through the recall campaign, headlines were based on Schwarzenegger movie titles like *Total Recall, The Terminator,* and *Predator,* as well as on famous lines like *"Hasta la vista,* baby" and "I'll be back." Arnold was bringing the two images together, that of the performing celebrity and of the leader. In the minds of the average California voter, the recall campaign, whatever it was about on a deep psychological or cultural level, was only tangentially about politics and governance, that was clear.

In the heat of the recall race, I asked Huffington—who was running for governor herself and at the very beginning of her own breathless, headlong recall campaign—what she thought it all meant.

"Oh!" she said. "You know, darling, I just saw this marvelous man, this shrink, he's a friend of mine's shrink, actually, and really has thought about it all. He's very smart, although a tiny bit deaf, you see. He made it all clear to me, really. It was such a relief. He explained everything—you know I was in such a muddle. But he told me why we are doing this, why it is so important. Go see him."

So I climbed the staircase that runs up the side of Dr. Leo Rangell's house—next to the treetop canopy of his junglelike front garden—to his aerie of an office. Inside Rangell's office are bamboo blinds and a 1950s-style décor that feels like a twiggy nest. Up here you feel as if you're floating in green. Rangell looks like a bird too, beaky and intelligent.

Unsurprisingly, it turns out that Rangell is a "shrink to the stars." Many people in Huffington's life do what they do "to the stars": hair colorist to the stars, valet parker to the stars, manicurist to the stars, internist to the stars (this one is a white man who wears white Hare Krishna wraps and a turban and comes to book parties), pediatrician to the stars, math tutor to the stars, and there are also gastroenterologists to the stars, herbal healers to the stars, acupuncturists to the stars, interior decorators to the stars, landscapers to the stars, handymen to the stars, caterers to the stars, mechanics to the stars.

Rangell is also a thinker, however. He's written books, which makes him a respected exotic in L.A. society—a genius, I have heard him called, but then that is a term frequently bandied about here. He calls Huffington "oh, yes, that woman, my neighbor," though of course he knows exactly who she is—not simply some neighbor lady. His face is unreadable, behind his glasses. Like any good psychiatrist, he keeps it remarkably straight.

"I'm not sure what she's doing in this election," he said, "but, well . . ." He sat back in his chair and gazed at me appraisingly over the top of his spectacles. Dr. Rangell's office has a couch and a chair, but also a wall of books, as if it were in Manhattan. In L.A., I miss books. When I see them in other people's houses, I feel as if they are beloved but long-lost relations, calling out to me from their shelves.

Rangell was thinking about what he likes to call "mass psychology." He lives and works two blocks from Huffington's house in Brentwood, so as he is quick to point out, the masses he analyzes are something he speculates about from a distance, a people whose emotions and cultural life he gathers from what he sees on the television, not during the normal course of his daily life. His mass psychology is mediated.

Naturally, as a psychiatrist of a certain age, Rangell tends to define the political situation in terms of masculinity. September 11, he said, was a profoundly "unmanning" experience for America. Americans' new, unaccustomed feelings of insecurity in the world quite naturally led them to a desire for a Terminator figure, and also to a revulsion against namby-pamby impotence as embodied by Governor Davis. (Davis was nicknamed "Gumby"—after the absolutely bendable, asexual 1960s toy—by the energetic, right-wing hosts of Southern California's most popular drive-time AM talk-radio show, John Kobylt and Ken Chiampou, more familiarly known as John and Ken.)

Roles in the "world family," Rangell said, were being recast. Is America still the dad? We want to be. The Terminator is an immensely comforting figure. If he's in charge of the house, we can sleep well at night. A man with muscle, an Atlas to carry the troubles of our world, who brooks no back talk from underlings. This was beginning to resonate with me as I sat on the patients' couch, feeling that this was where I belonged, with my inner backdrop of death, mayhem, and fiery destruction. A Terminator to take care of us all.

And as I thought about it, I *had* noticed that Schwarzenegger in reality *was* robotic. After a campaign event, he sometimes did a semi-formal press conference. But when he turned to look at a questioner, his entire head swiveled on his neck in a mechanical way, as if his eyes were stuck flat in their sockets and he could not shift his gaze. His face was strangely inexpressive, his smile oddly forced, mechanical, though nice to look at. My Hollywood friends said that all this was the result of steroids and plastic surgery and Botox. But I liked to think that Schwarzenegger really was the Terminator; he was bionic.

After talking to my new doctor, I realized that what was missing from my life in California was not books or rain or subways, all of which I'd left behind on the East Coast, but a Terminator: someone who—had we still been in New York—could have lifted up my inflatable boat in one hand like a feather above the heads of the crowd and brought it down to the river and dealt with it; someone who could inflate it with one hand while, with the other, fighting off the maddened marauders who would try to boatjack it. I needed a Terminator to carry us all to safety.

So after I left Dr. Rangell, I went right over to the Grove shopping mall and bought myself one at FAO Schwarz for thirty-six dollars. My Terminator is fifteen inches tall. He's precisely modeled on Arnold Schwarzenegger in the role, and he's dressed all in black. He has two detachable automatic weapons. ("Shotgun fits in left hand.") He's wearing sunglasses and leather and is standing in a rock-strewn, urban mini-landscape. He looks more like an SS advance guard in civilian clothes than a sci-fi figure, but he looks strong, capable of anything. Is he friendly or dangerous? Disturbingly, when I press a button on the back of the shattered wall behind him, my Terminator says, among other things, "I am unable to comply."

Why does he say that? It sounds more like a Herman Melville line, like Bartleby's "I would prefer not to," than it does something the tough-talking Terminator would say.

I suppose it's the Terminator's ultimate confession. Not every rescue goes off exactly as planned (the war in Iraq comes to mind) and not every rescuer is what you imagined he would be. "I am unable to comply." It's a funny, unsettling thing for my Terminator to say. Still, a step up from "fuck you."

Although his screen image is laughably easy to define, the real Arnold Schwarzenegger is a protean character, and harder to pin down. He's brilliant at structuring a deal in order to reap maximum benefit, but his genius is in marketing, and he has proven himself an adept salesman of the sport of bodybuilding, of Lifecycle stationary bicycles, of Hummers, of his restaurant in Santa Monica, of his movies, and—at the center of all these sales—of himself, his favorite product.

The character of the salesman in America is a familiar one, and hucksterism is a part of it, as is false sincerity, false modesty, and outright, downright lying. At various stages in his career, Schwarzenegger has practiced all of these methods, and his career has been much more visible, more public, than those of most actors—and more scrutinized, in part because he has gone from strength to strength in unexpected ways: as a bodybuilder, as an action actor, as a comic actor, as a politician.

In any community, when you switch your specialty so frequently, you become suspect. Hollywood is different, though, and in Hollywood, people were generally tolerant of Schwarzenegger and his moral foibles, his so-called high jinks, his bad-boy behavior. His success—and therefore his power—protected him from a lot of open nastiness. Nice things were said of him in Hollywood: He was a decent father and seemingly a plausible husband, of a certain kind; he was a good host who was a lot of fun, according to friends, if "a little vulgar," as one woman who knew and liked him delicately put it. He was smart, he was curious, and he was self-schooled.

The less nice stories about him were so numerous and so repetitive that no one in the movie business whom I talked to, friend or foe, had ever bothered denying them. In one story that was like many of the others, he was in his trailer, waiting to do an interview, sitting in an easy chair, smoking a cigar; two people entered unannounced; he looked up from the girl who was busy in his lap and said to them, "Don't tell Maria." But he didn't bother stopping the girl. The visitors scurried away.

This story was first told to me by a friend whose work is tied to the entertainment industry; when she told it to me, the story had two women interrupting Schwarzenegger in this compromising position. It sounded mildly plausible; later, when I came to write this book, I checked the story with her. I wanted to talk to those women, didn't like to tell a story secondhand. It turned out, upon closer recollection, that my friend had heard the story from her husband. It turned out, when I contacted him, that he had heard it from a third party, a writer. That writer, in turn, said *he* had heard it from a boom operator on one of Schwarzenegger's movies. The story was moving into that attenuated region called rumor, or even myth. Upon closer cross-examination, inspired by my questioning, the boom operator told the writer that he "didn't witness the actual event himself but may have heard it from someone who blah, blah, blah . . . ," as the writer put it. While I was finishing writing this very section of this very book, I found in Laurence Leamer's just-published Schwarzenegger biography a reference to a 1992 *Spy* magazine article that was one of the first places where sexual rumors about Schwarzenegger appeared. Here is the section of the unsigned *Spy* piece, as cited in *Fantastic*:

> There's the journalist who mirthfully tells of the star's back lot misdeeds—how he surprised Arnold *in flagrante delicto* during the filming of one of his blockbusters, and how Arnold said, "Ve von't tell Maria about dis"—but who will never commit the story to print.

The resemblance of this story—which was published almost fifteen years ago in a magazine my friend certainly had read—to the one that she'd told me was striking, to say the least. But I believe she spoke to me in absolute innocence of the *Spy* story. She didn't at all remember the article's existence; by now, this was just a story she happened to know about Schwarzenegger. It had become part of what was true about him. There were enough of these stories circulating in Hollywood and beyond, however, to reach a critical mass at which the average human says there must be some underlying truth. Broadly based rumors about someone, from a variety of sources, with many permutations, all on the same theme, generally (though perhaps not always) have some bearing on that person's conduct.

And so when the *L.A. Times* embarked on its painstaking Schwarzenegger "groping" investigation, its editors had plenty of reason to expect that they would find some people involved who'd be willing to speak on the record, and they did. The stories-as-rumor were based on stories from fact, but they were conflated and de- and reconstructed and had become a part of Schwarzenegger's local legend. The meticulously documented *L.A. Times* series was not about legend but about fact, which made the stories news, also.

The story about the trailer and the "blo-job"—as *Spy* said Schwarzenegger called this act—didn't circulate during the recall campaign. That girl, or whatever girl she was based on, did not come forward to talk to the *L.A. Times*. Possibly she was perfectly happy to be attending to Schwarzenegger. Possibly she's a Hollywood myth created to explain "Arnold." In any case, at the end of the campaign, many girls (former girls, now women) did emerge to tell their Arnold stories. For the record: they said, among other things, that he'd felt up one under her skirt; that he'd taken coerced photos of another's breasts; that he'd pushed a woman up against the back of an elevator. In every instance, he had used his unspoken but very real power to put pressure on women in one way or another, usually through public sexual humiliation. Often, the humiliation of a man associated with the woman in question was also a goal. The stories made him sound puerile, bullying.

But his supporters didn't see it that way, interestingly. People like John and Ken portrayed his aggression as "rowdy behavior on the set," the line put out by Schwarzenegger's campaign. Gumby's detractors felt it was all about masculinity, about a certain kind of

humiliating supermasculinity—even though the global image of the
California male is pretty metrosexual, like Jerry Brown, Steve Jobs, or
Jackson Browne, the rock singer from the 1970s. As Susan Faludi
wrote in the aftermath of the recall, "At a time of deep economic and
international insecurity, the easy power of the bully boy is a siren call
to the American male populace."

Schwarzenegger survived the groping charges, which were published by the *L.A. Times* in a series that came out on the very eve of
the vote. John and Ken, and talk radio in general, helped him get
through this moment by attacking his accusers, notably the *L.A.
Times,* as wimpy, left-wing, useless dishrags with an electoral agenda.
It wasn't that people didn't believe that Schwarzenegger had done
what the women in question charged him with. It was simply that
many people didn't see anything wrong with behavior in which
women were debased and the man remained above it all, laughing. In
addition, the big *L.A. Times* story was portrayed as a conspiracy to
attack Schwarzenegger's character in the week before the election,
when he would have little time to rebut. The candidate and later governor was a frequent guest on the John and Ken show, and once I
heard him tell John (or was it Ken?) how handsome he was.

"You missed a great career in the movies," Schwarzenegger told
him.

Schwarzenegger's public past, which was at least as raunchy as the
private stories that emerged during the recall campaign, also failed to
hurt his candidacy. Everything overweening, cocky, and unfeeling
about him seemed to add to his allure. He was a movie star: that's how
they *are.* Yet such stories, many of them told by Schwarzenegger himself to reporters in the proud, unashamed old days before politics was an
option, seemed to swirl only around Schwarzenegger and not, say, Warren Beatty, who, although a fabled Hollywood rake and a ladies' man,
was also reputed to like, even to love, women. Beatty had had more or
less serial relationships, not always of a very long duration (to put it
mildly), but still. Schwarzenegger remained untouched. His marriage
also protected Schwarzenegger from the kind of reputation Beatty had

before *he* married; for a long time, the Schwarzenegger-Shriver marriage—with its ongoing glamour and publicity—had diverted interest away from his past and hidden it from the public at large.

Schwarzenegger is exciting to watch, in spite of the rumors and stories, or because of them. His character helps to explain, to a large degree, his success and fame. He has complete confidence; he never seems worried, troubled, concerned. He's never timid, shy, or uncertain. Watching him, it's impossible to imagine that he's ever experienced a moment of self-doubt or, indeed, doubt of any kind. He believes in what he believes in, wholeheartedly: himself. And he cannot be embarrassed, because embarrassment only exists for those who have a layered sense of themselves. These character traits provide excellent equipment for Schwarzenegger as a politician, because politicians often end up doing things that are embarrassing, ridiculous, or completely inconsistent—and it is supposed to boost your popularity if you show no remorse or doubt when you're doing such things in public.

Schwarzenegger married into the right family. He behaves like a Kennedy, with that air of ownership, entitlement, and control that one assumes must be, for him, learned behavior, since he was a mere village boy to start with—unlike Maria Shriver, who was born into wealth and power. But there is something natural about his sense of self-worth too. Schwarzenegger always assumes he is the center of attention. It's not only because he is arguably the most recognizable man in the world, but also because he reflexively believes that people must be looking at him. In his own mind, he's the most interesting thing around. And he's right. He has natural narcissistic magnetism. Famous people get looked at, but Schwarzenegger is not just famous. Long before he became an icon (and he is one celebrity who deserves the word), he was a figure of fascination within his own circle. More than anything, he reminds me of Hercules, who killed snakes in his crib, and who had to be taught and taught again to have a conscience, to have second thoughts about the uses of his own power.

In every way, Schwarzenegger is remarkable. He has little physical grace and is not typically good-looking. He's a foreigner, notice-
ably so, never really having wanted to overcome the asset of his
accent. He's sort of an athlete, but not the kind we typically admire.
He has turned to his advantage all these negative or alien attributes
during a lifelong effort to mold himself into an icon or, more accurately, a product. Not only a product of his own imagination, but a
product, *tout court.* Something made, that can be sold.

It was a study in American moral duplicity to watch Schwarzenegger's past collide with his present during the campaign. There was
one standard of comportment for the entertainment industry, which
demanded outrageous behavior to feed publicists and tabloids and to
generate interest in imminent movie releases, and another standard
for politicians, which ruled such behavior taboo. Schwarzenegger was
caught flagrantly between the two; what was happening to him
couldn't have been more obvious. If you were even a slightly decent,
slightly humane person, you couldn't help feeling a little bad for him,
in spite of himself, and yourself. The standards of both his worlds
seemed so extreme, and so stupid.

For example, *Party in Rio*, a video with Arnold that was released in
1986 by the adult Elite Entertainment company, and re-released by
Playboy Video in 1992. In *Party*, Schwarzenegger plays a tour guide,
taking the viewers on a ribald, bawdy ride through Carnival. On the
video case, the copy reads, "Step into the heat of the action with star
Arnold Schwarzenegger as he parties nonstop. . . . Follow him to the
wildest, no-holds-barred parties in town." As reported by Chris
McGowan on CulturePlanet.com,

> Early in the program, Arnold visits the long established music-
> and-dance revue "Oba-Oba" . . . with sexy female dancers in
> revealing outfits. Arnold sits in the front row, ogling the women
> and making inane comments to a mortified Brazilian model act-
> ing as his "date." He learns the word "bunda" ["ass" in African-

ized Brazilian Portuguese] and goes on to say "I can understand why Brazil is devoted to my favorite body part: the ass." He is invited onstage and soon grabs the buttocks of the nearest showgirl and pulls her close. . . . At the end of the program, Arnold says to a woman, "I learned one word yesterday—*bunda*—that's good, huh?"

Well, the video was shot in Rio, after all, not in straitlaced Sacramento. Then there was Arnold's infamous *Oui* magazine interview of 1977—all this from a man who was now a candidate for one of the most important jobs in the United States, and therefore running as a person of "solid" family values, whatever that is supposed to mean. Here is one of the many outlandish things he told *Oui*—this about his early days at Gold's Gym in Venice Beach, California:

> *Schwarzenegger:* Bodybuilders party a lot, and once . . . there was a black girl who came out naked. Everybody jumped on her and took her upstairs, where we all got together.
>
> *Oui:* A gang bang?
>
> *Schwarzenegger:* Yes, but not everybody, just the guys who can fuck in front of other guys. Not everybody can do that. Some think they don't have a big enough cock, so they can't get a hard-on.

The most revealing part of this exchange is that wonderful moment when Schwarzenegger replies, "Yes, but . . ." to the question about whether the upstairs interlude was indeed a gang bang. At that moment, one thinks he is about to offer a justification for the gang bang, or a quibble about that characterization (*yes, but* she was into it; *yes, but* a gang bang would mean it was against her will, and it wasn't; *yes, but* we all knew her, we did this every Saturday, that's why she was there; *yes, but* I was not a part of it . . . *anything*), but instead he goes on to clarify how big the gang bang was, and to insist that only men who were qualified, who were man enough, could participate in it. Again, it's all about the men: the bangee has nothing to do with the conversation. The gang had to be able to bang. Of course, all the blather about size and ability is simply a way for Schwarzenegger to get into the dimensions of his own gear.

Three months before he became a candidate, Schwarzenegger continued to paint himself, happily, as an unregenerate misogynist. In *Entertainment Weekly*, he commented on a scene in *Terminator 3* where he battles the Terminatrix, an evil female counterpart. The battle begins in a bathroom.

> "As we were rehearsing, I saw this toilet bowl," says Schwarzenegger, an impish smile crossing his face. "How many times do you get away with this—to take a woman, grab her upside down, and bury her face in a toilet bowl? I wanted to have something floating in there," he adds. Apparently he was vetoed. "They thought it was my typical 'Schwarzenegger overboard,'" he says. "The thing is, you can do it, because in the end, I didn't do it to a woman—she's a machine! . . . We could get away with it without being crucified by who-knows-what group."

A friend of mine worked on the *Predator* set with Schwarzenegger in Puerta Vallarta, Mexico. One night, in the weeks before his wedding to Maria Shriver, the cast and crew had a bachelor party for him there, in a conference room amid Formica tables. The lights were low.

> Arnold was sitting at a table, smoking a cigar, surrounded as he always was and is by a group of his buddies, all big, rowdy men. On a little platform at the back of the room, a chubby older local woman was doing a strip-tease in ripped brassiere, panties, and ripped hose. It was very depressing, but Arnold didn't find it depressing. There were hoots and shouts, catcalls from him, and this woman was just trying to make a buck, probably had a big family. . . . She really looked distressed.

Schwarzenegger's candidacy survived all such stories; with the huge *L.A. Times* article—and the further allegations it engendered—

behind him, he had passed through his dead point and was soundly elected.

Up until the end of the campaign—when the groping allegations finally emerged into the mainstream—most of the arguments against Schwarzenegger were not about him, but were instead dry discussions about the sanctity of representative democracy and elections, and about the possible misuses of the recall mechanism.

Hardly anyone among Governor Davis's active backers supported Davis because they *liked* him or were enthusiastic about him as a politician; not many thought he was a particularly good governor, though equally, not many thought he was very bad, or even bad at all. Simply put, he *was* the governor, duly elected, and then duly reelected. For traditional Democrats and independents, the recall was like a formalized coup d'état. Democrats especially felt this, since Davis was a Democrat, a party regular who had been Governor Jerry Brown's chief of staff from 1975 to 1981. The recall also did not bode well for the future of American politics, they argued, implying as it did that elections were in some real sense provisional and that a celebrity of a high-enough caliber could trump any politician, if enough money and manpower were brought to bear on behalf of the challenger.

Two American academics had a theory about the recall. They did not think it was about the larger political issues, nor did they think it was about character issues, or about experience, or ideology. They thought it was all about "Arnold."

Not Arnold, but "Arnold."

Louise Krasniewicz, a UCLA anthropologist, and her coauthor Michael Blitz have been studying Schwarzenegger for more than twenty years, pretty much exclusively. After the recall, they published a book called *Why Arnold Matters*. In it, they explain what they think of as the Schwarzenegger phenomenon; they seem to believe that as a celebrity, he is unique. What follows is from an essay by the same name that Krasniewicz and Blitz wrote in July 2003 (the italics are mine):

Arnold's ability to insinuate himself into any discourse or any
metamorphic moment or any narrative thread is a remarkable
feature of his stardom. . . . Arnold Schwarzenegger is the name
we give to a collection of ideas which has spread in our culture
over the last 30 years.

The viral complex called Arnold Schwarzenegger is not just
referring to the actual person but to the entire collection of
ideas, images, actions, stories, metaphors, jokes, rumors, films,
websites, fan activities, magazine covers, *dreams*, weight-
training equipment, food supplements, t-shirts, interviews,
photographs, memorabilia, film posters, newspaper articles,
etc. that *spread Arnold Schwarzenegger*. Arnold's life, more
than any example we can think of, represents the trajectory of
an idea that spreads not because it is good or valuable or true,
but because a place is available for it in the culture at a particular point in time and because it can find new niches and hiding
places as it develops.

Schwarzenegger, Blitz and Krasniewicz claim, is what the two
Schwarzeneggerologists call "an idea virus." In spite of appearances,
much that is valuable is hidden behind their academic jargon—for instance, the idea that the Schwarzenegger life has no moral or intellectual content and represents nothing that is "good or valuable or true"
and thus cannot be compared to the Nelson Mandela life or the Ma-
hatma Gandhi life, to take two examples of other world-famous politicians. But there's a lot that's laughable, too, not least the insertion of
the word "dreams" inside that long list of fairly material, objectively
observable items: "magazine covers, dreams, weight-training equipment . . ." Also, the concept of "spreading" Arnold Schwarzenegger is a
difficult one to wrap the mind around. But the two professors go on, in
spite of their virtually French structuralist posturing, to make another
important point, and in a way to rescind their first argument:

Like other forms of shared cultural activities—myths, rituals,
symbols—idea viruses that are pervasive provide excellent

entry points into the structure as well as the fluid features of a culture. To look at Arnold Schwarzenegger is to understand what this culture has accepted right now as good and right and true. . . . Both the name and the idea [have] been used as an adjective, a metaphor, an adverb, and a simile for those trying to talk about things big, expensive, powerful, violent, tough, and successful. . . . What [the Schwarzenegger virus] points to is a model of behavior that values persistence, force, self-determination, physical strength, power, positive action, uniqueness, and destruction.

In another essay, called "The Replicator," Krasniewicz and Blitz assert that Arnold Schwarzenegger is what linguists, and some other academics, call a *meme,* a term they derive from the Greek *mimesis* and define as a basic unit of culture that is "transmitted by imitation and shared in the form of cultural identity." He is, they say, a "memorable unit."

One of the charming things about Krasniewicz and Blitz is that they are so blithely bogus: they use the contorted language of structuralism, literary criticism, and academic anthropology—enlivened by crude technobabble and by vulgar pop-psychoanalytic methods—to make what are essentially obvious arguments. One way they "prove" their point about the ubiquity of the Schwarzenegger meme—in a section of "The Replicator" entitled "Memes and Dreams"—is by relating their own dreams that feature Arnold, 154 of them, hence the strange inclusion of the word "dreams" in that earlier laundry list.

"We were studying Schwarzenegger and his films in the early 1990s when we began having a series of dreams about him and our research," they write. "Despite our awareness of Schwarzenegger's amazing reach into all aspects of the culture, we were nevertheless shocked when he began to appear in our dreams." (As, no doubt, Schwarzenegger would be if Krasniewicz and Blitz appeared in *his.*) The two professors then go on to document a few pages of their "dream collection." A few choice items:

Michael's Dream (February 5, 1993): Louise had found in a novelty shop a 78 rpm record of Arnold singing Elvis songs. One side was "Love Me Tender" and the other side was "Jailhouse Rock," which, she told me, when played backwards, was also the "preamble" to *Mein Kampf.*

Louise's Dream (June 3, 1996): . . . We are all younger. Arnold greets me like we know each other. Then we are backstage being interviewed by a sports reporter. She is a novice and nervous. She sucks a whole plastic water bottle into her mouth. I make her pull it out. We go view a re-enactment of a campus murder rampage. A man with a gun walks around and shoots people point blank. He goes up to one kid and shoots down his pants. The sports reporter asks us our theory about how this could happen. We say fear freezes people. Then the baby Arnold is holding has diarrhea and I change the diaper. Arnold is impressed.

Der Gropenführer, easily impressed. The Governator, the Terminator, the Predator, the Replicator . . . Although like Krasniewicz and Blitz, I think about Schwarzenegger a lot, even too much, I am sad to report that the meme Arnold Schwarzenegger has never entered my dreams. I await his coming, however.

But he has entered the governor's office in Sacramento, and hence, he has entered this book, as Krasniewicz and Blitz would be quick to point out. He's spreading himself. We're spreading him.

By the way, here's Arnold's dream (this from an outtake from *Pumping Iron*): "I had a dream, it was of me. It was me being on top of a mountain like a king, and there was no room up there for anyone else."

I was against the recall, and it was no act of courage or intellectual honesty or autonomy; this was the liberal line, the Hollywood line, Warren Beatty's line. It was dull but it was honorable. You couldn't be for recalling the governor because the governor was the duly elected chief executive of the state of California. He had committed no crime, not even a misdemeanor. There was no scandal surrounding him, no whiff of scandal. It was true that he seemed to have no personality, that he wasn't much fun. That wasn't a sin for a politician; why, even in fun California, there had been many unamusing politicians. A good, fat swath of the state was notoriously not too much fun (the Central Valley, the Imperial Valley, the Inland Empire . . .), and recalling the governor was not the mature way to be a democracy. The people had elected him and he hadn't even snapped an adulterous thong, that one knew of. There wasn't even anything screamingly wrong with his policies, although the state was certainly having problems: it was $28 billion in the red.

On the other hand, the recall was fun and added an amusement to California gubernatorial politics that would have been missing had the state been left to Davis. Even I—serious, beetle-browed, left-leaning Democrat—could appreciate Angelyne, L.A.'s billboard goddess, who was one of more than a hundred recall candidates and a meme fit for analysis by such as Krasniewicz and Blitz, if a local rather than an international one. In strategic places all over Hollywood and its environs, there were billboards featuring her in pink outfits and pink environments; these were not put up expressly for the recall but, like billboards for Schwarzenegger's latest videos, were accustomed landmarks on the local map. The billboards said nothing except, in small letters, "management," followed by a phone number. Angelyne's lips were pouting; her hair was blonder than blond; her breasts were preposterous, monstrous, pneumatic. It was said that she was at least sixty years old. Unlike some of the other candidates, she could afford the $3,500 required for filing. With all the publicity the recall would bring her, she must have considered it an investment in her business.

If we were going to have a governor who was not a politician, why not Angelyne, whose persona seemed so right for the state, at least to an outsider living in Southern California. Angelyne, like Schwarzenegger, was a tireless self-promoter. Like Schwarzenegger's "virus," hers represented nothing of value, good, or truth. She was the queen of meaninglessness, much more so than Schwarzenegger. Angelyne of the platinum blond hair, big breasts, and teeteringly, dangerously high heels, pink microskirts, and sunglasses. She was not a singer or really an actress or a comedienne or even a model, not a performer of any kind, although she was a performance artist in a sense—a public relations campaign for a public relations campaign. She couldn't be bad at what she did, because she didn't do anything. And at that, she was brilliant. Even publicity had no content in Angelyne's world. Angelyne was brash about her lack of meaning and substance. She promoted it on her website:

> Angelyne is a true star of Hollywood. Not content to be labeled a singer, actress, dancer or performer of any kind, her image and persona capture the magic of stardom in its purest form. Angelyne represents the power we all have within ourselves to reach our dreams and make anything happen. For those who come to Hollywood in hopes of catching a glimpse of some celebrity, an Angelyne sighting is an unforgettable experience. Driving through the streets of Los Angeles in her famous Pink Corvette, greeting her fans, ANGELYNE IS HOLLYWOOD!

"Stardom in its purest form." Mark Twain would have loved Angelyne, a natural huckster and showman, an honest phony. Warhol could have created her, her vamping, her empty eyes, the blankness. I saw the legendary Pink Corvette once, in the valet parking lot at the Beverly Hills Hotel. But I never had a transcendent sighting. Her meme did not intrude its reality into my life.

What was particularly engaging about Angelyne was her Internet campaign video. In these mini-snapshots—which Arnold understandably did not bother doing—most of the recall candidates tried to appeal to their focus constituency; I'm for business, they said, or immigrants, or young people, or gay people, or college students . . . They were wearing nice, neat clothes, for the most part, as if from a Talbots catalogue.

Not Angelyne. In hers, she was sitting cross-legged on the floor in front of an orangey velvet couch with pink, red, and magenta pillows strewn around her. Her hair was pulled back in a high, fetching ponytail. On the bottom of a poster that hung behind her, above the sofa, only the word "Governor" was visible.

She had a little dog in her arms. The speech, in its entirety, follows:

"Hi," Angelyne says to the camera in a breathy little girl's Marilyn Monroe voice. "I'm running for governor of California. It's just me and the dog. Will you please vote for us? We promise we'll be really good. The dog only eats a little bit, and I eat pizza and chocolate. Please vote for me. Good-bye."

Schwarzenegger could have done the same ad.

Arnold, in front of a Hummer 2, a cigar in his mouth and Maria in his arms:

"Hi," he says in his Austrian robot accent. "I'm running for governor of Caleefawnyah. It's just me and this Kennedy. Will you please vote for us? We promise we'll be really good. Maria only eats a little bit, and I smoke cigars and wear cowboy boots . . ." This strategy would no doubt have worked very well for Schwarzenegger, but instead his handlers had him run what looked, from the outside at least, like a traditional political campaign. The only difference was that everywhere Arnold went, for his carefully structured "town meetings," for television appearances, for press conferences, radio spots, and photo opportunities, and *all that kind of stuff,* he was mobbed. Perhaps the best demonstration of his enormous allure was the moment when the candidates had to register for the recall, file their papers, and pay their $3,500 fee. Huffington, who understands good publicity value when she sees it, carefully arrived at the L.A. County Registrar's Office at the same time as Schwarzenegger and his wife, and dashed over to them, knocking over a bank of microphones in order to ensure that her face was in the frame with theirs for the front-page newspaper photo. She was taking a piggyback ride on his stardom, in its purest form.

CHAPTER THREE

Dog Days

I T WAS EASY, AS THE EAST COAST and the Europeans did, to look at what happened in California during the recall and turn up the nose, roll the eyes, and say, "Circus." Reading the stories about what an embarrassing show it all was, I was reminded of the funny, snobbish memoirs that Charles Dickens and Frances Trollope (mother of the novelist Anthony) wrote about their visits to America— the rough and tumble, the absurd characters, the carny atmosphere, the fraud and quackery, the lack of aristocracy or a really *responsible* ruling class. Those writers looked down—sometimes affectionately— at the Americans. But all that junk and showmanship, that huckster-ism and blowhardism and loud raucousness, the lack of an aristocratic leading class is also what's *good* about the country and is the very stuff of Twain's lifelong portrait of America. Boorish, perhaps, but healthy.

By the end of the recall campaign, there were 135 candidates for the governor's office, which gave the election a barnyard, braying quality. One of the candidates, an independent filmmaker, called herself Abner Zurd, or Ab Zurd, even though her name was really Lorraine Fontanes. My personal second-favorite candidate (after Angelyne) was Trek Thunder Kelly, of Venice, who had worn only the color blue for a year and was running on a platform that heralded his "consistency." There was also Van Vo, who appeared in his campaign photo with his aide Thien Dung, who was wearing the traditional saf-fron robes of a Buddhist monk. The pornography publisher and First Amendment defender Larry Flynt was also a candidate. I also liked Ronald Palmieri, a very L.A., Gucci-belted, arrogant, smart-talking slicko who seemed to have had his teeth "done" and was very tan and was—according to him—the first openly gay candidate for governor of any state. (This was before Governor James McGreevey of New Jersey was outed and resigned.)

At one point, Jay Leno (in the interests of equal time, since Schwarzenegger had announced his candidacy on an earlier show) invited all the other candidates on, had them sit in his audience, and asked them to shout out their platforms simultaneously, in a wonderful moment of clarity for American democracy. It was a howling crowd of politicians, a menagerie of *101 Dalmatians*-style dogs, very different from Angelyne's actual anorexic dog. There were big-breasted, porn-star bitches (a porn star named Mary Carey was running); jowly, boring businessman dogs; silly, puffed-up publicity hounds; avant-garde, moviemaking dogs; performance dogs; surfer dogs; immigrant dogs with barking accents; student puppies; environmental tail-waggers, the whole lot, the whole kennel. It looked like democracy of a certain kind, but in reality, only six of the candidates at most were serious—meaning potentially able to defeat the governor—and of them not one came to the Leno 4-H fair.

In the end, only one candidate could bring an incumbent governor down, and that was Schwarzenegger. And the truth was that Schwarzenegger was not a rebel candidate or a candidate of the people or a candidate responding to overwhelming popular dissatisfaction with Davis; Schwarzenegger was the candidate of choice of the old Republican boss and former governor, Pete Wilson. So in the end, all that boisterous, chaotic democracy of the recall candidates, all the fun junk and showmanship, was nothing more than a front behind which a traditional machine was inexorably operating. In the end, it came down to a traditional choice between one Democrat (the governor) and one Republican. It was the fact of the recall itself—an unscheduled emergency election when no emergency existed—that was politically important, not the irrelevant crowd of contestants.

The historical responsibility for the recall circus lay with a surprising character. As governor-elect in 1910, Hiram Johnson, the Progressive who established the recall in California, cut a figure very different from Arnold Schwarzenegger. Johnson's was a different era, although the problems besetting the state were enormous even then. As that century turned, corruption was rampant and undisguised, perhaps not as common as it is today but more violent, more single-minded, and more explicitly disregarding of the voter and taxpayer. The state government had become a tool of the powerful railroad industry, and nothing more. Johnson proved a courageous and formidable opponent of the railway's graft, bribery, and embezzlement—and an unwavering, eloquent enemy of corporate ownership of politicians.

Yet you would not have known it to look at him. A photo of the era, taken on a sharply sunny day, shows him at Lake Tahoe with his wife, Minerva, who is wearing what seems, even for those times, an outlandishly outsized hat—a wide-brimmed sombrero that, glinting in the sun, looks as if it had been decorated by a drunken fisherman who simply tossed the catch of the day over it. Perhaps it is just an indistinct photograph and not a fashion statement.

In any case, the serious and bespectacled governor-elect, unsurprised by what seems to be a piscine exhibition on top of his wife's head, stands stolidly beside her, unsmiling as ever, in white trousers, a white shirt, a bow tie, a boater, and a dark, unbuttoned sports jacket nearly ample enough—if it were closed—to cover the expansive gubernatorial belly. He is carrying what looks like a small rug (possibly a newspaper?) and a very large book (possibly the state budget?). He's wearing white bucks. In addition to the apparent fish, Minerva is wearing a white dress down to her ankles and a lace collar and cuffs. (Kevin Starr, the California historian, writes that at age nineteen, Johnson had to marry his sweetheart Minerva in a hurry because of an impending child, leaving college early to begin his family and his career.)

In spite of his portly, conservative mien, Johnson had been a fiery prosecutor in the corruption trial of Abraham Ruef, the Tammany-style Republican political boss of San Francisco, who was a fixer and hatchet man statewide for Southern Pacific Railroad interests. During the 1906 trial, the home of a key witness was dynamited; the chief prosecutor was shot in the courtroom and nearly killed; his would-be assassin, a rejected juror and ex-convict, committed suicide in police custody; and the corrupt but indecisive chief of police mysteriously drowned as he crossed the bay on a police launch.

After he obtained Ruef's conviction, Johnson became an obvious and very popular Progressive Party candidate for governor and won easily, ending the era of Southern Pacific Railroad dominance of state politics in California. In 1911, as he had promised, he pushed through state legislation creating the recall, along with the initiative and referendum, all amendments to the California constitution. He wanted Californians to honor democracy, he said, and to beware "the smugly respectable individuals in broadcloth of pretended respectability who from ambush employ the thug for selfish political gain."

From Johnson's day on, California gradually and famously became a state of subversive and sometimes self-destructive laws, of legislation that encourages political rebellion, of tax propositions that undermine the philosophical basis of taxation, of appropriations mechanisms that subvert the budgetary process, and of all kinds of other interesting governmental chaos.

It all goes back to this rather eccentric man and his rebellion against the undemocratic corruption of his age. Johnson—who was the estranged, upstanding son of Grove Lawrence Johnson, a corrupt Republican state legislator and U.S. congressman (back in the days when the Republicans exerted unquestionable control over the state)—pushed through his packet of progressive legislation in a rapidly changing California, a California where abject, bootlicking politicians (like Johnson's father) followed the commands of the railroad interests to the letter. Johnson, in open filial rebellion, was absolutely opposed to those interests (and to any other powerful organization that wanted to co-opt government); he felt that the people themselves, counted vote by vote, and not organized into any kind of power-wielding group, were the best and only tool available to contain Southern Pacific.

Johnson's revolutionary concept was—as he said in his inaugural address—that "successful and permanent government must rest primarily on recognition of the rights of men and the absolute sovereignty of the people." As amended, Johnson's constitution provides for initiatives coming directly from the people, for popular votes on policy proposals (referenda), as well as for direct votes to recall public officials. Political scientists call this direct democracy. The initiative, referendum, and recall had already been incorporated into the politics of the Swiss cantons in the middle of the nineteenth century, to further the idea of direct popular participation in the affairs of state. In 1898, South Dakota became the first state to institute the initiative, referendum, and recall, shortly followed by eight other states in the Midwest and West. California was the tenth state to adopt the measures.

This is what Governor Johnson said on January 3, 1911: "I commend to you the proposition that, after all, the initiative and referendum depend on our confidence in the people and their ability to govern." If elections were bought, overtly or covertly, it was only right that the result be overturned, he reasoned. If politicians were corrupt, if they did not carry out the will of the majority, the majority could and should get rid of them.

There was a catch, however. Like every political weapon, recall could work both ways, as history has now shown. Just as a dirty vote could be undone by a clean recall, so could a reasonably clean election be undone by an underhanded recall. A recall could be bought, just like any election: this did not occur to Governor Johnson in 1911, at least not in any pressing way. Indeed, after recall was passed by the legislature in 1910, three state officials fell to its mechanisms, and then, in a hiatus of almost eighty years, it was not used again against any state official.

In 2003, almost a century after Johnson's liberating triumph, the California Republicans created the anti-Davis recall through a petition drive funded by Darryl Issa, a wealthy San Diego County Republican legislator and businessman (he made his money in car alarms, in a very good market: Southern California) who imagined he himself would become the recall candidate. A company was paid to collect citizen's signatures in shopping malls and mini-marts and supermarkets throughout the state. (These signature collectors were not idealistic student volunteers who *believed* in the petition.) It's estimated that in California, it costs a million dollars or so to get a recall or a proposition on the ballot. Some signature collection firms are known to scrounge up business by inventing a proposal themselves, test-marketing it, focus-grouping it, and then, if it looks as if it will fly, pushing it to possible proponents.

The Republicans were canny in their management of the recall. Fearing that the impromptu vote might permit a stronger Democrat than Davis to sneak into the governor's mansion, and also realizing that the short recall campaign was a chance for a cheap regime change with the right candidate, the GOP leaders went over Issa's head to Schwarzenegger, the unbeatable, who had made many noises in recent years about his interest in the job. He was a man who could be run as a people's representative, but also as a businessman's candidate who was friendly and open to old-fashioned special interests— for example, agribusiness, industry, real estate developers, and car dealers.

Business jumped to back Schwarzenegger, while he spouted crowd-pleasing rhetoric to the public in his town meetings and via people like John and Ken, about how he would not take money from special interests. For Johnson back in 1911, the monolithic special interest, and the only one that concerned him, was the Southern Pacific Railroad and its banker friends. For Schwarzenegger, special interests had a modern meaning, sort of a reversal of Johnson's "interests"; he took the term to mean teachers and public employee unions, who were big contributors to Gray Davis's campaign and to Democratic candidates in general.

"The opponents of direct legislation and the recall, however they may phrase their opposition," Hiram Johnson wrote, "in reality believe the people can not be trusted." When he said that, Johnson was trying to embarrass and delegitimize those who objected to his reforms, and given the political atmosphere of his day, his point was well taken.

But as both Hiram Johnson and Arnold Schwarzenegger knew, the central question at the heart of democracy is whether the people can be trusted, and if so, how much. The question is not antidemocratic. In fact, direct popular votes on policy issues can result in an incoherent set of policies, producing, as Peter Schrag wrote in *Paradise Lost: California's Experience, America's Future*, "a cycle of frustration, reform, and further frustration in which each initiative further constrains the ability of government . . . to respond to new conditions and set priorities." In California, for example, the voters chose not to raise taxes but also chose to increase spending in various ways. Undue influence and bogus political rhetoric can be brought to bear on representative democracy, and can also sway voters on policy decisions in referenda and initiative votes, in the form of partisan but seemingly objective broadcast advertising, or of fake endorsements of proposals by attractive-sounding groups invented by special-interest sponsors, or of radio talk shows with ideological agendas and corporate backers.

The traditional rebuttal to those who argue for direct democracy has always been its susceptibility to demagoguery. Hitler loved the national referendum, as did many other dictators. In part because Hitler wielded both fear and popularity, his four referenda succeeded with a 90 to 99 percent vote. In California today, not demagoguery alone but also corporate manipulation can taint the mechanisms of direct democracy.

"In Pop's day," says my uncle, one day when we're reminiscing about my grandfather, a Democratic machine boss in New Jersey, "Pop and his friends could go into a room and choose the candidate, and they'd make sure he won the primary, the Democratic primary, and that was that. He got elected." (The only case I know of where this did not work is the case of this uncle, who ran as a U.S. Senate candidate with

my grandfather's backing against an incumbent Republican and lost.)
The machine was a way of doing political business that was efficient
and accepted, and I'm vulnerable to the attractions of that method. It
gets the job done, and you know what's what, who's who in the hier-
archy. (Hiram Johnson would not approve.) I knew my grandfather
would have admired the boldness of the recall election and would
have been impressed by its result: how the Pete Wilson Republicans
managed to anoint their own new governor in the midst of another
governor's term, cut short the usual yearlong campaign, and all the
while make it seem that their man had issued forth from an open and
even a historic, even a *revolutionary*, contest.

Back in my grandfather's day, the someone who got the job done
was the "dad," as Dr. Rangell would say, and it was nice that in my
neighborhood, in my town, in my county, and even, often enough, in
my state, the "dad" happened to be my grandfather. *He* was always
able to comply. It was a comfort to be part of the boss's family. But I
also knew how much resentment such machine politics could create
both among party loyalists and within the broader electorate. The
undemocratic flaws of machine politics often ignite rebellions that can
take the form of initiative politics: that's what happened in Johnson's
California.

The people who crowned Schwarzenegger were not my people, so
I mistrusted them, and therefore him. Pete Wilson, the smiling business advocate and former Republican governor, was no grandpa of
mine. There were certainly political reasons to mistrust Schwarzenegger. His was a masquerade candidacy. Like so many political events in
recent years, Schwarzenegger's run was portrayed as the opposite of
what it was; the campaign pretended to be for the popular good when
it merely furthered the status quo, alleged it would help the little guy
when it was clearly intended to make things easier and better for business interests, used the mask of tax givebacks and a "no new taxes"
platform as a populist cover-up for its corporate underpinnings.

Schwarzenegger said he was going to "bring California back."
Back from where? It wasn't as if the state were hovering on the brink
of Communism or even Socialism, although admittedly, the sums in

the financial ledgers did not fill one with buoyant optimism. Back to what? (As Jay Leno said, "I love all these politicians! They all say the same thing: 'We'll give California back to the people.' Yeah, great. Now that it's not worth anything, they want to give it back to us.") My rescuer was pretending to offer me a deal: California back, for free! And no property taxes! No car tax! No new taxes! No *old* taxes!

Everyone would be happy. No problem. Schwarzenegger was approximating in his policy statements a campaign-trail trick that *New York Times* columnist William Safire calls the Irish Switch, a technique perfected in the old days by John F. "Honey Fitz" Fitzgerald, one of John F. Kennedy's legendary grandfathers. Schwarzenegger was good at this on the ground, as well. The Irish Switch tests a politician's physicality, which may be why it comes so easily to Schwarzenegger. The candidate steps forward into a crowd, and while shaking the hand of one voter, he talks to another and simultaneously, and almost secretly, winks at yet another. It's a three-fer. You connect with everyone, make everyone feel good.

Schwarzenegger was a feel-good candidate, I realized one day, while watching him glad-hand preselected spectators after he did the Sean Hannity radio show in a meeting hall in downtown L.A. And for a catastrophist like me, there is nothing so terrible as feeling good.

Many people in the entertainment industry in L.A. believe that Arianna Huffington's living room and the capacious round table in her dining room in Brentwood are the only informal places in Los Angeles where ideas are discussed, where there is actual content exchanged, where people congregate who care about political and cultural ideals. There is some truth to this (and in Huffington's office there *were* books, among which were several by her, including two she'd written in the past two years, while running for office, holding court, appearing on television and radio, giving parties, and writing her weekly column). Yet with the arguable exception of the hostess, Huffington's guests were not what most people would call intellectuals. They were high-energy types and some were quite brilliant, but they weren't often profound or deeply degreed. This was not the *New York Review of Books*.

Huffington herself, however, is a Genius, although whether she's a lowercase genius is still open for debate. A Genius, in L.A. shorthand, is a fellow of the Los Angeles Institute for the Humanities, a group of academics, achievers, artists, curators, and writers who meet twice a month for sit-down, white-tablecloth luncheons at the Faculty Club at the University of Southern California. The Geniuses group was established in 1998 by Steve Wasserman, then the editor of the *Los Angeles Times Book Review,* and Steven Ross, the chairman of USC's history department. Four years later, a competitive rump group (who invented the mocking nickname "Geniuses" for the Institute's fellows) was established by a bunch of malcontent would-be fellows. Among these were friends of Wasserman's to whom he'd spoken at length and in somewhat hushed tones about the Geniuses and how fabulous they were, etc., etc., yet who had not been invited to participate in the Institute. This group called itself the Morons and was cofounded by the journalist and blogger Mickey Kaus and the writer Ann Louise Bardach.

I personally am a Moron. The Morons have only two rules: If you're a Genius, you may not become a Moron, nor may you attend Moronic meetings. (Sean Daniel, former head of Universal Studios and now a film producer as well as a true Moron, once brought Huffington to a Morons meeting as a guest, rendering founders Kaus and Bardach "almost apopleptic," according to Daniel.) The other rule is, if you're coming to a Moron meeting, bring something good to eat. Moron dinners are not catered. The Institute, on the other hand, more secure in its identity and standing, welcomes Morons. If invited by a particular Genius, Morons may listen, in their uneducated, unenlightened way, to lectures by Genius guest speakers and may dine at the Genius luncheons. This is fortunate, because Morons are frequently lean and hungry characters in search of a catered meal and a free glass of wine. (In Manhattan, by the way, the intellectual set does not make such a separation between Geniuses and Morons, perhaps because in Manhattan they understand how really hard it is to tell the

difference.) Some other Geniuses besides Huffington are movie producer Lynda Obst, political commentator Robert Scheer, historian
Kevin Starr, and writers Susan Faludi, Carolyn See, and Mona Simpson. Morons include Kaus and Bardach as well as the director Taylor
Hackford, the actress Helen Mirren, the Nicaraguan writer Gioconda
Belli, the casting director Margery Simkin, and many, many ravenous,
garrulous, ink-stained wretches.

In October of 2003, just before the recall election, I went to a
meeting of the Morons in Pacific Palisades, in a house high on a hill
from which we looked down in the night through dark palms over a
lit-up slice of city to the ocean. Someone once said about Los Angeles
that it is beautiful—at night, from a distance—and this is true. There
were Morons all around me, and the honored guests of the evening
(Morons for a Night) were political consultants who analyzed the
recall race in terms a Moron could understand. Rob Long, a conservative humor writer who was once the executive producer of *Cheers* and
is a former Bostonian, was presiding in another room over the paella
he'd cooked and brought along. He and I were skipping the speakers
for a minute.

"There comes a moment for expats here," Long said, "when you
land at the airport in the middle of the night and get into a cab and roll
down the window and breathe and say, 'Okay. This is good.' Where
you look out the window at the palms and the cypress and the ocean,
and you don't notice L.A., per se. That's when it's good."

I was still waiting for this moment.

We moved back into the living room and listened to our hostess
make Moron of the Month nominations. Morons are sitting everywhere, on the stairs up to the dining room, on the terrace behind the
speakers, off in a smaller parlor to the left, on the floor, at the piano.
The living-room walls are red, and some lucky Morons are sitting on
red velvet wing chairs near the wall, others on café chairs near the
piano. I'm sitting on the Oriental rug along with four or five other
Morons, under a gilt triptych of naked angels. Crystal sconces light up
the scene; a cool ocean breeze is coming in through the open windows. Morons are very much into the real estate of Moron meeting

places. One e-mail from the founders trolled the list for a venue for an upcoming event: "Morons with Big Houses" was its subject line.

In the kitchen at the house in Pacific Palisades, two Mexican housekeepers are doing continuous cleanup. Sometimes I imagine it's the same two or three quiet Mexican women who are cleaning up after every dinner or party I go to in L.A. They're always there, with their heads bent over the sink, stacking dishes or drying wineglasses or filling Tupperware with leftovers, talking quietly to each other as they work, their long black hair done up in a braid or a bun.

I left the Morons early that night with my husband and went on to the Resnicks' house on Sunset, where Stewart and his wife, Lynda, were hosting a prerecall dinner. Everything inside seemed golden as the butler opened up the billionaires' big front door. We were ushered into the dining room, where a huge table was bounteously laid and the guests, about twenty of them, were beginning the main course.

Three boatlike bowls of low fresh flowers line the center of the table. It's all confusion as we are seated in the midst of the meal. The servants are almost as numerous as footmen used to be. They are all men. My husband sits up next to Lynda Resnick, and I am plunked down at the foot of the table with Stewart and a Mrs. Someone who looks like a long-dead thirty-year-old. A co-La Brea Woman, I think to myself. She has a thirty-five-year-old daughter.

At our end of the table, the conversation is about dieting and Kabbalah—the mystical Jewish creed that has been sweeping Hollywood for a few years now—and the pleasures of being what Stewart calls "comfortable."

"It's nice to be able to go to a good restaurant or have good wines, good food, but beyond that, what really does a person need?" he asks. I personally know from experience, however, that his Sun King-sized office is dotted with museum-quality statuary, that he has his own workout room, and that his foyer holds more than two hundred people. I happen to know also that at least some of his bathrooms have marble floors—not travertine, but very beautiful imported marble. Everyone listening to him knows this too.

While I'm brooding over "comfortable" and what it means, Stew-

art begins rhapsodizing about bittersweet chocolate. He has his foot-
man bring him one box, which turns out to be milk chocolate and is
summarily rejected; then another, which is too cold but bittersweet—
and meets with his approval. Stewart breaks up the bar so we can each
have a chunk.

It was another party of the political moment. After chocolate and
a ceremoniously served dessert wine, we all moved into the living
room for coffee. Among the guests that night were Norman Lear,
Albert Brooks, Michael York, and Mike Medavoy, the producer, who
has worked on several films starring Schwarzenegger. Jokes were
made about the allegations concerning Schwarzenegger and women.
Kinder jokes were made about Huffington and her candidacy. The
subjects changed in a desultory fashion but circled always around
politics. Michael York, who is British, said that the reason he was for
the war in Iraq was Tony Blair, but now he thought the war was
wrong. Most of the Resnicks' guests that night were moving toward
Wesley Clark for president; they'd dumped Howard Dean. Meanwhile, in a corner, Norman Lear was talking about his new project.
He was running a group that exhibits one of the few remaining 1776
copies of the Declaration of Independence at school after school, all
over the country, with the respectable goal of making students think
about what it means to be an American.

Lear and his co-investors bought the document in 2000 for $8.14
million. Perhaps *that* is part of what it means to be an American.

Although I'm a Moron, I'm also a fringe invitee of Huffington's, so I've
been to her place many times. You sit on the velvet bench eating
canapés, or in the big overstuffed couches, and listen to the talk. Rob
Reiner is a frequent guest at Huffington's. He's so nice and *haimish*,
big and bearish, bald, bossy, and bearded. He sits with his legs
crossed, and, like Beatty, pontificates about the presidential election,
the gubernatorial recall; unlike many in Hollywood circles, Reiner
seems to enjoy state politics as much as presidential politics; the rest
of the Hollywood crew—perhaps because they have so much money

that (Democratic) presidential candidates kowtow to *them*—seem mostly to prefer the national scene.

Huffington's living room was the place where I first heard that Schwarzenegger was contemplating a run for governor. When I heard Schwarzenegger's name mentioned this way, I thought it must be the punch line of a joke I'd somehow missed. But the joke about California is that the joke about California is not a joke.

To the people who make up her salon, Huffington serves as a court intellectual—always being clever in the presence of some king or other and his minions. She looks like an exaggerated Jackie Kennedy, and she talks like Zsa Zsa Gabor, but unlike most women in Hollywood circles who are not starlets and are therefore treated more or less as if they were La Brea Woman or La Brea Woman's spinster aunt, Huffington gets some respect and is listened to—to a degree. She matters; she's a figure—at least among a certain powerful elite group—even though she passed twenty-five years of age quite some time ago and is not married (any longer) to a rich and powerful man, is not even married, as it happens, and does not (yet) run a studio. She grew up in a tiny apartment in Athens, moved to England, won a scholarship to Cambridge, and by dint of her quick intelligence became the third woman president of the Cambridge Union, the legendary debating society of that university. But she's also a society girl and worked hard for her social recognition in England and later in the United States. Known in London as "the Greek pudding," a sobriquet coined by *Tatler* magazine, she slimmed down and turned herself into one of New York's most eligible bachelorettes and it-girls in the 1980s.

Now she is a rich divorcée, having split up with the Texas oil heir Michael Huffington in 1997 (he announced that he was gay) and dumped conservative politics as well. She lives with her two teenaged daughters in an eight-thousand-square-foot Italianate house on a leafy street. At dinner, her girls visit the table, but they don't eat with the guests. For Huffington, being home is like being out. She has even been known to leave parties she herself is giving at her own house, stranding her invited guests in order to attend another event.

Warren Beatty is part of Huffington's circle. When he comes in, he peers at me, a newcomer. His wife is there too, the actress Annette Bening. Warren gets right into gear; he talks rather unabashedly about Annette's recent medical checkup, going on happily, with only a bow to a blush, about colonoscopies and so on. (He is strongly in favor of the procedure—telling us how often he goes in for them and how he encourages Annette as well; older movie stars tend to be health-obsessed.) Beatty has a cheery, unmediated American innocence and often displays a studied lack of sophistication that is at odds with his checkered reputation.

One night at a big party up at Mike Medavoy's mansion above Beverly Hills, I watched Beatty listening with his usual seemingly intent, theatrical regard to Joseph Nye, the foreign policy expert from Harvard's Kennedy School of Government. This is what parties are like in L.A. among this group of powerful entertainment people. No one ever gives a party just to have fun, an occasion to gossip, drink, and wear nice shoes. A party here always has a money aspect and an informational aspect—as if they have to justify a party and prove that their heads contain something other than air. At this dinner, Dahlia Rabin, daughter of the assassinated Israeli prime minister Yitzhak Rabin, was a guest of honor, there to raise money for a library for her father's papers, and Nye was lecturing and answering questions about war with Iraq.

Nye talked on and on about the pros and cons of military engagement. The main course came to an end, and dessert was being served at the dozen or so tables. When the question-and-answer period came to an end, Medavoy, still standing as the emcee, asked Nye if he wanted a cup of coffee. Then you heard Beatty's voice, projecting well all the way from table number one to the back of the room, asking, "Or d'you want some ice cream?" He loves what is childlike and absurd, a sort of Huck Finn in L.A.

There is a marked lack of sycophantism in Huffington's circle. These are people who consider each other equals, and they don't show off for one another, they don't suck up, in a city famous for sucking up and brownnosing. No one is particularly respectful of anyone else— whereas in New York in such settings, the acolytes are always bowing to the mentor, the students hanging on the rebbe's every word. Here, Beatty's arrival doesn't stun the guests into worshipful silence, the way I've seen it do in Manhattan.

For a long time, I didn't quite understand. In my experience of simple, local politics, people were either leaders or followers or flat-terers. In *his* political world, my grandfather was the boss, not just the ward and county boss and the machine boss and the unofficial mayor of Perth Amboy and the local representative of the Democratic National Committee but also the boss of everyone. In his living room, people were office seekers or patronage lackeys or his employees or his servants or his little bubbly, darling, curly-headed, *obedient* grand-children. In Haiti, another locus of severe political sycophancy where I had lived for two years, leaders brooked no counsel, no criticism, and no opposition, meaningful or symbolic, and they too liked to sur-round themselves with cute, obedient followers. *Sou-sou,* which liter-ally means "suck-suck" in Haitian Creole, is often used there in political talk to describe a politician's relationship to a president or prime minister.

My grandfather and Haiti's presidents seemed omnipotent because they personally had control of all the money and all the power in their sphere, like a bully holding the piggy bank. In Huffing-ton's living room, the dispensation of money and power is different. Power and money there, especially money, are spread around liber-ally—as if at a meeting of corporate directors. Depending on who is at her house in Brentwood on any given evening, there can be much more money and power to go around in that baroque setting than there was in all Perth Amboy, New Jersey, in a month, or in the entire République d'Haïti.

Everyone at Huffington's is arrogant in his or her own private way, in his or her own private sphere, and that's part of the reason they all get along so well, I finally decided. They are equals. They are all very well aware of what they can offer. They treat presidential candidates as equals too, because they have a reciprocal power arrangement with them: each boosts the other's sense of importance, and of course, the candidates can raise money from the Hollywood people in exchange for the Hollywood crew's achieving a sense of political influence. These people at Huffington's are *backers,* and the subtext of almost all their conversations in an election year was, Who are we going to back? They are also enablers: they enable politicians to be with celebrities, to gain a certain kind of visibility, to meet other celebrities, to be associated and seen with celebrities, to receive the publicity perks of intimacy with celebrity friends, and to get more money from other celebrities.

Amid the playful, moneyed backers at Huffington's, the hyphenated transcendentalist John-Roger often materializes. The first time I noticed this odd guru, he was sitting amid a harem of eternally smiling women of incalculable age at a Huffington book-launch party one evening in 2003. It seemed extraordinary that a woman like Huffington, with a Cambridge education and an exalted status in American society, should need a quackish spiritual adviser. But again, we are back in the land of Twain and of *The Wizard of Oz.* Spiritual advisers like John-Roger have become a necessary Hollywood accessory, a lifestyle appurtenance. Who can forget Joan Quigley, Nancy Reagan's astrologer, an L.A. adjunct whom the first lady brought to D.C. from Bel Air? Or Hillary Clinton's flirtation with Jean Houston, the spiritualist who enabled Mrs. Clinton to have a chat with the ghost of Eleanor Roosevelt?

The spiritualist (much like the personal assistant, the acupuncturist, the herbalist, the masseur, and the yoga instructor) is an important member of the contemporary Hollywood staff. Stewart Resnick, that master of the universe, wears the little red thread of the Kabbalah Center around his wrist, has a Jewish prayer scroll or mezuzah over every door in his house (inner and outer, as if you were in a Hasidic brownstone in Williamsburg, New York), and receives regular home visits from the Beverly Hills Kabbalah Center's leader, Michael Berg. A woman at Resnick's dinner table told me it cost her $250 to buy the thread at the center; I do not tell her that you can get seven at the

Western Wall in Jerusalem for $5 from any number of itinerant believers. If everyone has a spiritual adviser—even Stewart and Lynda Resnick, who are undeniably strict materialists—Huffington too can be relied on to have one, just as she'd have a Kate Spade bag or a Wolf stove or Jimmy Choo shoes.

John-Roger and his associate, the unhyphenated John Morton (a former park ranger and author of the spiritual guide *The Blessings Already Are*, a favorite title of mine), run the Movement of Spiritual Inner Awareness, which includes Soul Transcendence, Mystical Travelers, spiritual exercises, the Light, and the TISRA TIL (a place allegedly at the center of the brain, not a place in Narnia). John-Roger has written of the "realms": the physical realm, the astral, the causal, the mental, the etheric, and the soul realm. Don't ask, although etheric is good, very good—a transition between mental and soul realms, it is "relat[ed] to the unconscious, in the sense that it is the gateway to the higher levels," according to the MSIA home page. According to its website, the sect holds gatherings in Santa Barbara (where Huffington used to live) and in L.A., in San Diego and Vancouver, in Ecuador and Colombia, in London and in Spain, and in Russia. Every year there is an MSIA campout for families at Lake Arrowhead in the San Bernardino mountains, a resort area that was almost entirely burned out in the 2003 fire season.

When you invite the Light in, you chant either the word "Hu" (pronounced "Hugh," the website tells you helpfully) or the word "Ani-Hu" (pronounced "An-Eye-Hu," though bizarrely, the words themselves seem to be transliterations of Hebrew pronouns). If you have RealAudio 4.0, you can download a recording of a gathering letting in the Light and chanting "Hu" or "Ani-Hu." Listening to this, it's hard to imagine Huffington, with her elegant pantsuits and her intense makeup and her dense, done hair, chanting and letting in the Light.

John-Roger himself is a Twain-worthy figure. He could so easily reach into his jacket pockets and pull out bottles and jars of ointments, baths, and cures. He beams, all the time, like an ageless cherub. His nearly unlined face has a lit-up sheen, as if it's had its architecture renovated several times, and then the marble's been polished. Outside the circle of smiling women who never take their eyes off him is a wider circle of beautiful young men, who never take their eyes off him. (Years ago, it was reported that Huffington had been baptized *twice* by his cult. More recently, she refused to say whether she considers John-Roger to be the personification of God.)

John-Roger completes Huffington's Hollywood entourage, though he is not as visible as Beatty and Bening, or Albert Brooks, or Larry David. Although her people were what boosted her up and financed her and kept her going, Huffington did not appear publicly with her Hollywood crowd as a candidate, not necessarily because *she* didn't want to, but because many of them did not want to appear with her. Beatty, for one, staunchly supported Governor Davis, and among Huffington's friends there were those who thought she was embarking on a career-embellishing but possibly embarrassing project. Her social trust—which in another place and time, with different dramatis personae, might have been called a brain trust—did not seem to take her candidacy very seriously, especially once Schwarzenegger was in the race. Many of them did help her out with generous donations, however.

Huffington was always more than unlikely to win the recall vote, and she pulled out of the race just in time to be able, if only tenuously, to attribute her low showing in the vote to the fact that she had pulled out. All along she'd been intending, before Schwarzenegger upstaged her, to be the fun candidate, someone who would offer sharp barbs and clever repartee and spice up the race while raising her profile in the state and nationally. With her money, media access, and connections, she survived the social stigma both of running and, worse, of *losing*.

What is remarkable is that only a decade ago, when Huffington lived in conservative Santa Barbara with her Texas oilman husband, she was an archconservative and a Republican herself. She's always been a quick study and seems to have realized in a half second that when you arrive in Hollywood as an industry outsider, you can't be conservative and a Republican and expect to have fun or standing or celebrity. Hollywood, in turn, has leaped to accept the revised Huffington.

Like Huffington, Arnold Schwarzenegger is a self-created phenomenon, a fast learner, and a charming host of some standing in L.A. society, though not typically associated with thoughtful conversation and
clever punditry. He's the opposite of Huffington in his pretensions,
though: he invented the Hummer as a personal vehicle; he smokes
fine cigars. Huffington drives and promotes the ecologically correct
Toyota Prius hybrid, and you have to go outside to smoke at her house.
When he was a candidate, most of Schwarzenegger's announcements
had to do with entourage, with the high-profile people he was inviting
to advise him, rather than with the policies they might have advised
him on. By contrast, Huffington was intensely issue-oriented—although always capable of dropping an offhand name.

One day, Schwarzenegger announced that former Governor Pete
Wilson would be his campaign cochairman, a fitting role for the man
who invented Schwarzenegger's candidacy in the first place. The
next day, the financial mastermind Warren Buffett stepped up to be
Schwarzenegger's financial adviser. (Schwarzenegger did dump Buffett quickly after Buffett suggested that Proposition 13, which
exempts California homeowners from property tax hikes, might be
considered for the dustbin. In *Paradise Lost*, Peter Schrag calls Prop
13 "the third rail of California politics—'touch it and you die.'") Two
days later, Schwarzenegger announced that George Shultz, the former U.S. secretary of state, would also advise the campaign—though
no one specified on what subject, since foreign policy was not an
essential aspect of the governor's job. Still, Bechtel, whose board
Shultz sits on, is a major player in California politics and economics.
Soon after Shultz was named, the actor Rob Lowe signed on too—
supposedly to organize the candidate's celebrity support.

It's all about who you know and who's at your table. On the face of
it, this would have made Schwarzenegger a more serious candidate
than Huffington: he had Shultz at his side, she had Larry David, cre-
ator of *Seinfeld* and *Curb Your Enthusiasm*. But the truth of all this
goes a little deeper—though not too deep. Schwarzenegger was certainly a more serious representative of his party; Huffington was running as an independent. Schwarzenegger needed heavier hitters than

Huffington did because, in spite of being a well-connected socialite and perennial gadfly and ambitious in the extreme (she was once called the most upwardly mobile Greek since Icarus), she had "serious" credentials. Huffington had already spoken and written at length about policy in a way that showed that she had a grasp of the issues at play in the governor's race and beyond, that she knew how to consider such issues, examine them, make decisions about them, even if there were aspects of her character and her past that made some consider her superficial.

Schwarzenegger, albeit overwhelmingly more likely to win from the moment he announced, hadn't done what Huffington had done, although once, in 2002, he managed to get a proposition of his own, the After School Education and Safety Program Act, onto the ballot and into California law, via Governor Hiram Johnson's direct democracy. The act, however, was never implemented because California has strict measures about budget appropriations and how much money must be available before certain programs can be funded; Schwarzenegger's program never served a single child, although that did not stop him from using it during the recall to try to prove that he had political experience, important-issue concern, and policy familiarity. To prove, in essence, that he cares "about families, about children, and all that kind of stuff."

In a state—and one might add, a country—where celebrity and charisma really matter, thinking about the issues is not too closely related to winning the election, as has been shown time and again. One of the main reasons policy wonk Bill Clinton took the presidency, for example, was that he also had charisma. Huffington is a celebrity here in Hollywood, of a certain kind, but small-time compared to Schwarzenegger. Her name is pretty recognizable here—and even nationally—in certain circles. But if you say "Arianna Huffington" in Zimbabwe or Saigon or Paris, or even—closer to home—in Monterey Park or Watts or Long Beach, you will get a vacant look. Then say "Arnold Schwarzenegger" and see what happens. There are degrees, wattages, of celebrity. Arnold's is a klieg light, Arianna's an appliance bulb.

———————

One day during the heat of the recall campaign, I went to a Huffington event at Will Rogers Memorial Park, a grassy knoll in front of the Beverly Hills Hotel. The press as usual was thirsty for camera-ready events, and they needed to show they were not covering Schwarzenegger exclusively, so perhaps it was not surprising that the media far outnumbered the public on this hot afternoon, even though the television crews and the newspaper reporters all knew that Huffington's candidacy was not really viable. A Huffington advance person was seen recruiting a family of tourists from Spain to hold placards behind the candidate. (They agreed to do it.) After all, who else would be out *walking* on this green part of Sunset Boulevard in Los Angeles except for innocent tourists? On her way from her hybrid Toyota to the makeshift podium, Huffington handed off her grande Starbucks latte cup to an aide, to keep it off camera. To one sector of the California electorate, Starbucks smacks of pretension and privilege; to another, it represents corporatism and globalization; you just can't win with that cup in your hand. In midwalk, another aide handed her a small bottle of water, instead. A photographic reflector shed a flattering, subdued light on Huffington in her beige pantsuit, while she attacked Schwarzenegger as a Bush Republican and crony of corrupt business. It was a very hot day, and she had arrived about an hour after schedule. The trees seemed to be melting under the sun, their heavy boughs giving some small relief to the mass of media people huddled below, watching Huffington. The bank of television cameras was recording. Huffington went on: Enron, secret meetings, Ken Lay, etc., etc.

From behind her, out of the window of a passing car, came a shout: "Publicity-seeking phony! Pay your taxes!" A story in the *Los Angeles Times* that very day had revealed the fact that for the two preceding years, Huffington had paid only $771 in federal income taxes. The story effectively destroyed what little campaign she had left in her in the wake of Schwarzenegger's entry into the race. A movie producer I know said laughingly that she'd immediately run to ask her own accountants and financial advisers whether it would be possible to imitate Huffington and have one column for regular, legitimate itemized business expenses, and then one for "Arianna" expenses, of the sort Huffington had liberally interpreted as business expenses, like hairdressing and makeup: "You know," this producer said, "for office décor, my new chandelier, my herbalist—that kind of thing." The accountants said no. Huffington's friends, many of whom say they do pay their taxes, were more irritated by revelations about her tax returns than by any other behavior.

That evening, Huffington hosted a barbecue at her house for her daughters and their friends and a few of her own circle. She told me beforehand that it was to be just a private, family barbecue. I interpreted this to mean that Warren Beatty would not be present, and I was right. I also imagined that there would be men standing over a fire, with tongs—to my mind, an integral part of the meaning of the word "barbecue."

But no, there is no outdoor fire. (The fire is in the kitchen, where the housekeeper is laboring.) Many skinny wives in tight jeans, their blouses diaphanous in the setting sun, come through the big doors of the Huffington breezeway out into the long gardens near the pool, bearing baked desserts which they did not bake and will not eat. Huffington's sister, Agapi, helps serve the food, alongside two servants. British friends from Huffington's Cambridge days are visiting from London. Harvey Karp, a pediatrician who has written two books (because no one at Huffington's is a normal *anything*; a plain pediatrician is not enough), sits in a corner, discussing the failure of the Oslo peace process in the Middle East, instead of talking—as he can, very intelligently—about how to make babies sleep and how ontogeny continues to recapitulate phylogeny even after birth (which, he argues, is why toddlers so exactly resemble Cro-Magnon man).

As I am consuming my second miniature Greek lamb chop, Rob Minkoff, the director of *Stuart Little* and *Stuart Little 2*, arrives. He also directed *The Lion King* and was an animator (at Disney) of *The Little Mermaid* and *The Great Mouse Detective*. He tells us he's working on *The Haunted Mansion* now, based on a Disneyland ride, a follow-up to *Pirates of the Caribbean*, also based on a ride.

Minkoff, who rose out of the ranks of Disney animators, is one of

America's infantilizers, or at least his works speak to the infantilism of Americans. Rides are *fun*. Movies made for ride lovers are for children, who bring along at least one if not two or additional ticket buyers with them when they go to the movies; if you tweak the child demographic upward a few years with teen-idol stars like Orlando Bloom and Kiera Knightly, Disney executives (and of course other studios have followed suit) figure *baby* movies will sell very broadly, and they do. Some adults I have met say that Disney's *Aladdin*, an animated movie, is their favorite movie ever made. It's like saying *Harry Potter* is your favorite work of literature. Schwarzenegger's candidacy in its most easily understandable form—Terminator for governor—simplifies politics and infantilizes the electorate.

I've forgotten my maxim, though: no one gives a party in Los Angeles just to give a party. Huffington is up and down, her face a mask of animated exhaustion. She's only been getting three hours of sleep a night, because she's been doing all the New York morning talk shows live at four in the morning L.A. time, harvesting maximum publicity during her short recall season. She disappears briefly from the table and returns, waving a piece of paper, with the triumphant announcement, "Our first ad!" (She has just hired media adviser Bill Hillsman—"Beeel Heeelsmahn," in her Greek accent.) She shows us the script, in which a diverse assortment of people each mouths parts of a Huffington stump speech, with her distinctive voice and accent emanating from each of them.

"Start with a white man in a suit," advises Karp.

"Let's talk about the big picture," Huffington says to me, leaning over as if confidentially. Karp also leans in, as if to listen. I am hopeful: perhaps she will say something illuminating or intimate, or revealing. She looks at me very seriously and says that perhaps, if we are lucky, out of "the chaos and destruction of the recall will come something creative, like the Indian myth of creation." It sounds as if her theory may originally have been John-Roger's.

In any case, it was her way of justifying her participation in the recall to her Hollywood friends, the population of her salon. If it was going to happen anyway, she reasoned, why shouldn't one among them be involved? She was staking out the high road, claiming that a kind of spirituality or altruism, an exalted hopefulness, motivated her, rather than—as many suspected and as she must have been aware they did—pure public relations and fame gathering.

"I think we really genuinely have no idea what will happen," she said, laughing. That's what she said, but by then, everybody knew that Schwarzenegger would win. Certainly everyone knew that Huffington would not. Schwarzenegger knew. On Labor Day weekend, a scant month before the vote, Schwarzenegger's schedule read as follows: "Saturday: No Scheduled Events. Sunday: No Scheduled Events. Monday: State Fair." With five weeks remaining, Schwarzenegger was visibly not worried. He was taking it easy. (He was to maintain a similarly laid-back pace as governor whenever plausibly possible.) Meanwhile, Huffington was visiting campuses, doing morning TV, radio spots, treating the campaign like a book tour, and maybe that's what it was for her, a prepublication book tour for her next big book, a groundwork laying, with a campaign fund—provided in large measure by loans and gifts from select Hollywood friends—to pay for it. The campaign fund was payback for all those nights in her living room, all those meals at her generous dining-room table, illuminated by crystal and the camaraderie of the like-minded.

Rob Minkoff tells a long story about how one day, four years or so ago, he received a call from a publicist he had once worked with who was now working with Schwarzenegger. The long and short of it was that Schwarzenegger was interested in doing a movie version of . . . Wagner's *Ring of the Nibelung*, with Minkoff as the director. ("I'd never indicated any interest in any such project," Minkoff says, but some middleman had dreamed it up, attributed it to Minkoff, and suggested it to Schwarzenegger.) So Schwarzenegger came to the set of *Stuart Little*, and Minkoff showed him around. Then—tit for tat—Schwarzenegger invited Minkoff to cigar night at Schatzi's, a Santa Monica restaurant that Schwarzenegger co-owned.

"So I went in and there was a lot of cigar smoke," Minkoff says.

Schatzi's had a cigar collection for its clientele, part of Schwarzenegger's shtick.

Knowing that his first jobs in film were as an animator and that now he's a Disney producer, I can almost imagine the scene playing out in Minkoff's mind. I see smoke in a corner of a dark, masculine, wood-paneled restaurant, and then the smoke clearing just a bit, and then a big, round table with a white tablecloth, spangled by glasses in various states of emptiness and a scattering of cell phones and a half-dozen ashtrays with stubs and lit stogies in them.

"And sitting around the table are Schwarzenegger and Pete Wilson and a handful of Republican hangers-on," Minkoff says. The political dogs, again. I imagine a big dog—a mastiff or a boxer or a Presa Canario, you've seen him in *101 Dalmatians* and in *The Aristocats*—a big dog with a broad, jowly chin and great, bulging musculature, sitting there in a nice suit, a cigar clamped in his jaw, surrounded by other dogs in tight, double-breasted business suits, neckties decorated with diamond pins, also puffing away. The big dog speaks with an Austrian accent. The other dogs are worshipful, nodding.

"That's when I realized Arnold had a future with the Republican Party in the state of California," Minkoff says. "I knew he would be Wilson's guy." I see toothy smiles of satisfaction on the dogs' faces, and the big one reaching for a phone.

I went up to Sacramento to watch the inauguration and to visit the Project Operations Center of the State Water Project of California. The center does not really have an address. If you manage to find its website, within the Department of Water Resources, listed under the Operations Center office, you will hunt in vain for a physical location, and yet of course, a system that distributes unimaginable amounts of water each year to a very thirsty state must have an actual place of operation, and it does.

I found the Project Operations Center one night, the night before Schwarzenegger was inaugurated. "Come any time," a fellow named Fred told me over the phone. "We're here day and night." Fred was nice and friendly. I never got his last name. From our phone conversation, though, I gathered that somehow I had reached someone who was on site, there at the Project Operations Center. I could hear a game on the television in the background. Unfortunately, although the Project Operations Center professed accessibility, it turned out that they were not really looking forward to my visit.

I took the freeway east out of town and drove down El Camino Avenue. It was a long strip, like a Southern California strip, with car dealerships and gas stations, fast-food places, strip malls, medical buildings, real-estate offices, funeral homes. I went through the number of lights Fred had told me to go through. El Camino was becoming semiresidential; night was settling down on neat patches of lawn along tree-lined streets. I peered out through the dark, trying to see the numbers on the houses and the buildings, because it turns out that the Project Operations Center *does* have an address, which I am not at liberty to divulge. I can say, though, that the Project Operations Center was at the time in the former offices of a dental partnership, in an ugly beige low-rise slightly set back from the road. (This description does not single POC out, since it applies to virtually every office building on El Camino.)

A couple of cars are still parked in the lot. Lights are on on the second floor. I ring the buzzer marked SWP. A man's voice comes over the intercom.

"Fred?" I ask, hopefully.

"Fred's not here."

"Oh, uh, he said I could come over this evening for an interview at the POC," I said. Already I felt my expectations dwindling.

"Well, Fred's not here," said the voice.

"But I am." One reporting technique I'd learned over the years was persistence. Just being there was half the game.

"Sorry," said the voice. Apparently this reporting technique was not always successful in Sacramento.

"Can you just ask someone if I can come up?" I asked. "Fred said it was all right."

I was beginning to think that Fred was a janitor or a security guard.

"One second," said the voice.

I stood there on the asphalt in the dark under the photosensitive security lights, waiting. On El Camino, the lights turned from red to green and then back again, and then, back again.

"Uh, miss?" came the voice.

"Yes," I answered.

"No possibility tonight," he said. "Call back tomorrow, this number."

And he gave me the number through the static of the intercom.

The inauguration of a movie star in the normally backwater town of Sacramento (California's capital, true, but provincial, nonetheless, like many other state capitals) brought in an unusually intense and enormous crowd. Because the new governor was also possibly the most famous living man in the world at the time besides Nelson Mandela or Osama bin Laden, the crush of media and communications vehicles and personnel was particularly severe; whole areas of the grounds of the stately Capitol building were roped off for satellite vans. Television cameras from all over the world obstructed the audience's view.

It was like a crowd scene in a Capra film, with old politicians and their aides doling out off-the-cuff interviews on the Capitol lawn while constituents of every shape, size, and color—some in furs, some in denim jackets—offered up their tickets or credentials to guards at breaks in the fence. The media too were Capra-esque, both skinny, blond, high-heeled television anchors and seedy, paunchy, cigarette-smoking beat-reporter types, crowded into a jury-rigged reviewing stand that threatened to collapse with every movement of its occupants. Everybody at the Capitol seemed eager and oddly excited.

An important-looking security officer walked past the foot of the press bleacher with a black Labrador, an explosives sniffer. Richard Riordan, former mayor of Los Angeles and one of Gray Davis's biggest rivals, was standing to the side of the press bleacher, collaring whatever reporter he could for live interviews, having his picture taken with passing fans. Mud was building beneath the bleacher from the endless foot traffic. I could feel us swaying. Finally, Riordan couldn't stop himself and climbed up *into* the press bleacher, hunting for interviews.

Media and crowd alike were watching two huge screens, where you could see the day's action, could see Arnold and Maria (as they are called in the media) coming down the hallway of the Capitol with the children, could see them on the screen emerging from the door of the Capitol onto the dais, and then, at the same time, see them in fact (in reality) emerge from the door onto the dais. And then you could decide which was better, the screen version or the live version. For many of the voters who elected Schwarzenegger, the screen version would have seemed more real, been more acceptable. Being larger than life is an important aspect of this particular politician.

Schwarzenegger took the oath wearing a Prada suit. (His wife was wearing a skirt by Valentino.) Some might not think this important, but aides to the new governor obviously felt it carried some newsworthy weight, because this information was embargoed by the campaign until the Schwarzeneggers made their appearance before the public. This was in the "attire memo," no doubt rapidly changing up until the last minute and delivered to the media as we sat in our rocking bleacher. I also received the attire memo, as well as something called the "luncheon menu" memo, by e-mail.

After the inaugural ceremony, the new governor and his wife retired to a luncheon in the Capitol rotunda, and I retired to Old Sacramento, where I had an appointment to talk with a former recall candidate, one of the 135. Old Sac is a place of gift shops and candy shops and head shops today, but it was once the center of the Gold Rush. The first California gold was discovered about fifty miles outside of town, in 1849. Eventually, about 75 percent of San Francisco's adult males left home to seek their fortunes in the gold mines near Sacramento and elsewhere, and the town during Schwarzenegger's inauguration had that Old Sacramento feel to it, of emerging power groups, of money, of the intoxication of a new era, fitting for a former capital of whoring, drinking, gambling, banking, trade, and financial speculation of every kind.

Here I met Cheryl Bly-Chester, loser. This was not the first time I'd met her. The first time, she was chairing a meeting in Beverly Hills of the "alternative" candidates, the ones who were neither Gray Davis nor Arnold Schwarzenegger nor the other semiserious candidates. About fifty of them showed up, many of the women wearing red, one of the men wearing an Uncle Sam suit—everyone desperate for attention, seemingly just because they wanted attention.

Bly-Chester was not like that. She was serious. The second time I met her was at the Jay Leno show, where she and all the rest of her peers were upstaged by Mary Carey, the porn-star candidate who was not Angelyne, and who kept lifting up her breasts for the cameras. Among the alternative dozens of candidates, Cheryl Bly-Chester was not a standout except in so much as she was not a standout, which made her, in the end, something of a standout.

This time, I met her at a bar in Old Sac. She's a tall, blond Republican, an environmental engineer from a naval family. To me, she looked like a California concoction. People sometimes think Californians are bizarrely eccentric, like Manson, or *characters*, like Jack Nicholson or Angelyne, but most of them are not weirdos, not at all, and this is especially true of Californians who are from California. (Manson, for example, was born in Cincinnati.) Bly-Chester was so direct it was hard for me to understand her points, so sincere it was hard to interpret her. She was in a business suit and sipping port while her briefcase sat on the floor next to her barstool, but with her long, straight, bouncy blond tresses and willowy bearing, I could imagine her with a surfboard, a real California girl. (She was probably imagining me in the stacks of a public library somewhere, someplace musty.)

Bly-Chester was forty-six, but she looked oddly young, more teenaged. She had the statewide lack of shading and nuance and edge, as if the gunslinging characters of the Wild West and of Twain's *Roughing It* had devolved over the generations into soap opera characters, but without the plot. Hard people without an edge; it's disconcerting.

Bly-Chester could also be a news anchor; she talks like one, with strong, flat enunciation, and her hair and makeup are good. "I do chemical, nuclear, biological," she says of her engineering consulting business. She's worked on bridges, water resources, alternative energy projects, nuclear power plants. Once when she was working on a nuclear plant, the trailer she was living in was flattened by a tornado. She was the Dorothy Gale of nuclear engineers, and, as she says, "I got out of there."

But the recall campaign surprised her. It was the first time that she was not taken seriously, she says. She likes to be taken seriously. Schwarzenegger was taken seriously, and she wasn't, even though, of the two, I would have to say that Bly-Chester is without question the more visibly serious. Even now, when the idea of pretending that she ever had a chance to win is just plain silly, she won't admit it.

"I was the real deal," she says. "If I didn't completely take on a persona as a person who felt she could win, and dead seriously, then no one would take me seriously." She was wrong on this score, of course, because she just does not understand the journalist's deviant mind, or even simply the comic side of things in general—doesn't take in what is absurd, and especially not in herself. Try as he would, Michael Lewis of the *New York Times Magazine* could not get Bly-Chester to admit she might not win. And this made her a target of his teasing, in print.

"Well," she says of Lewis's *New York Times Magazine* article, "the journalists had all passed judgment beforehand."

"You know," she says, "before the Leno show, Leno brought us all in, in sort of a preshow, and they asked us, 'Who wants to get up and dance and get a free T-shirt?' and so Mary Carey did almost a striptease; she had no underwear on, and she was doing splits on stage with her skirt up around her waist." Bly-Chester's eyebrows go up. "It was sort of unbelievable. But Leno's an entertainer, so I can't get too pissed off. I'm not an in-your-face person." She says she'd been hoping to represent the 70 percent of Californians who are not socialists and are not right-wingers, and who care about "education, the environment, business, jobs, health, law enforcement, and homeland security." This, of course, was also Schwarzenegger's target constituency. And it worked for him; it was a constituency he could put

together. And he was no wholesome engineer. He was something else
entirely.

During the inaugural ceremonies, I'd managed to get some of Fred's
higher-ups at the State Water Project on the cell phone. They were
less nice and less friendly. I spoke first to Pete, then Ted, Fred's bosses
(I assumed). I could tell that they were worried—that it was not normal for someone to want to visit the Project Operations Center. After
some back-and-forth, Ted finally agreed that I could visit POC. Ted
went over the directions to the center again. I told him I was already
well aware of the location. The appointment was for that evening; for
some reason, Project Operations seems to prefer the dark. After my
talk with Bly-Chester, I drove back out.

This time I'm buzzed in and accompanied upstairs by a security
guard who is not Fred. POC is where water distribution for all of
Southern California is planned and where most of it is executed. The
State Water Project also must generate for itself enough power to dis-
tribute that water. According to the gentlemanly, bearded Curtis
Creel, who was at the time chief of the Project Operations planning
branch of the State Water Project control operations office, there are
three people on shift "twenty-four-seven." Across a long wall in a
room that I am not permitted to enter—for security reasons—is a
huge map of California's water system from north of Napa down
through the Sacramento Valley and then further down, all the way to
the Cherry Valley Pump Station just northeast of San Diego. An edge
of the Mexican border is just visible. I can see into this room thanks to
the plate-glass interior monitoring pane inside the office.

Computers are clicking and blinking, keyboards jittering, and the
operatives are drinking coffee, one with his feet up on the desk. The
map dominates the room. It looks like a war room, with California as
the battlefield. Strewn across the map like lanterns on a string are the
names of lakes, dams, rivers, reservoirs, and pumping plants along the
Sacramento and Feather rivers and along the California Aqueduct;
they appear on the map above the lights that indicate which facility is

dispensing how much water at that moment, which are dormant, what is stored where, what comes on line next. From north (where the water comes from) to south (where it is consumed): Antelope Lake, Frenchman Lake, Oroville, Barker Slough, South Bay, Bethany, Los Baños, Dos Amigos, Pine Flat, Badger Hill, Bluestone, Devil's Den, Las Perillas, Buena Vista, Pyramid Lake, Pearblossom, Mojave Siphon, Silverwood Lake, Devil Canyon, Greenspot, Cherry Valley . . . More than enough poetry there to conjure up California. Creel calls it "a flyover shot" of the state.

The people who work in the command room develop and implement each day's water schedule. They oversee the movement of energy throughout the state and, as Creel says, "match things up, making sure that we generate enough resource to meet the load." The plants along the aqueducts lift the water and then release it, letting gravity make it flow. The pumping plant at Edmonston is what Creel calls "the highest lift plant," raising water two thousand feet and dumping it down to provide energy for 650 families.

Water flow is measured in acre-feet. One acre-foot is the amount of water it takes to cover one acre to the depth of one foot. The State Water Project delivers almost three million acre-feet to consumers in any given year. When the project is finally completed, it is expected to deliver just about twice that much, which neat multiplication gives some idea of how California's planners expect development to go in the next decade or so. The California State Water Project, along with the Central Valley Project (which is operated by the federal government), is one of the largest engineering feats ever undertaken by man. Together, the two systems can store 16.8 million acre-feet of water. Together, they supply water to about 22 million Californians, and irrigate about 4 million acres of farmland. Because the project takes water from the north and provides it to the south, it was not an easy measure to pass, but Governor Edmund G. "Pat" Brown (who called the project a "monument to me" and was the father of Governor Edmund G. "Jerry" Brown) managed to squeak it through the legislature and past the people of California by providing measures that he said he hoped would prevent "unjust enrichment" by thirsty and greedy agribusiness using public waters. Still, in spite of Brown's lofty intentions, smart farmers like Stewart Resnick, who owns hundreds of thousands of acres in Kern County, have managed to take control of and exploit huge water banks.

Normally, this would just be facts and figures to me: I'm not too interested in infrastructure or engineering, usually. But in California you have to be. For instance, it is the availability of this water that has meant that suburbs can be built right up into the canyons and ridges of the Simi Valley and the San Bernardino Mountains, which are two spots where the wildfires of the 2003 fire season threatened entire neighborhoods of new developments and burned them down in some instances. This water also comes down to me from Northern California and means that I can have grass—a great water consumer—growing in my backyard. It means my neighborhood can be green and lush even in a place that normally would be sagebrush, pine, and cactus.

When bonds to finance the State Water Project were approved by Californians in 1960, the then director of water resources, William Warne, said, "California . . . must always in the future be willing, as no one else is willing . . . to sustain growth and development." Whoever controls and distributes water has power—electrical, agricultural, political. Water availability also determines the broad outlines of California demographics, what the state looks like and who can live or farm where. Because the State Water Project has been so successful, Southern California faces an overpopulation crisis, aquifers all over the state are depleted, flatlands have become salinated, and the land of the Sacramento delta has collapsed about fifteen feet per decade as the water table has dropped. And a few clever men, throughout the state's history, have profited from all this.

I drove up to Bel Air the other day. On my way down Sunset, I bought a star map from two Latino men who couldn't speak much English. They'd just arrived in L.A. a few months before, from El Salvador; they get their maps of the stars' residences from a man who comes with a truck at the beginning of each morning and returns at around four to collect their earnings and to pay them a flat fee. It's a reasonable job during the week, when not too many tourists come to look for the stars, and so the flat fee of between $25 and $50 is greater than what the vendors take in from the tourists. But on the weekends, selling star maps is a losing proposition, because the street vendors sell between $200 and $300 worth and still get around the same base pay.

I took my map and drove off toward Bel Air. I'd been meaning to go to Bel Air. I'd seen astonishing houses in Brentwood and Beverly Hills, like the Resnicks' palace or the producer Lawrence Bender's white-clapboard mansion, where there was a policy forbidding red wine for fear of staining the carpets—this from the man who helped make *Pulp Fiction* and *Kill Bill*. But people told me that Bel Air was the ne plus ultra of swank.

It's a gated community, in a sense. That is, the entrance to Bel Air, off Sunset, has an enormous iron gate. (I've never seen it closed, but they say it was closed during the 1992 riots.) There is no guard asking you to present your identity papers and state your destination, but just beyond the gate are two or three private security trucks. This reminded me that the name of the security firm that supposedly watches over my neighborhood—in its seemingly lackadaisical way—is Bel Air Security, meant to give us that Bel Air feeling of rich, protected, empowered exclusivity.

In Bel Air, you are being watched. Video cameras are posted at the bottom of every driveway. These people must be even more skittish than I am. Climbing up the soft curve of the hills of Bel Air in my secondhand, not-spanking-clean Volvo station wagon, I feel like an intruder, a suspect. I'm passing the Reagan house on St. Cloud, driving past high, high hedges and thick walls—cement walls, brick walls, stucco-covered walls, all grown over with ivy—and I can see hardly any bit of house from the road. Around every bend up here, you'll come upon a handful of Latino gardeners or car washers, wielding hoses, squeegees, and rags, or leaf blowers and weed whackers; from a distance I am constantly mistaking gardeners, with their leaf blowers in hand and motors on their backs, for soldiers with machine guns and radio packs. (I've definitely spent too much time in the Middle

East.) Near one property are security guards in sunglasses with translucent wire curls of communications equipment sprouting from behind their ears. Down that driveway, someone is making a movie. These are the only people visible in Bel Air: gardeners, car washers, security, and a few construction workers putting together the rudiments of a new palace.

I keep thinking of Bel Air in Haiti: it's also the name of a neighborhood in the capital, Port-au-Prince. Haiti's Bel Air is often called a slum in American newspapers, but it's really just a normal Haitian neighborhood of cement-block houses, shacks, and shanties. That Bel Air is on something of a hill too, and the roads wind past low pink and blue walls; the houses that can be seen from the street are made of painted cement block. Behind the visible houses lies a maze of little shanties, a warren of collapsible shacks with corrugated tin roofs, and in the alleys between the houses runs sewer water that is sometimes used for laundry and personal hygiene as well. But like L.A.'s Bel Air, Bel Air in Haiti is not an unpleasant place, at least during quiet political times. It's just . . . different.

In Haiti's Bel Air, people are out on the street day and night, playing dominoes, selling fried food, sweeping their tiny cement yards, drinking pineapple wine and telling stories, combing each other's hair, chatting, flirting, eating ices. Men walk through the neighborhood selling expired prescription drugs left and right. Unlike its namesake in California, Haiti's Bel Air offers little security, or at any rate, security has been mostly left to community leaders and toughs, so when there's a rumor that security is on its way, in the form of police or U.N. peacekeepers, everyone rushes inside and bolts the door, because after that, the shooting begins.

Still, I miss the streets of my old Bel Air as I drive, in a sort of a criminal's crouch, down Bellagio across Copa de Oro to Saint Pierre. It seems sad to live in a place so bereft of life, so immune to real life's little inroads, so regally, resolutely detached. Money will do that to you. Here there is no stench of sewage to remind you of the human condition, no neighbor to make a meal for your sick mother if you have to go away, no grandmother living in the lean-to or the other room, if there is another room, no humble straw pallet on the floor for the cousins, no clicking of the dominoes to fall asleep to, no storyteller on a roof going on and on toward midnight for the benefit of the whole neighborhood, no cockfights in the secret arena back behind your brother's house, no radio blasting merengue, no drummer practicing down the street out in back, no friends popping in unannounced at any time of day or night, no babies sitting on the sidewalk with their big sisters, no one fixing tires with tar on the street corners or rewiring the electricity with paper clips; just the hired help serving you day in and day out, the cook and the nanny, and the charming Vietnamese au pair, the driver, brunches at the Hotel Bel-Air in the pretty open-air dining room up above the pond with its vicious swans, and then the nice Salvadoran pool man on Wednesdays, with his fluent English, and the handyman (a former actor) who's putting in the screens, to say nothing of the eternal mowers and hedge trimmers and tree men, and, of course, the *landscapers* (another caste entirely! People with *diplomas! People with certificates!*) arriving with trucks full of trees, and the upholsterer, the seamstress, the decorator, the swim instructor, the fellow who does the sprinkler system, the boys' basketball coach, and the caterer for Thursday's party. The florist will be coming in the morning. Huffington, who lives in far humbler quarters than these, has been known to hire people to come in and decorate the Christmas tree for her and the girls.

In an attempt—one of many during the recall—to show how normal his life is, Arnold Schwarzenegger told Oprah Winfrey that he and Maria insist that their children do their own laundry. He and Maria, Schwarzenegger said, have put up signs all over the place to achieve this. You would think that the signs would read, "Katherine, Christina, Patrick: *do your laundry!!!*" But no, Schwarzenegger went on to say, with no trace of understanding or embarrassment (as if he had not lived the first nineteen years of his life in a small farm town in Austria in a lower-middle-class family), the signs are positioned throughout the house to tell the servants *not* to do the children's stuff.

There is almost no community in America as alienated from reality as Hollywood, and Hollywood in its broadest sense includes Bel Air, Pacific Palisades (where Schwarzenegger used to live in an $18 million compound), Beverly Hills, Santa Monica, Malibu, Venice, Brentwood (where Schwarzenegger now lives in a $12 million house in a gated community, and where Huffington lives in her more modest $7 million home), and all the other communities where entertainment money rules.

My favorite example, possibly apocryphal: Newly wed a decade ago (for the fourth time), the actress Melanie Griffith was eager to buy something special for her husband, the actor Antonio Banderas. His birthday was approaching. Griffith was thinking of art, and more specifically, she wanted a Rothko. A certain gallery in Beverly Hills was contacted, and one day, the gallery took several of its Rothkos and placed them outside in front of the gallery's door, with security guards watching. A few moments later, a limousine with smoked windows began to drive by. As the car passed, slowly, the back window rolled down, and Griffith, barely visible, examined the paintings from within. Then, through the window, like something in a Chandler novel, one finger emerged and pointed at the picture she had selected. After making her selection, Griffith shut the car window with her elbow, so as not to spoil the manicure she had just had done. And the limousine drove off.

Griffith's elbow on the window button is a nice symbol of the Hollywood disconnect, like Schwarzenegger's laundry note for the servants. The elbow on the window button, as the Rothkos stand to attention for review, is about entitlement, coddling, luxury. The laundry note for the servants is an attempt to conform to the celebrity profile cliché that tells us, disingenuously seeking our empathy, that all celebrities are somehow *just like us*.

A little black dog came to my door the other day. He wore no collar. He was a puppy. He looked up at me appealingly, with the wide-set eyes, snub face, and broad skull of a pit bull. I should have marked him for a huckster immediately, but I am that sucker every huckster must have. The puppy was what the French call *joli-laid*, which translates into "ugly-pretty." My Welsh spaniel did not love him, but the rest of us did. He was so cute.

At least for the first day, until he got his strength. The vet told me he was part pit bull, part Lab. I got him shots, I fed him choice puppy food, we named him Freddie, I bought him a little bed. Then I went around the neighborhood and put up signs announcing he'd been found: did he belong to anyone? But it seemed that Freddie was a dumped dog, brought onto our street by someone who thought the area looked friendly, like a pauper who leaves a baby on the steps of a mansion.

Freddie had his own ideas about how his life should be run. As he emerged from our front door, he would begin barking in a proprietary way. He was my little Arnold. He didn't want his own bed, he wanted the spaniel's bed; he didn't want his own little bone, he wanted the spaniel's big bone. And after two days of good food, what he wanted he took. My spaniel, three times bigger than Freddie, cowered before him. Still, Freddie was a smart dog who slept through the night in my spaniel's old crate and who got himself house-trained in a matter of days.

I didn't realize in the beginning of our connection that Freddie was to be a racial bellwether, but it's amazing how fast in L.A. a little thing like a stray dog can become a window on the culture. No one in my neighborhood would own a pit bull on purpose, because a pit bull is perceived as dangerous, unpredictable, violent, a drug dealer's dog, a felon's dog, a ghetto guard dog, a dog of the underculture, a dog for insecure places.

That's why I knew—even as I patiently pasted up my cheerful signs on the poles of streetlights at the corners near where Freddie had appeared—that no one would respond. Although Freddie was—I did include this on my signs—also part Labrador (as Maryann, a dog adoption amateur who saw his picture, said, "Yeah, about two percent"), no one in my neighborhood would have lost him, because no one would have owned him in the first place, and no one would want him, because he was the wrong kind of dog. Although the nice Vietnamese mailman perceived my galumphing spotted spaniel as "a guard dog" because the dog barks very angrily and the man is a mailman, the closest thing to a real guard dog in the neighborhood was a pair of large, exotic Rhodesian ridgebacks. Otherwise the dogs were dachshunds and poodles, sheepdogs and collies, Labradors and retrievers.

I put pictures of Freddie up on the Internet at a site recommended by Maryann. I splayed myself across the floor with the camera, trying to find a flattering angle, trying to make him look cute and huggable. When I examined the results, I thought he looked adorable, but then I was no longer objective: I thought Freddie was a nice and intelligent puppy, with a slightly aggressive personality; my neighbors jokingly called him the alpha male.

I sent the pictures to Maryann for vetting. She was not entirely pleased. Freddie's fur was a little sparse on his stomach, she pointed out, and for some reason no matter how I caught him with the camera, his bald chest and genitals were largely featured, as well as those flat eyes and his teeth. "He looks menacing," she said. "We need cute. Maybe if you shoot him in profile?" She was happy that his ears had not been clipped; the flop somehow detracted slightly from his air of menace.

I was panicking. Freddie was taking over my life, and my dog's life, and it didn't look as if I was going to be able to unload him "humanely." Maryann didn't call me back. I supposed that the photograph had been discouraging to her: she had been thinking that I had a puppy, but what she got was a pugilist. She was imagining Freddie as Oliver Twist, but he turned out to be the Artful Dodger.

All day long he scooted around my backyard; he liked to bother Joe, who was fixing the deck, doing something called "hardscaping." Joe took to Freddie, which was nice, since Freddie liked to stand there with his ears perked up and watch the men work. Then one day Joe told me that his friend Jesus wanted the dog, if I were willing to part with him.

And so it was arranged. Jesus's friend Abraham, who was helping with the stonework, would take Freddie to Jesus that very afternoon. Jesus, Joe said, was a family man whom Joe had known for years, a construction foreman with a big backyard and two teenaged boys and another dog; Freddie would have a great time.

I packed up a bag for Freddie, not without regret. I sent him off with the rest of his food, some special vitamins to make the fur grow on his bald stomach, his rejected little dog bed, some toys, and his veterinary records. Abraham took Freddie in his arms and sat down with him in the passenger seat of his friend's pickup. I watched Freddie's little intelligent face in the window as the truck disappeared down the street.

About a week later, I called Maryann. I felt I should tell her the good news, even though she hadn't called me to share any leads or to commiserate.

"I just wanted to tell you I found a place for Freddie," I said, expecting a delighted reply. Instead, there was a moment of silence on the line. I do not know dog people.

"Oh," she said finally. "Well, I hope it's not with a Latino family." I was stunned.

"It *is* actually," I said.

"We don't have a very good outcome with Latino families and Staffordshire terriers," she said. "Staffordshire terrier" is the politically correct name for pit bull.

"What?" I asked, since a Latino family was the only family I'd found who had shown any interest in having a pit bull. "Why not?"

"Well, they tend to use them as guard dogs," she said. "Actually, I did have someone who was interested in your dog."

"Really?" I said.

"Yes, I was just going to call you," Maryann said. "She's a very nice woman who works at home." There was another pause. "She has a PhD."

This was too much for me. I thanked Maryann for her work and told her she should tell the nice lady that Freddie was already adopted. But I did feel guilty all day long because in my haste I had deprived Freddie of a home with a doctoral degree.

And then I decided to thank heaven for Jesus, and I'm sure Freddie did too, because what would Freddie do with a lady like that? It would be worse than Huck and Aunt Polly. There were many things Freddie wanted, but a PhD was not one of them.

Finally the movie cameras were coming to me. Someone had decided to use my house as a location. True, it happened to be a Scandinavian bank, but I'll let that pass, although why a Scandinavian bank would come all the way to L.A. to film a commercial with a "Scandinavian" look was mysterious in the extreme, especially considering that so many Hollywood movies are now filmed in Romania, Canada, Ireland, Mexico, and Bulgaria in order to save money. A friend of mine said it was for the technological know-how, the talent, and the braggability, but in the event, it seemed that all the important people doing the shoot were actual Scandinavians: Danish and Norwegian. Plus in my opinion my house looks as if it were in Connecticut, not in Stockholm or Oslo.

Some people wisely do only high-end shoots, but after having been rejected even by the ant people, I realized high-end was not to be my fate. After repeated rejection, I was eager for anyone who was willing to use me; like a wallflower at a party, I was now determined to be happy with the first dweeb who asked me to dance. Hence the single-day Scandinavian bank shoot, which was far from the glamorous, star-studded, two-week, major-studio, five-digit event I had been imagining.

By the end of the day, a teacher—who was in fact a retired teacher hired by the production company—was "teaching" three small, strawberry blond child actors on my front steps: they were playing with blocks and drawing pictures. It's the law that with school-aged kids, a movie production has to keep them up-to-date with their classroom work, although what these kids were doing would not really qualify for any curriculum but pre-K, certainly not in the days of No Child Left Behind. Dining tables for fifty people had been set up in my driveway, with red tablecloths and roses in vases, and a full buffet, including vegetarian options, out front. Big macho techies were eating marinated chicken; the Scandinavians picked salmon. The household was allowed to partake also, the director told me. His name was Martin.

At the end of the driveway, cables ran to two video monitors where you could see what the production was attempting to create. The set builders also erected a huge steel construction across the entire backyard, to hold up an old-fashioned, wide, wooden plank swing for the nice Scandinavian-style boy to swing in. The commercial, Martin told me, as if he were the next Bergman, was about "a fantasy of homeownership"—exactly what California was for me. At least forty people were wandering around in my small backyard, eating, pointing with forks or glasses, and making comments on the proceedings. I watched them from my office window while I tried to write.

It was a bright, sunny day. A tired-looking assistant in T-shirt, khakis, and sneakers was holding up a huge, clear Plexiglas sheet on which a horse had been crayoned in a childish fashion: this was the elder daughter's fantasy. I couldn't quite seize the story line, but I believe the final fantasy belonged to the littler daughter (with braids like Pippi Longstocking's), who stood in front of the Plexiglas sheet on which an extra roundness to her mother's stomach had now been drawn (the horse had vanished): a new sibling on the way. Meanwhile, the boy was swinging, kicking his stout little legs. Cut!

The bedraggled assistant took to the drawing with a sponge: the curved top of the mother's belly was not right, Martin decided. Artists with special crayons came running out to the center of the lawn to redo the thing. The children rushed back to their teacher and their Legos to get a little more education in. I typed a few more sentences and went out to watch the monitors. The director and assistant directors were sitting on stools behind the monitors, commenting.

My reward for the day: a check for $1,100 (I was new to all this and did not know what to ask for; still, it was free money) and a wooden swing that the techies put in my garage on a shelf next to the powdered milk and bottled water. As he was leaving, Martin turned to me.

"Your house will be famous in Scandinavia!" he said, with a big white smile.

It was not my intention to contribute to the Prostate Cancer Foundation. But at Christmastime, a donation was made in my name to that charity—by Stewart and Lynda Resnick. One day, I arrived home to find a big, heavy, yellow-and-red-striped box, shaped like a Gypsy circus wagon, inside my front door. Within were pomegranates—large, perfect ones, globular and magenta, unlike any I'd ever seen—as well as almonds and pistachios and a little carousel horse ("The Fabergé Golden Carousel Jumping Horse"), courtesy of the Resnicks' Franklin Mint. A big, square holiday card accompanied this gift.

A banner on the front of the card, written on a buntinglike overlay, read, "2004: The Greatest Show on Earth." The setting for the family photograph that the banner adorned was the inside of a colorful circus tent. Astride an elephant, there was Lynda, wearing a sparkling golden décolleté circus mini-outfit and golden pumps, with three pink ostrich feathers emerging from her bouffant. She is tossing pistachios from a bag into the elephant's trunk. (The bag is labeled Pistachios to make sure you do not confuse these nuts with the more common kind preferred by elephants but not grown by Resnicks.) There was an unfamiliar, slighter Resnick relation on the trapeze; below her on the ground were some tiny children of the Resnick brood, one of them juggling oranges (another Resnick crop) and pistachios, and two others, lesser Resnicks, wearing tutus, pink tights, and yellow feather headdresses. In front of all this commotion stood Stewart, the master of ceremonies and impresario, wearing red tails and a top hat, smiling broadly, gesturing with a black walking stick, and spreading one arm wide to show off this improbable scene, as if to say, "Step right up!" Inside the card, the message read, "From our Three Ring Circus to yours." An insert informed us that a gift had been made in our name to Prostate Cancer, to Breast Cancer (covering all the bases), and to Conservation International ("to protect life on Earth," CI says on its website).

Those pistachios and oranges under the happy, innocent big top come from somewhere; they are not just props. They come from Kern County, where the Resnicks are one of the biggest landholders (and where California City is also located, almost a hundred miles east of the Resnick lands). Paramount Farming and Paramount Citrus, the Resnicks' huge agribusinesses (which together constitute the largest farming operation in the United States), now have a controlling share of what has become the privately owned Kern Water Bank in Kern County, the state's enormous water stockpile, which is a part of the State Water Project. Intended by the state of California as a safeguard against drought for both agricultural and municipal/industrial use, to be stored in wet years for public benefit in dry, the water bank has, under the Resnicks' control, "allowed Paramount farming to double its acres of nuts and fruits since 1994," according to a report in the *L.A. Times*. Paramount is no relation to the studio of the same name.

As anyone knows who has seen the movie *Chinatown,* water is traditionally California's most controversial commodity, because it is— simply put—the basis for everything, and yet there is not enough of it to support both the state's growing population and the state's growing agriculture. Since the beginning of its modern development, there hasn't been enough water in California, and hence major fortunes in the state have famously (and infamously) been made on water rights, water infrastructure, water banks, and water control. Control of water has been—as is true for all civilizations—the sine qua non of all development, especially agricultural and municipal. It is almost a cliché about California even to open a discussion about water. But it was without question the irrigation security provided by the Resnicks' gaining control of the Kern Water Bank that made it possible for their operation to become one of the biggest agricultural ventures in the world.

I'd been here for a year, and still I was missing the torrid, struggling mass of Manhattan's humanity. In New York, every day is filled with chance encounters with fellow men, thousands of them in transit: on the subways, the sidewalks, the buses, the elevators. Every day there brings an opportunity for close study of the species. Best of all, after you spend twenty minutes watching a man and woman of indecipherable ethnicity bickering and sniping in an unfamiliar tongue, and a mother with three children filing her nails, and three teenagers giggling as they scrabble through their bags, looking for something—and what that thing might be arouses your intense curiosity—after all that, you can get off at Twenty-eighth Street secure in the knowledge that you will never have to see any of them again.

In L.A., by contrast, anyone you're watching so closely is probably a friend or a family member or is sitting across from you at a dinner party. No encounter is unplanned, and in the end, you will definitely find out what it is they are searching for in their bag, and it will invariably be an anticlimax: lipstick, keys, cell phone.

In Los Angeles, the closest encounter I have on a daily basis with strangers who might surprise me is in street traffic. I'm turning left at a light, and a car from the oncoming traffic is also turning left, at the same light. My opposite, my counterpart, my mirror image—my partner in the dance. We are both waiting for the through traffic to slow or pause and allow us to turn, and we are facing each other in the turning lane. Often the encounter lasts for a full minute or more. I try to make the most of it, try to make eye contact, almost always unsuccessfully. Usually the person is talking on a cell phone or adjusting the radio. Sometimes the person is smoking a cigarette or fixing her hair in the rearview mirror. Today, one oncomer was an Asian man with a pencil mustache and an unlit cigarette, and another was a teenaged blond girl who was talking to a dark-haired woman in the passenger seat. I don't learn much from these chance encounters; no theories of human behavior can be elucidated in such short spurts, and with no audio input. But I'm thirsty for them anyway.

At the beginning of his term as governor, Schwarzenegger decided that he ought to do the right thing. He announced that it was his intention to initiate an investigation into the recent reports of his sexual misconduct to find out, one assumed, if there was any truth to them. You couldn't help wondering if he was going to interview himself and ask himself some very tough questions. Understandably, the probe never went forward, and there was never any further mention of it from Sacramento. The *Los Angeles Times* is still working to develop leads in the story.

But a later event took place involving the governor's bodily fluids that must have pleased Krasniewicz and Blitz, the two Schwarzeneggerologists. At a police memorial, the governor was reportedly seen tossing a cough lozenge he'd been sucking on into a trash bin, from which an alert garbage picker/fan fished it out, as fans used to do with the Beatles' chewed gum. Soon after, the cough drop appeared for sale on eBay, with a starting bid of five hundred dollars, under the category "Schwarzenegger DNA." It was certainly a strange item: "Own a piece of DNA from the man himself," read the description.

This would no doubt qualify as "spreading Arnold Schwarzenegger," although who was to say it was authentic? The listing pictured a semisucked yellow drop on a black background, as if the glistening throat lozenge were a rare Oriental topaz. "Like many people who collect items from international stars this is a must have," the listing continued, cheerfully and ungrammatically. "I've heard of people going through trash cans of the stars trying to find items such as this, but . . . witnessing this was amazing and this is why I'm offering this to the fans and collectors of memorabilia to the stars and no one is bigger than Arnold Schwarzenegger!!!" Possibly, I thought as I read this copy, the lozenge had been posted to eBay *by* Krasniewicz and Blitz.

In any case, the DNA sale turned out to be a violation of eBay's stricture against selling human body parts on the site, and the cough drop was removed from play. Later, eBay told the *Los Angeles Times* that if the seller reclassified the candy as a "collectible," it could be reposted. As if it were something from the Franklin Mint. But I never saw it again.

Two days ago, there was a microearthquake four kilometers from Malibu. I could swear I felt it, a little rumble underfoot. I was walking past Le Petit Greek, a restaurant on Larchmont Boulevard, near my house,

and I'd stopped in my tracks in order to see what everyone was looking at. It was another bloody sunny day, naturally. I wouldn't have felt
the rumble if I hadn't stopped, not that anyone else seemed to notice.

I looked where everyone else was looking. At a sidewalk table at
Le Petit Greek sat a very pretty girl, a remarkably beautiful woman,
and it began to dawn on me, slowly, that I was having an actual
celebrity sighting, my first. This woman was clearly the object of
everyone's attention, microearthquake or no. The eyes of all the
passersby, all the restaurant patrons, the waitresses and busboys, people at the shoe store and the Japanese restaurant and the pizza place
next door, and all up and down the street were turned toward her: it
was like a moment stopped in time. She was smiling at her date and
taking no notice of the attention. Her hair was long and perfectly
styled and chestnut brown, and she had upturning, very green eyes,
and excellent cheekbones, and a lovely flush in her cheeks and ruby
red lips, really, and good, summery clothes.

And I have no idea who she was.

The Malibu micro that day took place just south of Northridge,
where the really big macroearthquake of 1994 originated. Among
generalized mayhem and destruction, the 1994 earthquake also
broke apart large sections of the Santa Monica Freeway (also known
as the 10), and created a mountain more than thirty miles away from
the quake epicenter. The mountain is known as La Montaña, because
it rose up in Huntington Park, a Latino municipality south of downtown L.A.

La Montaña is a five-story-high, 5.4-acre pile of rubble and debris
made out of the broken-apart slabs of the 10. The freeway rubble was
carted to an empty lot behind Cottage Street in Huntington Park after
the earthquake. Its carter allegedly intended to recycle it and sell the
concrete for use as roadbed, a not uncommon practice for concrete
rubble. Instead, however, he just left it there in Huntington Park for a
decade, and refused to heed a number of court orders demanding its
cleanup.

More than a decade after its creation, small trees and bushes are growing on La Montaña, dandelions are sprouting, and fine particulate matter, blown from the earthquake detritus by the winds, has been embedding itself in neighborhood lungs for years, to what effect no one knows. The great gray thing broods and seems to shudder like an angry, barnacled Leviathan behind the very modest brown and yellow houses of Cottage Street, and I can't help wondering, as the dust blows by me, how La Montaña would look behind my house or, better, behind Stewart and Lynda Resnick's house—how long such a mythic geological apparition would remain there, looming over the conservatory and the trellised walkway, and spreading dust and debris in the empty lot that backs on their magnificent palace on Sunset Boulevard.

PART TWO

Sunset

CHAPTER FOUR

Theories of Relativity

C ALIFORNIA IS ON EDGE around me now, like the country itself. Rain—rain!—is coming down on the formerly drought-stricken south in record inches. I'm wet all the time: who remembers an umbrella here, who thinks to look for leaks, who has a damn bucket? (I do, but there's a boat in it.) It's too much—too much rain after too little rain, too much rain after too much fire. Too much is how things are happening here now.

Excess is visibly part of nature where I live. It's part of what the California writer Mike Davis called the ecology of fear. The rain beats down in its relentless dull drumbeat, and people are nervous. They're not relaxing or saying, "Water—we need it." That's because it doesn't just rain; it does something more. It floods, it deluges, it sweeps away. The hills are falling down, taking houses with them into the mud. Laurel Canyon is blocked by a fallen house, a nice white modern house completely toppled, with trees coming out of its sides. There are sinkholes in Pasadena. My friend Cassandra's pool is filled with rock and mud from a slide. My friend Keith's house is buried two stories deep in Studio City, red-tagged, condemned, evacuated. He and his family are living with friends. Natacha says, "Don't say this to Keith, but what if there's an earthquake on top of all this rain?" Brilliant catastrophizing, Natacha, I think. Californians are worrying about apocalypse because the Western world, including George Bush's America, is undergoing a spasm of millenarianism right now, and the earthly harbingers of apocalypse seem to be particularly evident in the chaparral and canyons.

It's not weather that can be taken lightly. In La Conchita, a tiny hamlet under a cliff on the way to Santa Barbara, five members of a young family die under a slide while their dad is out buying ice cream for the children. Months later, when it was finally dry again, landslides created by the rains continued to undermine foundations and push houses down hillsides. In Laguna Beach, carried by the slides, one house's first floor lay on top of another's roof. The hillside, strewn with roofs and lattice and porches and gates, looked like a cubist painting.

I'd been away from L.A. for a trip east, a mental-health break, as we used to call trips home when I lived in Haiti. There was weather in the east. It rained all over New York for days; the sewers were over-flowing; it was the kind of thing the *Los Angeles Times* loves to put on the front page of the paper ("Third Day of Torrential Rains on East Coast"), because this is traditionally an aspect of the East Coast that Angelenos offer as a reason, perhaps *the* reason, to live in L.A. "How's the weather?" they always ask their friends back east. ("Back east" is another term; you never hear someone on the East Coast say "back west." It's "out west" and "back east." The east is seen as back, still, because everything started from there. The phrase denotes direction, but is also temporal. Back is in the past; California is now.)

The thing about rain and water in Southern California is that it is usually miraculous; a storm is looked on with all the matter-of-factness with which you might receive manna from heaven. Long after I am sick of precipitation, Californians will say, I love the rain, I love June gloom. A cloudy day is something special to them. So when it started to rain here and never stopped, there was an initial period of ecstasy. Isn't this fabulous? Followed by the inevitable Los Angeles complaint: My pool is overflowing.

The governor, making the most of disaster, as usual, rushed down to La Conchita to be with victims of the mudslides that temporarily destroyed the small makeshift community. Although the houses of La Conchita were red-tagged as too dangerous for human habitation, Schwarzenegger counseled residents to move back in and stand firm. Standing firm is an expression he reverts to when he can't think of any other exhortation, when conditions are too grim.

All along my usual hiking grounds in Fryman Canyon and Beachwood Canyon—the canyons being the only place in L.A. where I experience natural nature (as opposed to lawns, decks, plantings, medians, landscaping, pools, and fountains)—pieces of the dirt paths had simply fallen away into huge, sagging heaps of mud and grass. In places, the roadbed was almost impassable. A dried riverbed, which I'd always thought of as a desert wadi, was now a real rushing stream. A caked bed at the bottom of the canyon was now a broad, deep pool with dogs swimming in it. Waterfalls burst out of the ravine in spots where you'd never suspected that water lurked, and plunged down the canyon, as in the famous romantic landscape paintings of Yosemite from the early days of California settlement. Someone had taken a warning sign and put it down flat so runners could use it as a platform to get over a mudslide crevasse along the path. Even though it was still overcast, a bright, lush, green, junglelike splendor had overtaken canyons I'd always thought of as brushland.

Still, some things remained the same. From the top of Beachwood, with heavy vegetation behind me and mud beneath my feet, I could see the huge iPod sign down in the southern reaches of Hollywood, near the corner of Highland and Santa Monica. The iPod sign has overtaken the Warner Brothers and Paramount Studios water towers as one of the great landmarks of L.A., its cultural import equal to— and perhaps, these days, greater than—that of the Hollywood sign. (If you hike up close enough to the Hollywood sign at the top of Beachwood Canyon, just as you come around a curve, you'll notice that the sign seems to say "Ohllywodo," because of the angle. For me, this was an unnerving, demystifying display.) Like the Empire State Building, the Eiffel Tower, or the Hollywood sign, the iPod sign represents its culture and its era without even trying. Perhaps municipal officials will find a way to make it permanent.

I have finally seen a celebrity I recognize. I heave a sigh of relief. The sighting took place at the Center for Yoga on Larchmont, across from the Greek restaurant where I saw my first but unidentified celebrity.

This time, the celebrity was so celebrated that even I could not be unaware of who she was. Her very blond hair was pulled back like a dancer's; she was tall, thin, and brittle, and there came that moment legendary in celebrity sightings where suddenly and out of the blue the realization comes to you that a person you are seeing is someone you have formerly only seen on videotape, on film, or in magazines: that moment of recognition when image becomes flesh. I turned to check into my class and it occurred to me: this woman next to me is Nicole Kidman, actually.

Then we went in to an hour-and-a-half class. She put her mat down next to mine. But sadly, yoga class is not a good place for observation of anything other than, say, your own nostril breathing or your own left heel. It would be interesting, for instance, to see Nicole Kidman in the fish position, but in the fish position, your head is strictly looking one way, which is not to your right. When she's in crow, so are you, and if you look to your right in crow, you will quickly discover that your head has hit the ground, if you ever managed to get it off the ground in the first place. This was the class in which I discovered that your gaze in yoga is usually straight ahead. Occasionally, I would be lined up behind her, and then I could see that she was very beautiful but not too flexible. This was not a person who would easily place her ankles over her shoulders.

The teacher, however, *did* get to look at her the whole time, and to interact with her, and he did more than his usual minimal interacting and adjusting during this class. There was a lot of Nicoling from him: That's good, Nicole. That's right, Nicole. A little wider stance, Nicole, etc. She had that semicatatonic look on her face that people can get when they are the center of attention: it's like a trance that they go into.

At Starbucks immediately after class, in a gaggle of women talking about Nicole ("She must be shooting nearby"), I learned two new things. One: that the Center for Yoga is, according to the women who go there every day, extremely famous. And two: that today's yoga instructor was not just a yoga instructor but someone who had *played* a yoga instructor in the memorable opening scenes of *The Anniversary Party,* a movie about actors in L.A. Later I found out that almost all the yoga instructors there were actors, or screenwriters.

We sit and look out our windows at the rain, or drive along at a crawl on the freeways in the rain, listening to the radio as the rainfall reaches near-record levels, day by day. Clouds sit low over the hills, the fog comes in and out. By February, the area had beaten a record for winter rain set back in the 1889–90 season. And the rains continued through the spring. Today, it's raining again, a bleak May day. Looked at from a wise and experienced perspective, all the wet is good. But because water consumers here are usually protected and distanced from the real environment by infrastructure—the water bank, the State Water Project, the dams and overflows and reservoirs, the aqueducts, the canals, the diversions—we are only grateful for the latest downpour by rote: no one feels happy.

Anyway, rain can carry the public mood only so far. The state's economy is still evaporating, the housing boom is slowing, the state's job growth lags behind the national numbers, other indicators are down, and the governor has borrowed millions in order to keep the budget going. The advantage California once had, ahead of everyone in everything, is gone, *and* the weather sucks. Where's the edge, the California promise? A terrible sense of insecurity pervades the state, and—as do Americans in general—Californians worry about their new vulnerability: have they brought it on themselves?

It was hard to assess the governor's plans for the state. Schwarzenegger was still courting the mainstream national media like a presidential hopeful, and they returned the compliment by covering him like a movie star rather than a Sacramento politician. A *Vanity Fair* cover photo showed Schwarzenegger and his wife, somewhere on the California coast, astride a motorcycle—him in front, her behind, of course. ("After all these years," the governor revealed in a pull-quote on the magazine's cover, "we are still engaged with each other, hot for each other, into each other.") He's in jeans and a leather jacket, and she is in a long white evening gown with Jackie O earrings on, sitting sidesaddle with her arms around his shoulders, his hand reaching across her thighs to hold her by the calf. She's his prize. It's hard to remember the bright-eyed, round-faced Kennedy girl Maria Shriver was when the two of them got married back in 1986, though Schwarzenegger doesn't seem to have changed much since then.

Even if you're not going to buy the magazine, there's the governor smiling out at you from the newsstand racks on Larchmont or San Vicente or Laurel Canyon, with all his moneyed, well-groomed power, from atop his superstud cycle. You might like him, you might want to emulate him, or have him like you, but no matter what, you're bound to feel that this man, dressed even in real life in an outfit that approximates the Terminator's (though more costly, less ripped), might not care too much all the time about the little guy, the guy whose wife does not have a perfect French manicure or blinding white teeth, a four-hundred-dollar (at least) hairdo and lots of diamonds.

The age of Schwarzenegger is clearly a time for reevaluating what it means to be a man in California, in America. Do you stand tall, or back down? Do you torment prisoners, or report their tormentors? Is a proper man the one on the Harley in leather with a skinny, bejeweled heiress riding behind? Arnold was supposed to be a real man, another in the line of Charlton Heston, Clint Eastwood, and the Marlboro Man, a macho version of the California story. He showed what might be achieved by someone who projected the ability to inflict injury, someone always ready for an armed response, an affect that Schwarzenegger has always projected, that Krasniewicz and Blitz would agree is synonymous with his name. In shaky times, a politician who projects power, decisiveness, and a measure of violence can win big with the American people. President Bush was such a figure for a time. When an old friend of his disagreed publicly with Schwarzenegger about not returning $2 billion he had borrowed from the education pot and about changing the rules of teacher tenure, the governor called his friend up on the phone and told him that his position was "pussy." The governor's friend argued that there had to be some give-and-take on both sides.

"Come on," Schwarzenegger repeated, "that's pussy."

Pooossy.

Someone is defining things in terms of masculine and feminine.

In California, however, there are other options besides macho for the male of the species. To all evidence, this is a state filled not only with all-American males but also with more than its reasonable share of girlie men, and by this phrase, no matter what Schwarzenegger may have meant when he used it, I mean metrosexuals. The Bay Area is filled with them. Silicon Valley too. Hollywood.

And the Apple Store at the Grove shopping mall in L.A. is another magnet, possibly the best venue in L.A. for girlie-man watching, the most reliable agglomeration of heterosexual and also homosexual male non-Schwarzenegger voters in Southern California. They come to the Genius Bar at the Apple Store to ask questions all day long. They do not have normal day jobs.

This non-Schwarzenegger-voting girlie man can be an architect or a landscape artist, a software designer, a network developer, an Internet hobbyist, a video streamer, a composer, an acting coach, a teacher, a would-be rock star, a freelance mathematician or scientist, a yoga instructor (who is also an actor and a screenwriter), a museum curator, a restaurateur, anyone with a website, or, of course, an assistant producer, a special-effects designer, an animator, a personal assistant, an agent, a director (though agents and directors often fall into the hypermasculine category too), or an actor. He's the new, techno-savvy man, the Steely Dan man, the opposite of a NASCAR dad, not reliant on caveman methods for his professional or sexual powers. He wears flawless black jeans or blue jeans with at least one ragged, fashionable hole in them; a black T-shirt; sometimes a sports jacket if he's doing well or wants to appear as if he is. His hair is fairly close-cropped but not *too* close-cropped. His sideburns are subtly decorative. Sometimes he has a facial piercing or an earring or two. He wears sneakers or flip-flops. He's usually white—although he can be Asian, black, or Latino—and often a little too thin.

Another, darker side of masculinity, the failure side of macho, is well represented here in Los Angeles too, and always in the news. These are the men who provide the material for current and future crime thrillers, for Michael Connelly and lesser mystery writers. The fertilizer salesman who was convicted of killing his pregnant wife in order to run off with his new girlfriend. The singer in the shower with a little boy (exonerated); the down-on-his-luck actor charged with the shooting death of his fortune-hunting wife (also exonerated); and the drug-addled 1960s record producer charged in the point-blank murder of a has-been (or never-was) actress and music club hostess he picked up one night for a little action. Also the man who used his nineteen-month-old daughter as a shield from the police. Also the LAPD officers who, in an excess of armed response, killed the man and the little girl.

I'd arrived in Los Angeles in the middle of a season of celebrity trials, with breathless news stories detailing bizarre acts, all of them—at heart—about sex gone wrong, about unacceptable versions of manhood, trials that were clearly about what is allowable to American men. On a grander scale, while these trials were unfolding in Los Angeles, Redwood City, Alhambra, and Santa Maria, Specialist Charles Graner, the chief defendant in the Iraqi prisoner abuse scandal, provided an international example of what it could mean when American masculinity went awry. "One night in October," the *New York Times* reported, Graner told his then girlfriend Lynndie England "to pose for photographs holding a leash tied around the neck of a naked and crawling detainee [at Abu Ghraib prison in Iraq]. He e-mailed one home: 'Look what I made Lynndie do.' The now infamous pictures of detainees masturbating, he said, were a birthday gift for her."

Completely unfair, of course, but I was inevitably reminded of our governor, my rescuer—the not-so-subtle element of pornography, the taking of pictures, the absolute need for humiliation, and how Lynndie is "told" what to do. Graner's vicious antics had the ring of Schwarzenegger's "rowdy behavior on the set," with the added S&M props of leashes and dogs. Both Graner and Schwarzenegger had been represented by some as "fun-loving" or "playful." Equally, the ex-soldier's bragging contained something of the reflexive bully's shit-eating grin, reminiscent of Schwarzenegger's self-congratulatory smirk that was so prominently and disconcertingly featured in *Pumping Iron*.

Now I'm building a pool house in my garage, and everything's a wreck. Naturally, I would be building a pool house during the worst rainy season Southern California has seen in a century. But I'm in California, and if I can't build an empire, or buy up a county, or perform an engineering miracle, erect a dam or divert a river . . . the least I can do is reconfigure a garage. There are problems, however: leaks, cracks, rebolting against future geological turbulence. And amid all the displaced bats, balls, mitts, and bikes, I can't find my blue boat in its bucket.

It has put me in a bad mood. I don't know why I'm so sad about losing it. Even though this year the California catastrophe was rain, it still doesn't seem as if the boat could really ever be useful to me here. But who knows: for two months, it's been raining.

A few weeks after the rains begin, the cars on my block come close to floating away. No one can believe it. A neighbor calls the police, although what the police are supposed to do about floating cars no one is sure. In the end the police don't come, and yet the cars are also not carried away.

But somehow my boat has been. Someone must have moved it. I feel nostalgic for it. I wonder where it's gone—over to the city dump along with pieces of my cement driveway that have been removed to make way for plumbing? Or, like an old broken microwave I recently put out at curbside, into the trunk of an interested drive-by snatcher, a trader in relics and questionable goods?

So much of what I've had has been lost in my moves back and forth to Haiti, to Jerusalem, and around the country. Things I've forgotten are in storage in places I've forgotten; in Albany during an evening snowstorm almost a decade ago, we simply gave up on one huge storage crate, abandoned it and its contents to an unknown fate, and now I imagine all sorts of things were in it: my dead father's love letters, my dead mother's crayon picture of her dog, my Beatles album collection, a form response from Mrs. Kennedy to a condolence letter I scribbled out after the president was assassinated—a form letter, but still, from Mrs. Kennedy. Oh, well . . . And now my boat too I consign to this wretched, scattered pile of lost things, lost memories.

Probably the boat in its blue bucket got put in the Dumpster with chunks of wall and a pile of rotting firewood, and carted away, like the concrete refuse of La Montaña—forgotten things that are always on the move, objects in a life-size shell game. Over on Cottage Street, haulers have finally been taking load after load of La Montaña away from the neighborhood to "an undisclosed location." The man in charge of the haulers told me, "We're going to keep that a secret." Perhaps that secret place is also where my boat went. Maybe La Montaña has been moved to a landfill somewhere out on the 5, on the way to the Central Valley.

Or nearer by? The other day I noticed a new road project by the side of the 10, with an impressive hill of rubble next to it, waiting, it seemed, to be reused. The 10 was the freeway whose collapse during the Northridge earthquake created La Montaña's debris. I wondered, Have they simply carted the wreckage back?

Deep down, I'm hoping that perhaps I'll find my boat—along with my earthquake emergency supplies—under the enormous, puddle-punctuated blue tarp beneath which we've stored what was once in the garage, including old warped tennis rackets and a bug-infested tent. Maybe after the rains have stopped, should that moment ever come. Peeking under the blue tarp the other day while the rain was taking a breather, I did find two Rollerblade skates overflowing with rainwater, a sneaker in which a family of spiders had taken shelter—and two optimistic, hopeful oars.

———

I seem by accident to have become a perfect Californian, like an emigrant traveling across America in a covered wagon, or like Mrs. Brier and the forty-niners in Death Valley: with a trail behind me of lost homes and possessions, lost family too. When she had to cross Death Valley on foot, one Mrs. Barrett left everything she had from back home by the side of her abandoned covered wagon (furniture, books, kitchen things, toys, family heirlooms, a spinning wheel, and such) and put on her Sunday best, including ribbons and petticoats, crinolines and furbelows, and an indescribable hat—probably not unlike Mrs. Hiram Johnson's hat a half century later—and thus made her way, with her three children, across the harshest terrain, just to get to California. To think that I took a plane over what had seemed to her an endless wasteland and crossed it in just a few minutes' time, in blue jeans and a T-shirt, drinking a Diet Coke—even more unimaginable to Mrs. Barrett than her hat and her ribbons and her unbearable thirst are to me.

A trail of losses, and now, starting up fresh. That's what is special about California, but I don't like it: this loss of past, this starting up fresh. I like antiquity. I'm used to Jerusalem, an old city with an older city in its midst—the ancient or antique city, it's called in Hebrew. In Jerusalem you can't avoid history, the history of several entire peoples, no matter whether you seek it or flee from it.

But by the time you end up here in California, it's not only that you can become whoever you wish to be or that you can assume a new persona, it's that you *are* by now, almost by virtue of having arrived in this place, a different person. There is a strong parallel with the Puritan transit to the New World: a fresh start was what they sought when they came across the Atlantic. And simply by virtue of that tumultuous, murderous trans-Atlantic trip, by the time they got to Plymouth Rock and the Massachusetts Bay Colony, they were no longer a dour, oppressed religious sect but rather a boatload of hardy voyagers and settlers. By coming to the New World, they had escaped social opprobrium and political oppression and changed their fate. California is the New World's new world, America's America.

Funny, then, how the new promised land of California turned out to be a direct counter to the Puritans' dark, depressed, perfect human community in New England. Instead of snow, cold, and a lowering sky, Americans in the new new world would find themselves in what looked like a land of perpetual warmth, eternal pleasure and ease. I like that idea. Instead of scrabbling against hard earth to eke out a harvest of tough black and red corn, you'd put a pan in a river or thrust your fist into the dirt and—if you were lucky—bring forth handfuls of brilliant, valuable gold or silver. Unlike his stern, penny-pinching New England counterpart, God here would be friendly, generous, a big help, a nice guy, his messenger no thundering Cotton Mather or Jonathan Edwards but instead a best-selling L. Ron Hubbard or Huffington's smiling, shining John-Roger.

I am meeting the Resnicks and their friends at the Einstein exhibit today. They and many of their friends whom I'll be seeing this evening have something in common with Governor Schwarzenegger: they are happily deracinated, and they treat California like a rich, benevolent, beloved old aunt who has agreed to save them from financial mediocrity and anonymity, and to set them up in new lodgings. Such people (newcomers, of course, first-generation stock) believe that, as Schwarzenegger always says, they "owe everything to California": their family (their *new* family: spouse and offspring, not the extended, embarrassing one abandoned back east), their friends, and especially their possessions, their real estate, their business. These are people who are glad that what they've left behind has been left behind— unlike Mrs. Barrett with her furniture and spinning wheel. They are shockingly unsentimental about the past. Nostalgia does not figure into their emotional makeup; they're not casting anguished glances back over their shoulder, looking for their blue boat and their Beatle cards. They're forward-lookers, like the governor.

And who wouldn't look forward if what they'd left behind was Thal, a village (population about two thousand) a few kilometers from Graz, Austria's second-largest city? In this, Schwarzenegger, while pretending he's a California dreamer, is just a realist. Opportunities in

Thal, or even Graz, were not many for the son of a former Nazi Party police officer. One measure of how little opportunity there was is that it was bodybuilding that ended up providing the young Schwarzenegger with a way out.

People whose backgrounds are like Schwarzenegger's assume that whatever the future brings is likely to be better than what went before. They retain no pastel-tinted memory of bliss. They are always striving to put childhood's nightmarishness, penury, or despair behind them, taking hope from every new day.

Schwarzenegger is like that. You can see it in his eager eye: he greets each new experience with expectation of profit and amusement. There's a sequence of him on video receiving the city of Graz's Ring of Honor from the elders of the town. It's a lovely scene. It's 1999; he's a big movie star, definitely the most famous son of Graz. The council members are not only happy but, as you can see in the video, they're enthralled by his celebrity. They are literally all smiles. And he's at his best too, relaxed, delighted, charmed by the fact that he, Arnold Schwarzenegger, a policeman's son from the nearby village, has seduced the politicians and the council from the cosmopolitan center—important notables, to the younger Schwarzenegger. The Ring of Honor is a bespangled oddity, but somehow one imagines it might sit well with the rest of Schwarzenegger's jewelry. He's got a bit of a beard and mustache; he's looking almost hip, for Schwarzenegger, and laid-back in a nice way.

He calls the mayor Herr Burgomeister and speaks German (in which he has only the slight Austrian lilt, compared to the heaviness of his Austrian accent in English). He seems to feel right at home and to harbor no doubt as to the city council's good intentions concerning him. For a kid like Schwarzenegger, with the childhood baggage he had to carry into his successful adulthood, it must have felt like an important victory.

Schwarzenegger is an optimist, and why wouldn't he be? In the narrative of his life, things have always gotten better and better. For him,

America, and more particularly, California, has been not just a backdrop for his success but an essential element in it. This sunny coast of the American imagination (Kevin Starr calls it "the coast of dreams") has traditionally and legendarily attracted the formerly forlorn, the financially bereft, the victims of drought and economic depression, the lonelyhearts—people seeking a better ending for their story, searching out fortune because they haven't had any so far, or those who are running away from anonymity or notoriety, from poverty or theft, or from any bad situation. It's a refuge.

Although internal emigration demographics are changing, California still attracts people who come from all over the country to settle here. This is especially remarkable because all Americans who are not from the country's poorest regions are now, very broadly speaking, from the same homogenized place, a place not so different from much of California.

This American homogeneity, however, was not always the norm. (Sometimes, especially in California, I still wonder if the United States is just *one* country.) In the days when the country was still growing geographically, and there was no television, little or no radio, and only a smattering of electricity and automobiles, we were each of us a local breed. During the emigrations westward in the late nineteenth century and on through the first three decades of the twentieth, Iowans really were Iowan, Bostonians Bostonian, and California another world; up until the 1940s, there were state societies in Southern California for transplants from all the other existing states, societies that held picnics and potlucks and provided California information for new settlers from the home state.

One of the first of the state societies, and perennially the largest, was Iowa's, which was established in 1887, with 408 Iowans attending its first picnic, about which the Southern California writer Carey McWilliams wrote with great eloquence and humor. The motto of the Iowa Society, not intended as irony, was "Hog and hominy." Many of the physical attributes that are now taken for Californian are really Iowan—that blond, square-toothed, strong-boned farmer face. At one point, according to McWilliams, the Iowa state society in Southern

California included at least 150,000 members. By this time, the annual Iowa Society picnic had become known as Iowa Day.

Contrasting societies called Native Sons of the Golden West appeared a little earlier, mostly in the northern half of the state, for Californians who were among the relative few at that point to have been born in the state. Still, unless they were of Native American or Mexican origins, the Native Sons could not go back very far in their genealogical line before discovering that their forebears came from eastern trapper or logger stock, frontiersmen all (pioneers, as the Native Sons called them), or were Gold Rushers; the institution itself, which still exists and has many of the secretive, paranoid trappings of Freemasonry, was organized in 1875 by Albert M. Winn, a Virginian who had come to California in the Gold Rush, and who wanted to memorialize and perpetuate the values he felt were embodied in that era. (Many observers of that time believed that the highest values of the era were greed, ruthlessness, and license, but let that pass . . .)

Today, however, no assimilation or dispute over who really belongs in California should be necessary after one's arrival at LAX. Such distinctions are now theoretically unimportant—although for me, every day in California will always be to some degree New Jersey Day, without the picnic.

Even if you've just deplaned, and it's the first time you've seen the colored lipstick lights at LAX, if you're an American, you've already lived in California. Received wisdom is that American culture comes from Boston and New York, from Washington, from the East Coast. From back east. But the real landscape through which the American mind wanders is Californian; it's out west. Californians who feel culturally inferior (or New Yorkers who feel culturally superior) are locked in the earlier days of the republic, when things like European style and culture, new books, fashion, new industries, did filter from the east to the west, just as ideas and culture had previously floated into New York Harbor from Europe.

But now time is running backward, from west to east, and the direction of culture is reversed. The background in catalogues, the scenery in TV car advertisements, the physical types of our actors and actresses, the locations where the movies we see and the ads we watch are filmed (my backyard comes to mind), the mentality of our culture producers—all of these come in large measure from California. I grew up thinking Brian Wilson, Charlie Manson, Jane Fonda, Jerry Brown, Joan Baez, and the 1960s were American, when actually they were Californian creations.

Although I come from Perth Amboy, New Jersey, I really grew up in California, like all Americans.

Then why do I feel so unreal here, as if the land were breathing around me, waiting for me to do something? As if I were a dark, unfinished patch in the middle of a bright, forgotten landscape painted by someone else?

I found that dark patch at the Einstein exhibit at the Skirball Cultural Center, up in the heights of the chaparral over the 405, the exhibit the Resnicks had invited me to tour, along with a handful of equally deracinated Angelenos, some from as far away as London. The Resnicks' guests were shepherded around by museum people, as well as by astronomers and physicists who knew something about Einstein and his theories.

The exhibit was crowded. The public was here, as well as the friends of the Resnicks. It's rush hour, and people have come from work, in their nice work clothes. Couples are meeting up for the evening in the museum lobby. The show is called *Einstein* and the poster for it has a breezy Albert Einstein, riding a bicycle, his hair flying out around him in all directions, a look of ecstasy on his face.

The exhibit I notice first displays light beams being split and traveling around a maze of tubes and poles that look like a virtual map of the New York City subway system. Another shows Einstein's report card (surprise: not so bad at math). Another reveals—I believe, but this is *my* interpretation, and I got a D in simple physics—that light is bendable, and shows in a literal way, using black foam, that the universe is made up of some kind of theoretically mushy material that can be bent, not just vast emptiness. Over in a corner, inexplicably, is a mirror.

All the visitors are filing past this mirror, looking at themselves—not surreptitiously but quite boldly inspecting their makeup and their evening attire, tossing back a chestnut mane, straightening the waistline of a sweater, checking, checking. I watch them flow past. I'm not paying much attention when I come up to the mirror. I'm thinking instead about Einstein's girlfriends (he had quite a few), and the atomic bomb and the H-bomb, and how after Hiroshima, Einstein wrote that man could now expect either a new paradise or universal death, which seems to about sum it up from where we're thronging through his life's work, up here in L.A., high above Sunset and the unmoving rush-hour freeway.

Ahead of me, Stewart Resnick is reading something on the wall, and I hear Lynda mentioning to a friend that luckily she bought two pairs of the shoe she'd just scuffed under a museum door. One of her guests over near the bendable space-time exhibit is reflecting out loud on research he's done on stress alleviation, and I hear a snatch of conversation from my group. "Oh, Michael and I have been homeopathic for thirty years now." As I pass the mirror, I too check myself (still short, dark, poorly coiffed, visibly self-conscious), only to find that as I am approaching the very edge of the looking glass, I disappear. I have to do a double take, but still, I'm gone! I look around: Lynda up ahead, Stewart still brooding, someone laughing behind me, a childlike tinkle. I wonder, Is this happening just to me?

Somehow the mirror has suctioned me right out of the picture. I'm astounded. In the space-time continuum in the canyons above Sunset Boulevard, I no longer exist.

The exhibit was called Black Hole.

CHAPTER FIVE

Modern Luxury™

T HE RESNICKS' HOUSE ON SUNSET is far away from my neighborhood near the La Brea Tar Pits. The house, located on the stretch of Sunset where the boulevard becomes a leafy grove instead of a neon extravaganza, has a high, automatic, wrought-iron security gate and a semicircular driveway. Within the gates, a sweeping front staircase, down which Fred Astaire and Ginger Rogers should have danced, rises up from the driveway. The house is old-world, imposing and majestic. On the wide landing at the top of the staircase is a marbled mosaic with a grand, scrolling *R* in the middle, really too noble for humble feet to tread upon, but there it is nonetheless, a couple of yards in front of the house's regal double door.

One evening, I head up La Brea Boulevard for a visit to the house on Sunset. I always feel that I'm really going to see not the *people* who live there but rather the house, because the Resnicks themselves are almost obscured by the grandeur of the building in which they've chosen to reside.

It is once again pouring rain. Looking through the windshield at the sodden landscape, I remember my original California self, ecstatic in the hot January winds of the Santa Ana, swimming in winter, incredulous about weather so perfect. That first winter convinced me that I was in eternal vacationland, the Southern California that was originally sold to all those nice Iowans when it began to be settled and developed, the one that attracted all those shivering midwesterners and northerners. Rain never occurred to me. As I drive through the downpour, I think fondly of my bucket and boat, which I'd finally found a few weeks before, after some desperate searching, hidden in a pile of trash behind the broken-down garage. I'd stashed the boat away for the moment in our tiny "California basement," a bear-sized cave big enough only for a hot-water heater, where—during this season—there had been occasional waterfalls, spouting from the wall on the lawn side.

At least it's before rush hour. My route goes up away from the tar pits toward the hills. The rain is coming down, dropping on us in curtains, again. On the east side of the street in front of a string of hip La Brea art galleries, a black-haired, bearded man is squatting at curbside, between two parking meters, washing his hair and face in the energetic stream that is coursing down La Brea. His clothes are soaked. His crouched position and the way he scoops up the water in his hands and shovels it over his face and head remind me of the people I used to see bathing hungrily and doing their laundry in the murky sewage streams of La Saline, a waterfront slum in Port-au-Prince. Luckily, the stream down La Brea is cleaner and more salubrious than its Haitian counterpart. From the bracket of the streetlight above the bathing man hangs that publicity banner for the Skirball exhibit, streaming rain: old Einstein on his bike, his hair windblown.

I cross Doheny and pass through the Strip, deserted at this hour. Soon the foliage of Beverly Hills begins, and I'm at my destination. A few minutes early for my appointment, I don't go in. The Resnicks' Little Versailles, as I call the house, looks as if it were made for this rain, dripping amid its gardens and tall trees like Miss Havisham's mansion in Dickens's *Great Expectations*. It definitely could be seen as sinister—large and dark and looming, like the house in the noir Billy Wilder movie *Sunset Boulevard*—especially in the rain; it isn't what normally comes to mind when you think of the California dream.

Nonetheless, this was the L.A. house that Stewart Resnick set his heart on, the first time he saw "this dominatrix of dwellings," as Lynda called it in a little article she wrote for her friends, explaining the purchase and the adventure of owning such a house. On the other hand, Stewart is from New Jersey; I understand his esthetic: "Don't bother me with talk about good taste. Big is good; impressive is . . . impressive." Not that he would ever state it in these terms.

In L.A. there's a sense of unreality that's very like déjà vu, and I'm having it now as I continue down Sunset. Everything looks studied and virtual, with the precise, exact reality of a movie set. All along the boulevard, there is an eerie metaphoric quality. Not a house but "like" a house. "Like" a castle in Scotland, a palace in France, "like" a fortress, a chalet, an ivy-covered soap opera mansion. Not rain but "like" it. One reason so much in L.A. looks like a set is that—in many cases—the thing you're looking at *was* the set for a scene in a movie or a television show. Almost any corner of the city reminds you of something . . . something . . . , and then it turns out that the something it reminds you of is itself, that very corner.

I continue on past the Resnicks' and turn up Mountain Drive toward Loma Vista and onto Schuyler Road. At number 1005, a huge American flag sags down, dispirited. Then past more mansions almost hidden by their oaks, magnolias, and spreading elms, the high hedges heavy in the rain, a new pink chateau going up, flanked by Portosans for the workmen, but no workmen because of the weather.

A block away, huge gates open up to a public park that used to be the private grounds of Greystone, one of the estates of the Doheny family, who were the most profitable American oil producers of their era and the first to inaugurate an oil well in Los Angeles proper, in 1892. At the end of his rope at age forty, having prospected for gold and silver in the most desolate areas of the West and come out with empty hands, Edward Doheny had seen terrible days of destitution. One day, he was sitting outside a hotel where he and his family were living in a room he could no longer pay for. Quite by chance, a cart hauler passed by "hauling chunks of a greasy, brownish substance," according to a possibly apocryphal but still telling story in *Dark Side of Fortune*, by Margaret Leslie Davis.

> [Doheny] ran after the dray, calling out, "What are you haul-ing?" "It's *brea*," the driver replied. . . . "Where does it come from?" "A hole out near Westlake Park." The driver slowed to a stop and allowed Doheny to scoop up a handful of the dark brown gunk and examine it. It felt viscous, slimy and tarlike in

his hands. . . . Doheny decided to hop aboard a streetcar and visit Westlake Park. . . . He had nothing better to do. Once there, he easily located a great hole oozing with gobs of the brea. . . . When he asked a nearby worker what it was used for, he learned . . . that, when mixed with soil, [it] could be used as a velvety-black combustible oil. . . . "My heart beat fast," Doheny later recalled. "I had found gold and I had found silver and I had found lead, but this ugly-looking substance . . . was the key to something even more valuable that any or all of these metals."

From that day on, it is said, Doheny became an oilman. His oil fueled America in the First World War. In 1928, Ned Doheny, the young scion of the family, along with his wife, Lucy, and their five children, moved into Greystone, which was a new, fifty-five-room, forty-six-thousand-square-foot mansion that had cost the family more than $3 million to build, a stunning sum in its time, the equivalent today of about $34 million. Much of the Resnicks' neighborhood is built on former Doheny land. This evening, in front of the Greystone gates, a blue Starline tour bus sits idling in the rain.

I can just make out the foggy silhouette of the tour guide within, lecturing to an audience who can barely see out through the steamed-up, rain-drenched windows. I can guess at the information being imparted. The mansion, like many others in Los Angeles, was the site of an infamous murder, one of those era-defining crimes Los Angeles seems to engender, like the Manson rampage or the O.J. Simpson killings—neither of which took place so very far away. Greystone—which looks like what its name suggests—seems a good house for a murder. It's been used as a set and a backdrop so many times, it's practically a part of the American subconscious: in fact, it's open only for special-occasion rentals and movie shoots. There is a reason why Raymond Chandler, with his crimes amid magnificent real estate, dense corruption, depraved sex, and scandal, is the archetypical L.A. writer.

The Greystone murders had in all likelihood to do with oil and bribery in the highest corridors of power in the United States, though on the surface, the killings were portrayed as the possible result of sexual jealousy or money differences or sheer insanity. In the earliest morning hours of a February night in 1929, Ned Doheny and his personal secretary, Hugh Plunkett, were found dead at Greystone in what was portrayed at the time as a murder-suicide. Both men were in their midthirties and had been shot through the head. Doheny was wearing only his underwear and a silk bathrobe. By the time the authorities were called in, Plunkett's dead hand was holding the gun. The Doheny family claimed Hugh Plunkett had been behaving like a mad man in the weeks leading up to the deaths. Since the ostensible murderer was already dead, supposedly by his own hand, speculation about the murders was easily hushed up.

Years earlier, Plunkett, Ned Doheny's friend, had come out of Kansas to L.A., where he found a job working for a service station. The young Plunkett worked on many cars belonging to the Dohenys. After Ned Doheny married, Plunkett was hired as the family mechanic, and he quickly rose to manage the construction of Greystone and the entire household of the younger Dohenys. He himself was unhappily married and spent most of his time with Ned and Lucy. He was their chief houseman, as well as Ned's valet and personal secretary. A personal assistant par excellence: so many of the people in these neighborhoods today employ a Plunkett equivalent, or several. (One movie producer I know has a fellow on hand for the sole purpose of dealing with the family's electronics, and also has a family handyman *on retainer.*)

At the time of the two killings, Hugh Plunkett, Ned Doheny, and his father the oil entrepreneur were just months away from trial for their involvement in the Teapot Dome scandal, in which it was alleged that the elder Doheny, with his son's help, had bribed Albert Fall—the secretary of the interior and an old friend of the elder Doheny's, from his silver prospecting days—in order to gain control of the U.S. Naval Petroleum Reserve No. 1 at Elk Hills, in Kern County, California, near Bakersfield.

"With his son's help" perhaps does not make it clear enough: the elder Doheny had Ned, then twenty-eight years old, travel to New

York via train and withdraw $100,000 in cash from Ned's own bank account in Manhattan. Ned's confidant Hugh Plunkett accompanied him to New York, and further. With the money in a leather satchel, the two adventurous, untroubled young men went down to Washington, D.C., where they hand-delivered the cash bribe (or was it just a loan between friends? as the elder Doheny later claimed) to Secretary Fall in a room at the Wardman Park Hotel.

Four months earlier, Estelle Doheny, Ned's mother, had written cozily to Secretary Fall:

> We are resting midst the flowers beneath the fig tree and we are wishing that you could be here. There is a hammock in the . . . shade and a rocker, and a lounge is there too. There is a pool within the Palm House waiting. There is rest and recreation. Won't you take a real vacation and come spend it here with your friends? Do come.

This all took place during the notoriously corrupt Harding administration, possibly the last time in American history that business and government have worked together as closely as they have done during the George W. Bush administration.

Doheny's $100,000 was not the only bribe Fall was accused of taking for naval reserve contracts. The most infamous concerned Naval Petroleum Reserve Number 3 at Teapot Dome, Wyoming, which Fall granted to a New Jersey oil magnate, after an even more generous gift than Doheny's was delivered. Fall eventually served time in prison for the corrupt deals, but Doheny was exonerated, in spite of the fact that it was Fall's acceptance of Doheny's $100,000 that sent Fall, a less well-connected, less respected man, to jail.

In the end, many plausible scenarios were offered for what might have happened on that murderous night at Greystone in February, 1929. Perhaps Hugh Plunkett, fearing incarceration, wanted to make a deal with prosecutors that would have compromised the Dohenys' defense, and Ned Doheny shot him, then killed himself. Perhaps the two young men were victims of a double assassination intended to protect the elder Doheny and the remnants of his scandal-shredded oil company. Various respectable forensic experts testified at the time that the gun had been cleaned of all fingerprints before the police were summoned, that the gun had been warmed in order to make it seem to the authorities that the killings had occurred later than they had, and that Ned Doheny's wounds were not consistent with a murder-suicide in which Plunkett was the murderer. The worst thing, the tragedy, was that no matter how the crime had been perpetrated, by whom, and by whom covered up, only one man was likely to have been responsible for it. In all likelihood, his only child ended up dead because Edward Doheny Sr. couldn't keep his hands off oil.

The Starline van pulls away. Up at the top of the Greystone expanse, which rambles up past the mansion and over the hillside, the faint, moony light of a movie shoot is still glowing through the dark afternoon air. I turn down the hill toward Sunset. As I pass by the Resnicks' house once more (intent on driving around the neighborhood until five minutes after I'm supposed to arrive), a long, black stretch limousine pulls slowly through the mansion's enormous wrought-iron gates and on into its circular driveway, like a silent reptile creeping through the wet, like wealth made visible. But as I find out a few minutes later, it's only Lynda Resnick, chauffeured back through rain and traumatic traffic from her ladies' lunch in Santa Monica.

I didn't realize that the distance between the buzzer and the Resnicks' gate would accommodate the nose of even the most expansive car, so I foolishly get out of mine to press the button and announce myself. By the time I park in the circular driveway, climb the zigzagging outside staircase, and walk over the big *R* to the huge door and the umbrella stand, I'm very wet. I note that the umbrella stand is filled almost to overflowing, and yet aside from assorted housekeepers and assistants, only two Resnicks live here, and only one of them is at home right now.

A butler opens the door and takes my umbrella and coat. Lynda emerges from the back of the house to greet me. The house seems empty but I know from that telltale umbrella stand and from past experience that it's filled with staff in the kitchen and pantries, and with Plunkettlike people who lurk with dust mops or BlackBerrys in back rooms never seen by me. Lynda is wearing commanding three-inch heels and a contemporary version of a beehive hairdo that adds to her height, but she's still the slightest bit shorter than I am, and I'm not tall. She's shaped like an hourglass, a figure from a different American era, someone men would whistle at. She brings to mind antiquated adjectives like "buxom" and "curvaceous." She's not plump or fat or zaftig. She's compact. She moves with an assertive composure you'd associate with a much taller woman in much less precarious shoes.

Much of the money that bought and furnished this palazzo came out of the Franklin Mint, of which Lynda and Stewart Resnick are co-owners. Before their advent, in 1985, the mint made only collectors' spoons and commemorative coins for the masses, but under Lynda Resnick's marketing leadership, it branched out into collectible dolls and other cultural artifacts, such as the "Save the Eagle Proud and Free Fine Art Print," the "I am the Resurrection and the Life Plate," the "Official Vietnam Veterans Collector Lighter," and the "Duke John Wayne Collector Teddy Bear."

You would not guess that these products would issue forth from the same sensibility that chose this house, which is overwhelmingly French, of both the pre-Revolutionary and Empire eras: fleur-de-lis ironwork, enormous formal living rooms; a vast gilt office, like a king's receiving room, for Stewart; a cavernous foyer big enough to hold hundreds of guests; gilt and inlaid Empire ceilings; gorgeous Italian and Hungarian chandeliers; a naked gold cherub over one downstairs toilet. (Perhaps this last jibes with the Franklin Mint, somehow.) Large and brilliant rococo canvases from pre-Revolutionary France hang in the east wing living room, although the theme of much of the other artwork around the house is Napoleonic, perhaps in acknowledgment of and homage to Stewart's stature. A huge alabaster statue of Napoleon at Elba, brooding on his terrible fate, dominates the living room, sitting in solitary despair amid the frivolous revelers of today.

The Resnicks, less heroically, started out in interior decoration, burglar alarms, and janitorial services, and subsequently bought the Mint. They also own Teleflora, a national and international floral service, and recently bought Fiji Water, on the island of Fiji. After buying the Mint, they expanded into California agriculture. Though they dominate their sector of agribusiness in California, the Resnicks are absentee farmers, not hayseed farmers. They are what Richard A. Walker calls "agrarian capitalists" in his book about California agribusiness, *The Conquest of Bread.*

As Stewart Resnick puts it, "I became a farmer because I was looking for a passive investment." Not a lot of sentimentality for the land there. It's more about making the land produce according to market demand. The pomegranate in particular has become, under Resnick stewardship, a boutique fruit, as well as a juice producer that satisfies a demand artificially boosted by creative marketing, a Lynda Resnick forte. Pom Wonderful is her brand, with its sexy, curvy juice bottle and its antioxidant claims.

In other words, although the very corporate Resnicks fit well into a segment of California farming (oil companies have always had agricultural holdings here, for example), they are not exactly traditional western farming stock. Both are East Coasters originally, Jewish (not generally the religion of the average California farmer), and—to put it mildly—not inheritors of California lands. They are not linked to the land by family ties. Overall, about 97 percent of the state's farms are family-owned or owned by partnerships of families. Around 6 percent are under corporate control, but many of those corporations are family-owned. The categories are fluid, however. One could argue, for instance, that Paramount Farming, which is privately held, is a family-owned business, since Lynda and Stewart are a family.

Still, it's hard to think of Lynda and Stewart as a mom-and-pop operation. Ah, well. My city-girl dreams—of knowing hard ranchers who drive tractors over their vast terrain, or men in overalls with pitchforks and straw in their hair—are fled. A Japanese gardener and a Salvadoran landscaper who work in my neighborhood are closer to my farmer expectations than Stewart, who, when he is casual, wears wide-wale corduroys, butter-soft loafers, and—on occasion—elegant, fine-spun "workshirts." And Lynda: "farmer" and "Lynda" have nothing in common. Yet she is one, if a farmer can still be said to be someone who *owns* a farm. Maybe Lynda is a farm owner, not a farmer.

I've only been at the Resnicks' a few times when they did not have Crystal Valet parking the cars of their guests. This means that when you arrive and pull up to the front door of the house, a line of handsome white, Asian, and Latino men in white suits with lavender ties, almost like a kick line in a Broadway show, is waiting to whisk your car away, possibly to the nice piece of land next door on Sunset, which the Resnicks also own and use, improbably, as a parking lot, the parking lot next door on Sunset being the real-estate equivalent of, in New York City on Park Avenue, an extra empty apartment next door—proof that there is more than enough money to waste. As you are leaving, your Crystal Valet valet hands you a white rose with a Crystal Valet business card attached to the stem and pulls your seat belt halfway around you for your convenience.

In other words, Little Versailles is not the kind of house you normally go to in order to hang out there or to lounge around, although the Resnicks themselves must do that. Still it's hard to imagine Lynda and Stewart, in his-'n'-hers bathrobes, fussing over the Sunday crossword puzzle in one of those rooms. Or sitting around the pool in their bathing suits under the bougainvillea arbor behind the conservatory. Everything is grand—bedroom, sitting rooms, dining room—even though the Resnicks are tiny, exquisite people, almost miniature, like dear little forest creatures, certainly too small for their echoing residence. But then, almost any human except for a fabulous figure from history would be dwarfed by this place. As Lynda says with a disarming mixture of pride and self-awareness when we begin to wander around the house, "It's not home, but it's much."

Who have I seen at the Resnicks'? All of the customary hard-core liberal Hollywood establishment: Huffington (Lynda is her daughter's godmother); Mike Medavoy and Lawrence Bender; Norman Lear; Albert Brooks; Rob Reiner; Michael York; Gore Vidal; Beatty and Bening; the television writer Aaron Sorkin; the humorist and writer

Bill Maher; the actress Leigh Taylor Young; the comedian Larry David and his activist wife, Laurie David; the columnist Robert Scheer; the television writer Lawrence O'Donnell; and a rotating, ever-changing cast of characters who are too numerous to remember or whom I was, in my ignorance, incapable of recognizing. Usually, as far as I'm concerned, these people could be anonymous straphangers, I am so unrelated to their world; this is when I feel like La Brea Woman, struggling through tar. They are forced to say things to me like "Oh, I'm an actress on *The L Word,*" and I still have no idea what that means until I get home and Google them. To them, I am a strange alien observer, at best. Or simply nonexistent. Once, when I saw Stewart Resnick—whom I'd already met and talked to half a dozen times, and next to whom I'd sat at a dinner at his own table in his own house only a few weeks earlier—I was again reintroduced to him. He said, "Oh, when you came in tonight, I thought you were my industrial psychologist."

Walking through the rooms downstairs with Lynda Resnick is like taking a tour of pre-Revolutionary France. As Lynda wrote in her vanity essay, the house "is topped off on all four sides with rows of balustrades through which a queen might peek out and utter: 'Let them eat cake.'" These are modern-day Dohenys. It's no surprise that Lynda and her husband are about to buy a "very significant" portrait of Marie Antoinette. Perhaps the tragic queen can look across the living room at Napoleon in his Elba agony, and smile.

Lynda guides me up the kind of staircase that Scarlett O'Hara descended in so many memorable ways. Scarlett is a heroine of hers, it turns out. (She had the Franklin Mint begin a series of Scarlett items, including a doll, that generated revenues of $35 million.) The stairway Lynda is ascending rises from the echoing front hall up a lovely plantation-style curve to the second-story landing.

Like Greystone, Little Versailles, early on, was owned by oil people, by Dolly Green, whose father, Burton Green, founded Belridge Oil, with pumps in Kern County, near Bakersfield, among other sites.

Burton, a Texas wildcatter, came to California in the 1920s for the oil, and bought up a large tract of virgin land—now Beverly Hills—in order to drill. When he discovered that there was very limited oil beneath his land, he sold much of it to developers. What wasn't Doheny's in Beverly Hills was Green's.

And the concentric circles among the wealthy continue to spin out from Beverly Hills. Like other lands previously owned by oil companies, some of Green's Belridge property in Kern County now belongs to Paramount Farming, which is owned by the Resnicks. As Stewart Resnick describes land transfers in Kern County, two of the largest landholders there in the days of oil exploration were Getty and Superior Oil, which later sold off their fields to Mobil and Texaco. Those two companies became "the biggest farmers there." Eventually, Resnick says, "Texaco and Mobil wanted to get out, and we bought both of those operations."

Lynda Resnick's father, Jack Harris, was a Philadelphia man, so she's another one who's not from here. She was a teenager when she arrived in Los Angeles. Her family came here because after her father, who started out making religious movies, had a surprise success with *The Blob* (filming on a microscopic budget in Chester Springs, Philadelphia), he wanted to be nearer the center of the movie business. Before they came out west, Lynda had starred on the *Horn & Hardart Children's Hour,* an early television show. She describes her childhood performing self as astonishing, gifted, charming, brilliant, and funny. "By the time I was nine, I was washed up," she says, with characteristic self-deflation.

But by the time she was nineteen, Lynda Sinay—she was married at the time to her first husband, Hershel Sinay, an L.A. publisher— had already started her own advertising agency in Los Angeles. She entered the annals of U.S. history by offering the use of her office photocopying machine to her friends Tony Russo and Daniel Ellsberg, who came over with Ellsberg's teenaged children one autumn evening in 1969 and spent the entire night photocopying the Pentagon Papers (a seven-thousand-page Defense Department report on American involvement in Vietnam from 1945 to 1968) in secret, excising the words "Top Secret" from each page so that they could then take the cleaned-up document to a commercial photocopying store and make further facsimiles. The papers were leaked to the *New York Times,* and Lynda was eventually brought before a federal grand jury to testify. Although she and Stewart are billionaires, she remains a serious liberal politically, a committed Huffingtonian. Lynda says that recently, the Vatican canceled a big order from Teleflora, which she and Stewart own, because she gave money to Huffington, who supports the legal right to abortion. Lynda also has served on the executive committee of the Aspen Institute, a liberal thinktank.

Lynda Resnick's accomplishments are the stuff of American myth, combining shrewd know-how, an intense gift for marketing, and brilliant, good-hearted, reflexive salesmanship. Like Arnold Schwarzenegger, Lynda Resnick is more than anything else a salesman. The Franklin Mint gave her scope to display her abilities because it manufactured tchotchkes, whose sentimental value Lynda understands implicitly, and also provided a platform to market them to hundreds of thousands of Americans, whose psyche Lynda easily grasps in an elemental fashion, which is remarkable, because she is a child of privilege who has only extended that personal and social sense of entitlement throughout her adulthood. Nothing in her résumé— besides her father's creative role in *Blobs* I, II, and III and her move to California—would indicate that Lynda Resnick would somehow have a profound understanding of Middle America.

Except, perhaps, for her thorough commitment to gaudy extravagance. It's an odd thing. The self-denying taste of the old WASP establishment doesn't seem to have filtered out to the sybaritic coast, at least not to today's generations, even if they came from the East. Frayed chintz, chipped paint, unmatching dishes, and hand-me-down furniture—the staples of old haute WASP and wannabe-WASP décor—do not figure into the California home.

Newness and the latest mass trends are attractive here. Joan Didion—that Old California social critic and arbiter of the correct—

condemned Ronald and Nancy Reagan to the outer reaches of civilized society because of the new gubernatorial residence the Reagans had had constructed for them by their corporate friends. The Reagans' house ("dream house," Didion calls it, ironically, since of course there is not much evidence of any "dream" about it) was open and contemporary, words Didion uses in quotation to show their empty, real-estate-broker provenance. The worst for Didion, possibly, is the "wet bar," with a "long vinyl-topped counter."

"This vinyl 'resembles' slate," Didion writes. The house isn't even really in Sacramento, and besides, no governor ever did really live in it; Reagan, a Hollywood type like Schwarzenegger, lived instead in rented quarters. A person on the current governor's personal staff says that whenever Maria Shriver comes up to Sacramento to house-hunt, Schwarzenegger preemptively instructs the brokers she uses not to show her anything she'll like, so that no Schwarzenegger Sacramento house will be bought. He doesn't want to live there with his family, reportedly. He prefers solitary hotel life during the working week.

In the old days, under the Reagans, two governor's mansions were empty at once: the new Reagan residence, which was not finished until after Reagan left office, along with an older Gothic Victorian gubernatorial residence downtown, which Didion herself used to visit as a girl. After Reagan, Governor Jerry Brown—the original California metrosexual—continued the tradition, eschewing both houses in favor of a $275 apartment rental, where he slept on a mattress on the floor.

The old house, which Reagan and his wife abandoned in 1967, is a fantasy gingerbread structure. It has been designated State Landmark 823. From Didion's essay it is possible to assume that the only reason to run for governor of California is to have the chance to live in this house. According to literature from the California State Parks, of which the residence is a part,

> The Mansion . . . stands much as it did when vacated by the Reagans. . . . "Walk through history" and see the furnishing and personal items left by each family, including Governor Pardee's

1902 Steinway piano, the plum velvet sofa and chairs purchased by Mrs. Hiram Johnson in 1911, hand-tied Persian carpets acquired by Mrs. Earl Warren in 1943, and the official state china that Mrs. Goodwin Knight selected in the late 1950's.

You will also see marble fireplaces from Italy, gold-framed mirrors from France, and exquisitely handcrafted hinges and doorknobs, all of which are reminders of the Victorian era.

Moving on scathingly from room to room in the modern Reagan house, Didion says that, in the entire place, "there are only enough bookshelves for a set of the *World Book* and some Books of the Month, plus maybe three Royal Doulton figurines and a back file of *Connoisseur.*"

The kind of taste Didion is condemning here—Middle American, uneducated, incurious, untraveled, unintellectual if not anti-intellectual, ahistorical, bland, and vulnerable to marketing—is exactly what Lynda Resnick embraced at the Franklin Mint. Like Royal Doulton sculpture, or Royal Copenhagen, of which my grandmother had many pieces, these are all examples of culture selected by people who prefer art without ambiguity, philosophy without doubt, history without skepticism, politics without ambivalence. They are comfort objects, like the Twin Towers memorial in California City. Like the tiny Twin Towers, and like the Franklin Mint's commemorative plateware and other mass-manufactured and mass-marketed *objets,* the Reagans' *World Book* and figurines represent politics, history, and art that do not threaten, and that—within a certain social spectrum—confirm the "taste" of their possessor. Such artifacts are selected because they expressly avoid the eccentric, the idiosyncratic, and the eclectic: they could never be considered effete or foreign.

It's a measure of Joan Didion's alienation from California, and her essentially nostalgic, East Coast character, that she (of course, explicitly, knowingly) equates empty taste with "moral decline" and wishes for houses that have "stairs and waste space," with bedrooms that "are big and private and high-ceilinged and . . . do not open on the swimming pool," houses with "sewing rooms, ironing rooms, secret rooms . . . two pantries, and a nice old table with a marble top for rolling out pastry."

In many ways, its history and geography can account for California's architectural and decorative tastes. From the Gold Rush through its petroleum century, California has been a land of literal arrivistes, including its grandees, its giant farmers, its huge railroad robber barons, its enormous media tycoons, its colossal oilmen, its gargantuan studio heads, who have created with their sudden, massive wealth—often taken right out of the ground beneath them—new and grandiose standards of bad taste. After Edward Doheny (of Wisconsin) and his wife, Estelle (from Philadelphia), bought a beautiful house on Chester Place in L.A., they added a bowling alley, a music room, and a wildlife menagerie. The house is the kind of building that can be and has been described as "French Chateau*esque*," although it also incorporates elements of English Tudor, Gothic, and mission styles. Sometime between 1906 and 1913, the Dohenys, at the height of their wealth and social prominence, added a domed octagonal room they called the Pompeian Room, which includes Wedgwood medallions lining gold- and bronze-accented walls, stained-glass panels, gilt ornamentation, and a geometrically paneled floor. The dome itself shimmers with gold: it's made of 2,836 pieces of gold favrile glass, which was cast in the kilns of Louis Comfort Tiffany on Long Island, and it is magnificent in the way a palace *should* be magnificent. The Dohenys also removed many old-growth trees from the yard of the original house and planted new, more fashionable ones; they refurbished the great hall in a hunting-lodge motif. Finally, they decorated the Wigwam Room, which was Doheny's study, in frontier style.

Cut off from the rest of the nation by the country's biggest mountain ranges, on the other side of which were arid, sparsely populated states, California was virgin cultural territory, a place to choose your own culture, to invent your own provincial Weltanschauung from a catalog of all that was available within your economic means. For people like the Dohenys or the Resnicks, that catalogue was enormous—only limited by their own education and tastes, and, as social critic Reyner Banham has pointed out, the movie business nearby did not help quell the architectural fabrications. "Stemming from the impetus given by Hollywood," he writes in *Los Angeles: The Architecture of Four Ecologies,* " . . . Los Angeles is the home of the most extravagant myths of private gratification and self-realization, institutionalized now in the doctrine of 'doing your own thing.'" Although their great houses are very different, both the Dohenys and the Resnicks in their separate American eras were attracted to royal and imperial France. There was an untouchable and seemingly endless luxury to the Sun King's reign, and to the subsequent reigns of his heirs, that appeals to masters of the universe. But such an age could not and did not last forever.

One of Lynda Resnick's exploits as vice chairman of the Franklin Mint was the episode of Jackie Kennedy's faux pearls. Lynda purchased these at a legendary Sotheby's auction in 1996 for $211,500. Sotheby's had listed this triple-strand necklace of fake pearls at $700. Back in the 1960s, the necklace had cost the first lady $275, and she wore it in several well-known photographs. Having bought the original fake, Lynda mass-produced the pearls and sold them from the Franklin Mint at a cost of $200, which buyers could pay in easy installments of $39 a month. They were hugely successful, and the originals were displayed at the Franklin Mint Museum: yes, there was once such a place, but it closed recently. Eventually, the Resnicks gave Mrs. Kennedy's original costume pearls to the Smithsonian museum in Washington, D.C.—a tax write-off for the Resnicks, after a fabulous run.

Lynda Resnick calls the products of the Franklin Mint "aspirational" and has said that they are "things people want to need."

"All of our businesses," she told me, "either entertain or do good. We made a commitment to that. Our flowers make people smile. The Franklin Mint is part of the fabric of America." Of her brand of pomegranate juice, Pom Wonderful, made from pomegranates grown by Paramount, she says, "It is the top seller in high-end juice, and it is saving people's lives." Stewart Resnick swears by the stuff and drinks a jigger of it every morning with breakfast. (He also has a personal medicinal pomegranate concoction about which Warren Beatty says, "It is the single worst thing that I have ever tasted.")

Lynda Resnick believes, she has said, that "there exists a basic human instinct to collect . . . to possess things that will last . . . to surround oneself with things of value and beauty," and she herself lives by that instinct. But the Franklin Mint is not where she buys her collectibles. Her own personal taste is at the opposite end of the spectrum, but it too could be called aspirational—or by its more old-fashioned names, hung with Didionesque class opprobrium: arriviste or nouveau riche. Anthony Trollope, the Victorian novelist and social critic, would have been quick to recognize what the Resnicks' house is: an investment, of course, with all the fine art and antique furnishings, but also a tool for increasing social standing.

Out West, not just excessive decorating or visibly lavish entertaining but all kinds of behavior that might be considered outlandish by people in places with more established norms can be socially acceptable. The Resnicks are not beyond their own brand of cultural antics. In 2006, Lynda started to write a column for the glossy shopper *L.A. Confidential*, in which she dilated with self-conscious coyness on the glories of her social standing. Meanwhile, Stewart—perhaps self-mockingly—agreed to model nude for his friend Pat York, Michael York's wife, a photographer who spent several years taking naked portraits of people in the workplace. More than anything else, the Resnicks seem to want to be interesting, different, cultured—not just financiers and philanthropists, but arty, intellectual, involved. Like the Dohenys before them, they use cultural involvement to increase social standing. Touchingly, money turns out not to be everything.

Here is Lynda, describing the party she had at the house before the architects and decorators descended:

> Just before major renovations began, we invited 400 of our nearest and dearest to come to the Sunset House. . . . Called for

four o'clock, the party lasted well into the night. Guests reveled in the bacchanalian quality of it all; the food was hearty and medieval, gypsy minstrels played flutes while floating from room to room. The highlight was a ravishing semi-nude belly dancer eating fire in the entry hall.

After the house was finished, Lynda called her mother to complain about how big it was, how small it made her feel. (Stewart once told a friend that they almost did not buy the house because the ceilings were so high, and the Resnicks themselves so small.)

"Obviously you are not ready to grow up!" her mother said. "You have been groomed your entire life to live in a great house and be a legendary hostess. Now get it together and go meet your guests." Lynda has risen to the challenge, although, as she says, "I couldn't have done it in any other town, in any other state. I had no credentials with the Eastern Establishment." Here, in Los Angeles, the Eastern Establishment—and even the western establishment—was really of no account.

"It is now twenty-eight years that we have lived at Sunset House," Lynda Resnick wrote in her little 2004 memoir. "We have had so many wonderful parties, entertained presidents, future presidents, all manner of politicos, movie stars and movie star-makers, pillars of society . . . and an array of fascinating houseguests."

Very few people in Hollywood society like to talk publicly about the Resnicks' house. When I asked Huffington what she thought of the house, she just smiled and shrugged. She has gone to so many parties there, been celebrated at so many. As the Duchess of Stevenage says to her son in Trollope's *The Way We Live Now,* "Of course they are vulgar, so much so as to be no longer distasteful because of the absurdity of the thing." The population of Huffington's salon often migrates contentedly from its comfortable nest in Brentwood, north of Sunset, where valet parking conditions are tight, to the much more spacious Resnick residence, with its convenient and unseen parking lot that cuts to almost nothing the time you must wait to retrieve your car when you're leaving. (This has its disadvantages, though. Sometimes if it takes long enough to get guests' cars at the valet after a dinner where parking is difficult, the wait itself can turn into a rogue social event, like an afterparty, or a postparty debriefing.)

None of these people, including lesser lights, will talk much about the house on Sunset, because the Resnicks are likable, genial hosts and their guests all want to be invited back. The meals at the Resnicks' are very good, served with great professionalism by the staff, the wines very fine, the conversation sparkling, the guest list excellent if eclectic. (I once had dinner there with both Jared Diamond, the Boston-born evolutionary biogeographer and best-selling author, *and* Yvette Mimieux, the right-wing French-Angeleno blond bombshell actress from the 1960s.) The table setting at the Resnicks' is regal, all golden Empire, with heavy silver, glittering crystal, and the most beautiful plates, no doubt of far better provenance than the official state china Mrs. Goodwin Knight bought for the old governor's mansion in Sacramento. To have dinner at the long table under the huge chandelier in the dining room, knowing that coffee and desserts will be offered in the music room after, is to feel *as if* one were a part of some kind of modern aristocracy, of an entitled few. It's like dining at the table of the Sun King. But it becomes clear as you look around that nobody here is really *a part* of all this, not Jared Diamond, not Yvette Mimieux, certainly not me, and not even the host and hostess, really. The money is the most important guest at the table; it's what Didion would call the unspeakable thing.

"California wasn't set in its ways," Stewart Resnick says, when explaining how he was able to do so well so quickly here, after leaving New Jersey and going to school at UCLA. "There was nothing established in place. It was so easy to open new things. I was able to build a new business without much trouble. And we could eventually do things socially that would never have been open to us on the East Coast. We were accepted easily."

"Shortly after we moved in [to the house on Sunset]," Lynda wrote, "we realized we were quickly becoming everyone's new best friend. . . . We were invited to parties given by people we didn't know. We soon tired of the sort of friends that love you for the wealth they think you have."

But what has given that "sort of friend" the idea that the Resnicks have such wealth?

I stick by my theory that California has a dark heart. Down at the Salton Sea—on the way to Mexico—you are a long way from Sunset Boulevard, but you can still feel chambers of this dark organ pulsing. The way down is flat and dry. You take the same roads you would take to get to Palm Springs, but Palm Springs is a natural oasis in the desert: the Salton Sea is not. The sea comes into view; it too is as flat as a mirror. Like so much in California now, it has a creepy beauty, the kind that is created when man meddles too much with nature. You come upon it suddenly, with no introduction, and yet it's vast, spreading out so far that you can only assume it continues on beyond your sightlines. Sometimes the sea vanishes clear past the horizon, disappearing in mist or under a very local cloud cover. As you drive down the west side of the sea, bony hills rise to your east, and a sandy outcrop extends to your west up to the sea's bank. You are driving right along the San Andreas fault here, which is the geological reason that a giant sinkhole formed in this place and eventually became the Salton Sink and then the Salton Sea.

Then you get to Bombay Beach on the shores of the sea. People live here, you remind yourself; it's as arid as California City, except that it's sitting at the edge of a huge basin of water. Looking out toward the sea from the grocery store in Bombay Beach, I recall that the crew of the *Enola Gay* dropped dummy atomic bombs in the sea before dropping the real one on Hiroshima. It's a good spot for dummy bombs. Except for the sea, it's as ashen and empty as if a real one had already found its target here. Bombay Beach is a place for the scrawny and the starved, for roadrunners and coyotes, and for nonnative species that are passing through, migratory birds and planted fish, when these last two don't have a die-off season in which Salton

Sea pollution—a toxic mix of agricultural runoff and military waste chemicals from the surrounding region—kills them all.

As in California City, the human population here resembles the local animal population. Snowbirds, retirees, elderly adventurers, misfits, and freedom-loving tax dodgers from all over the country come to roost in these hard salt flats in houses that look as if they were made of tin foil, paper clips, cardboard, paste, tar, sail canvas, shoe leather, and extension cords—and that probably are. Antennae and satellite dishes gather on the roofs, in the yards, like flocks of exotic alien birds. The VW van, on last legs and last paint job, is still a popular car here. Another popular vehicle is the golf cart, but not for playing golf. The houses are laid out in small, dusty grids up against the sea, in cities with names like titles of Robert Stone novels: Bombay Beach comes to mind, and Niland. To get to the Salton Sea, you cross over the dry Bug Wash and Z-Drain Wash. You go through the towns of Thermal and Mecca, past a sign with a huge cross on it that reads God Loves You *THIS* Much—Repent and Believe.

It's very dry near the water. In Bombay Beach, old vans and car parts and bits of roof were overtaken one recent year by rising waters, and parts of them stick out at odd angles from what looks like a distillation of salt and refuse just past the shoreline, like signals of a forgotten emergency. It doesn't smell just right, here.

The Salton Sea is an example of the kind of thing that can happen when men decide that a dry area ought to be an irrigated one, that a desert ought to be cultivated fields. All around the southern edge of the sea is the Imperial Valley, a developer's name for the southernmost tip of California's agriculturally productive lands; before irrigation, not much would grow in what was then called the Colorado Desert, although water historically came in irregular bursts.

These flash floods were infamous to the Cahuilla, a Native American tribe in the area, whose "oral tradition included tales about the sudden and dangerous appearance of a lake in the desert," according to William deBuys and Joan Myers in *Salt Dreams*. In *Roughing It,* his

first-person memoir of prospecting in the West, Mark Twain wrote
about a desert flash flood. The day before the inundation, he tells us,
the Indians who worked in the area started packing up, muttering,
"By'm-by, heap water!" The prospectors, not from these parts, at first
did not understand and then disbelieved them.

"The weather was perfectly clear," Twain writes, "and this was not
the rainy season." He and his friends went to bed at seven, only to
wake an hour later to the sound and then the sight of the river overflowing its banks and filling up the whole basin around the hill on top
of which they were staying. Only swift action through waist-deep
floodwaters saved Twain's horses. A few seconds' greater delay, and
the animals would have been swept away. By eleven that night, "our
inn was on an island in mid-ocean." This was one of the West's fabled
"hundred-years'" floods—which can happen every forty years or so.

The flood that re-created a prehistoric lake at the site of the dry
Salton Sink, however, was anything but natural. It arose because
developers—attempting to prove that their irrigation schemes would
work better and faster than proposed federal improvements—hastily
dug a new canal from the Colorado River to the Colorado Desert, the
southern quadrant of the Mojave. "It was a ditch," deBuys and Myers
write, "nothing more, connecting one of the most powerful arid-land
rivers in the world with a stretch of desert where by now . . . some
seven thousand too-trusting settlers had staked their fortunes." On
November 29 and 30, 1905, pushed by a warm cycle of El Niño, the
Colorado rose ten feet in approximately the same number of hours.
The waters plowed through the new canal and debouched (as water
people like to say) at the Salton Sink. The flooding did not stop, nor
did any of the attempts engineers made to halt it prosper. Instead, all
the dams and blockages and moats and stop-water gaps that were
slapdashed together by the desperate engineers were dragged down,
overwhelmed, and obliterated by the sheer force of the Colorado.

By this time, the Southern Pacific Railroad, soon to be Governor
Hiram Johnson's archnemesis, had gained control of both the devel-
opment and damming projects. The Colorado's spur to the Gulf of
Mexico—abandoned by the river in its diversion to the Salton Sink—

was now a dry wadi, while the Imperial Valley lay under a vast blanket of water between eight and ten miles wide. On its way, the water destroyed the Mexican town of Mexicali and almost swept away Mexicali's California twin town, Calexico, too. All of this water was on a mindless journey to the Salton Sink—the lowest point in the desert lowlands at 227 feet below sea level—because water always wants to head downhill. It filled the sink and turned it into a sea. Finally, on February 10, 1907, after more than two years and six failed attempts to contain it, the Colorado was diverted back to its natural course, leaving the Salton Sea behind.

The enormous salt sea—which is thirty-six miles long and 25 percent saltier than the Pacific—is a fitting tribute to the developers' incompetence and greed that filled it. The sea provides a particularly sharp instance of the inevitable environmental degradation that follows on the heels of rampant, unchecked development, whether agricultural or municipal. Today, those who live nearby are the country's economic outcasts and those hardy types who want to live outside the radar of government awareness, to say nothing of taxes.

(Although I did receive a letter of solicitation just the other day from a business called Dr. Nedwed Real Estate, advertising land for sale at the Salton Sea. "SALTON SEA—," it read, "the NEW upcoming area in SOUTHERN CALIFORNIA—brand new developments on the West Shores of the biggest lake in California. Buy land now—ready to build—all utilities are on the property!!!!!!!!!!! . . . Build your dream home or make a great investment into the future. Prices rise fast!")

There are certain things about the Salton Sea that are hard to believe when you look at it: that five hundred years ago on this spot, there was a freshwater sea one hundred miles long; that today, some 380 species of birds are accustomed to visiting here; that four million tons of salt makes its way into the sea every year, and that there is no outflow. The Salton Sea is what is called a "terminal sea."

A wildlife refuge was established on thirty-seven thousand acres of marshland here in the 1930s: birds whose habitat in the Colorado River delta had been destroyed by the diversion of the river made a new home in the new marshes created by the Salton Sea. In 1998, after his untimely death in a skiing accident, the protected area was renamed for Representative Sonny Bono, the former mayor of Palm Springs who, as a congressman from the Imperial Valley's Forty-fourth District, worked to restore the Salton Sea and its wildlife, even going so far as to persuade Newt Gingrich, then Speaker of the House, to come and give a speech on its shores. Once an enormous refuge, the Sonny Bono Salton Sea National Wildlife Refuge now covers only twenty-two hundred acres of marshland. The rest has been covered over by the floodtides of the sea.

One more fact: although "tourism" is down by half since the 1960s, hundreds of thousands of people visit the sea every year, generating millions of dollars annually for the local Imperial and Riverside county economies. Why do they come here? When you look at the sea and its shores, what you see is salt and a destroyed infrastructure and environment where only the most hard-bitten and hard-boiled of any species, including human, can survive. It is to the natural what California City is to the urban. On the shores of the sea are yacht clubs erected in more hopeful times that are now shells, with empty swimming pools, broken docks, torn chain-link fences. Maybe they come for the birds. Birders will go anywhere.

About a mile to the east of Bombay Beach, rising improbably from the flatlands, looms a man-made mountain. This is God Never Fails Salvation Mountain, built out of painted hay bales and other cast-off items by a white-haired outsider from Maine named Leonard Knight. The hay bales are donated; the paint is donated.

In any other landscape, Knight would be a homeless religious ranter, a doomsayer speechifying on street corners about end days, but the arid wasteland near the Salton Sea and Niland has given him a platform on which he can happily build his fantasies. The striped and flowered Salvation Mountain is a real desert rat's confection: it zigzags upward in a riot of scrawled design, topped with the message God is Love, and its apparent concomitant: Repent.

I am repenting coming to the Salton Sea, but Knight is a gentle soul. We're standing under a kind of grotto he's built next to the mountain. There's a little shade; I feel a little human. I can't help buying a jigsaw puzzle from him that shows the mountain. And I praise his pickup truck, which is a krazy kart, a house on wheels (complete with tin roof) painted with a folk design that reminds me, I tell him, of the little painted buses in Haiti.

Although like any artist Knight is susceptible to praise, Haiti does not impress him.

"I prefer desert to islands," he says.

Some people do not care for water. I say this to him.

He says, "I prefer paint," and smiles because this is, to him, a great joke.

Knight is Slab City's unofficial gatekeeper. You pass him and his mountain of repentance before entering Slab City. ("Welcome to Slab City," says a makeshift sign, as if it were Bakersfield, as if it had that kind of municipal chest-swell going.) Here's a spot where more old people have set themselves up. It's an old U.S. Naval facility, with the Chocolate Mountains behind it, and the slabs referred to are the barracks' foundations, though they're mostly covered now with dirt, dust, and scrub. Since Slab City is the name of the shantytown or the Hooverville or whatever you want to call this municipal gathering, I suppose I shouldn't be surprised to see a makeshift edifice with the name Rat's Nest written over it. I like that: it's unpretentious, and it names the unspeakable. Next door to Rat's Nest is a house made out of a truck, with a big old American flag hung out from it, and a burlap canopy stilted up from the side like an awning over a front porch. I like that too; the American flag a nice flourish, a commentary.

This land is owned by the state of California, so what's on it can be seen as state-sanctioned; these people are living on land they don't own, don't pay rent for. A permissive state is what these people need, because if the place were private property, the owner would boot them off If it were private property, they wouldn't be living here—or anywhere else they had to pay for. Slab City is a squat. It represents poverty but also freedom, freedom from rent, freedom from a mortgage, freedom from property taxes—indeed, freedom from property. Just behind a bunch of shanties, I can see a blue slapdash church, some kind of prefab, modular Sheetrock-and-tin slap-up. It's called the Slab City Christian Center, offering a pancake and ham breakfast, free. The pastor's not in; his wife died last year and he tends to wander.

There are no streets in Slab City; it's an urban rung or two down from Bombay Beach—more like a campground than a village. At what might pass for the town square (an empty patch of dust near the middle of the shantytown) a sign is up for the Slab City Talent Show: Musicians, Singers Wanted. Toward one end of the square sits the Range, a sociable place with a sign in front of it, strung between poles and decorated with hubcaps. Live Music at Sunset, the sign advertises. A lot of drinking gets done in Slab City, with most of the liquor purchased—along with prescription drugs—across the border in Mexico, where such things are considerably less expensive.

Two older men with walking sticks go by. They tell me that they're just back from fishing in the canal. I haven't seen a canal, though they assure me there is one, just over there, and one points. They also do not have any fish. They're heading toward the Range. I meet another man in the square. He's grizzled and well-spoken.

"I used to run an electronics assembly factory in Shanghai," he tells me.

I suppose this is possible. Why not?

"But I got tired of that," he says. He leans over toward me intimately. I'm not sure I want his secrets. "I was bored, you see.

"Then one day I was more disgusted than usual, and I was surfing the Internet in Shanghai, when what do I come upon?" He looks at me with a canny eye, one eyebrow up. "Slab City. On the Internet, I swear." He's been here for going on three months now, he says.

"What was it about Slab City that attracted you?" I ask.

"The economics," he says. "What are *you* doing here?" His eyes have a suspicious cast.

"I got lost," I say. "I was just visiting Salvation Mountain."

"Nice, isn't it?" He looks as if he might not mean that. "Well, don't stay long," he says. "People here don't like strangers. Be sunset pretty soon." The light is slanting now, casting long shadows from the low shacks and shanties.

He is headed over to the Range, himself. He's a broad-shouldered man who reminds me of Hemingway—a whiskery, wide face, with eyes that glint with hidden meaning.

I'm beginning to think the Range looks pretty good.

Sunset is always a happy time in the desert.

I can't believe this. It's raining on the way back from the desert. I'm leaving the southern part of the Mojave, heading through Palm Springs—the oasis—toward home. In my mind, metaphorically, I'm taking an old route, one I often took when I lived in Jerusalem. I'm returning from the Dead Sea, another of the world's great below-sea-level saltwater lakes, to the city of Jerusalem via Jericho, an oasis town. Always comparing geography, I have envisioned an easy trip through desert and past oasis and over mountain until I reach the blessed city.

Instead, rain. A living, breathing storm. It hammers down on the car. It's like a tropical storm in the islands, sudden and shattering. The night is inky, the traffic at a standstill. In some places, the rain has turned the highway into a lake, and our cars are not amphibious vehicles, not meant for traveling over rushing waters and stony desert in one day. Cars are breaking down by the side of the road. Mine battles the rising waters gamely enough, but I can see nothing of substance, only white lights and red lights, and their shimmering, streaking afterglow.

I feel a little panicky: in California, I'm always stuck in my car in dramatic weather. I'm either all alone on deserted highways or isolated among thousands of others in these twisting, miles-long jams. I turn on the radio but there is no solace on the airwaves: the classical station plays movie soundtracks. The windshield is fogging up, and although I'm not moving and my vision is useless to me, I still have that human desire for visual reassurance—for an indication that I still am *somewhere.* Defrost helps for a minute.

You can't tell what movie it's from, always, but you can recognize a soundtrack from the mushiness, the sentimentality, the sheer overwhelming emotion and melodrama that it's trying to convey, like the Franklin Mint of music, and I can't handle all that right now in the blackness. I scan up to the next station, and the next. Golden oldies compete with hip-hop, and then Spanish pop and *banda* music from Mexico. Further up, there is country music and Christian rock (a contradiction in terms). This last, the announcers tell me, is Music That Points Us to the Cross, these are Heavenly Sounds of Praise. "I want to love you with a passion / I want to serve you with abandon / I'm on the altar / Send the flame."

I press the button again. Some so-called commentator is hyping Governor Schwarzenegger's girlie-man speech to the Republican Convention. The phrase "Governor Schwarzenegger" still sounds jarring. The slapping impotence of my windshield wipers adds to a sense of helpless comedy.

By the time I reach L.A., the rain has stopped, just as suddenly as it began. I'm back on the comfortable, familiar Hollywood Freeway, coming through the Cahuenga Pass. Up on a hilltop on the left is a giant illuminated cross the size of the Hollywood sign, at least. I have yet to figure out to whom it belongs and why it is there; when I look, I see no building that goes with it, no church, no mission. Just the cross, looking down on all of us going about our evil business in secular, materialist Hollywood.

As I approach the Gower exit, the illuminated tops of the eccentric Hollywood skyline whizz by: Snow White, in her pretty yellow and blue dress, curtsying in her gentle way, advertising Disneyland; the Knickerbocker apartment building; Storage USA; Hollywood First Presbyterian; and the round Capitol Records building, with its impressionistic needle and disc that disappeared so apocalyptically in *The Day After Tomorrow.* An SUV cuts in front of me, attempting not to have to exit from the Vine exit-only lane. It's a Ford Explorer and it has a vanity plate that reads END DAYS. I'm passing the Hollywood Tower to the north.

I'm getting off the freeway.

La Brea Woman was not a part of the tribe that lived in the environs of the tar pits, where she quite literally ended up. Where could she have come from? But then, California is a place for foundlings, whether disconnected by accident or free on their own recognizance. La Brea Woman wandered in from nowhere. She's in a drawer now, in a dingy room. Why does this not surprise me? Like so many in L.A., she turns out to be not entirely what was represented. About two years ago, the tar pits museum removed her exhibit from in front of what is now an emergency exit between the "Invertebrates" case and the "Asphalt and People" case. Her exhibit was removed because the curator, John M. Harris, was worried that this display of historic remains might give offense to Native Americans or attract their attention to her remains. So many relics are disappearing from public view for reburial on the reservations.

La Brea Woman had been an old-fashioned exhibit, a sort of archaic special-effects phenomenon, and painfully inauthentic. Such exhibits are called "Pepper's ghosts" after their nineteenth-century British inventor, Henry Pepper, who designed the illusion for the stage. Using mirrors and spotlights, the La Brea Woman exhibit let viewers see her skeleton and then, as if by magic, the actual woman herself, a dolled-up mannequin.

Then back to the skeleton. And so on.

Today, La Brea Woman's alleged skeleton hangs from a hook on an old wooden coat rack in the museum's curating office behind the research lab, and the mannequin stands next to it, virtually shoulder to shoulder, near desks and file cabinets. It would be creepy to have your body looking at its skeleton in this way, but it turns out that: (1) that is not entirely the actual whole skeleton of La Brea Woman, and (2) she would have looked nothing like the mannequin, who is a very young, attractive, sensuous, tanned brunette, with long, long hair that strategically covers her nipples.

Although the skull attached to the skeleton is a cast of La Brea Woman's actual skull, the rest of the skeleton belonged to a modern Pakistani female, according to officials at the tar pits museum, and was purchased by the L.A. Museum of Natural History from Ward's Biological back when Ward's still sold actual human remains. The Pakistani woman's skeleton was then colored to resemble the dark bronze coloring of all bones that have aged in tar, and the femurs were broken, shortened, and put back together to achieve an approximation of La Brea Woman's small stature.

So from start to finish, the person I knew as La Brea Woman was a phony, a creation of fabulists and liars, a woman put together to entrance men, with her perfect adolescent breasts and her lithe waist and her little loincloth, and her pretty little face, like the young Elizabeth Taylor's.

"Actually, she had an ectopic tooth," Christopher Shaw tells me. He is the collections manager. He has opened the file cabinet labeled Artifacts Pit 10: La Brea Woman, and removed a skull from an old wooden box that was tied up with rope and upon which is written Fragile, Handle with Care. He shows me an indentation to the right of the skull's top jaw, where the tooth would have shown above her lip.

"Also we believe that she had a small brain, possibly a cleft palate too. And she had lost many teeth by then," Shaw says, turning the skull in his hands to show La Brea Woman's various defects. "The molar in her lower jaw is impacted." Though she was between eighteen and twenty-two years old when she died, La Brea Woman may well have been considered middle-aged, according to Shaw: an elder in those days was someone who lived to around thirty. It was a long time ago. La Brea Woman is approximately nine thousand years old, the oldest known Californian. Paleontologists' belief that she died a violent death outside the tar pits and was then tossed in has been bolstered by the failure of the missing piece of skull to turn up in any of the thousands of digs in the area over the years. In the end, not much of her at all was found, and in the 1970s, when she was in transit from

the Natural History Museum to the new tar pits museum, one of her
femurs was stolen.

One would not know from the wealth of information provided to visitors to the museum that the La Brea Tar Pits are at the center of a per-
fervid religio-scientific controversy, one that has been tormenting
many souls in this problematic, antiscientific, fundamentalist era. Cre-
ationist scientists (another contradiction in terms) have recently been
asserting vociferously that the tar pits provide evidence of a global
flood, commonly known as the Flood, the one Noah got caught in.

Paleontologists have always assumed that the La Brea Tar Pits
were simply tar pits dating back some forty thousand years, large
pools of asphalt, possibly covered over with a layer of dirt and dust,
that when stepped on by an animal of any weight would suck him
down and asphyxiate him. This murderous aspect of the tar pits
explained the presence of a cornucopia of fossil remains. It also
explained why the ratio of carnivore to herbivore remains is far in
excess of what the ratio would have been among the animal population living in the area at any time during the accretion of the fossil
record.

It is believed that groups of carnivores, including carnivorous
birds, would be attracted to the pits by the smell of the decaying flesh
of another animal—herbivore or carnivore—who had been trapped in
the tar, and, descending on the carcass, singly and in large groups,
would become entrapped themselves. The huge collection of remains
of an extinct type of wolf in the pits—which no other postulate could
explain—is one of many long-acknowledged proofs of this theory.

But there are certain scientists today who do not accept this
received wisdom about the tar pits. These scientists, or pseudoscien-
tists, have turned the tar pits into an unprepossessing but important
battleground in their muscular attempt to drown out the voice of
rational, non-faith-based science. Part of the creation science movement, they claim the earth itself is younger than the generally
accepted age of the tar pits (since Scripture describes at most, accord-

ing to their calculations, only ten thousand years). The fossil remains in the tar pits, they assert—with much grave pseudoscientific data, and many charts and drawings to accompany their assertions—were carried there by a huge flow of water, providing absolute proof of a global flood. Only this, for them, can explain the presence of such great numbers of carnivores: they were swept there by the Flood.

Such thinking has its roots in the work of the mad genius, pseudoastronomer, and friend of Einstein, Immanuel Velikovsky. In his best-selling book *Worlds in Collision* (1950), Velikovsky posited that Venus broke off from Jupiter thirty-five hundred years ago and caused massive environmental disasters on Earth, disasters that were documented in their day in various religious myths around the globe, including flood, drought, and plagues of locusts.

Those who have followed Velikovsky are called catastrophists, so of course I feel threads of sympathy with them. Unlike me, however, these catastrophists are trying to cobble together a key to all mythologies, which seems to fit in with the way much of the world's population is thinking right now. What was the Flood but a giant tsunami, like the one in December of 2004, but bigger? We saw the way the tsunami threw all the bodies together in a heap: that's the tar pits, the catastrophists say, sort of ignoring the tar part. We are bad and God will punish us—so goes the thinking. (Actually, the new catastrophists do not think that they themselves are bad, only that the rest of us are.)

For the catastrophists, the flood that (they believe) filled the tar pits with carcasses in one day gainsays the theory of evolution, which they call gradualism. Wayne Jackson wrote in *Christian Courier* in 2000,

> According to the evolutionary scientists who "interpret" the data (and make no mistake about it, "interpretation" is the key word), the La Brea record goes back at least 40,000 years. Those who respect the testimony of the Scriptures would not agree with this protracted chronology. The question is, therefore: to what sort of conclusions does this fossil evidence point—evolutionary *gradualism*, or biblical *catastrophism*? . . .

These discoveries generate a special interest for creationists, because they lend considerable support to the concept of catastrophism. This is the view that the fossil record in general is explained better in terms of the universal *Flood,* recorded in Genesis 6–8, than it is by means of the evolutionary ideology known as [gradualism], the notion that the fossil record was laid down, *ever so gradually,* over millions of years.

In recent years, earthquake, flood, and terrorism have led people to worry about the End Days, even to go to the extreme of sticking them on their vanity plates, like the plate I'd seen the other day coming back from the Salton Sea. They've even, perhaps, led some people to the extreme of electing a superhero governor, someone with the strength and tenacity to wrench us from a bad destiny. As a friend of mine said to me over dinner one night, "I'm a Democrat but I like Bush because he's decisive. Clinton always wanted to think about every issue from every angle. I can't stand that, all that doubt and worry, that constant questioning. I want a decision maker." It's the same principle that caused Californians to vote for Schwarzenegger, the same thing that made me hope he was a rescuer, the same principle that makes the creationists want to fit the tar pits into a prearranged scheme. People feel comfortable with certainty.

Here is Wayne Jackson again, at the end of his piece on natural disasters in *Christian Courier,* published in the aftermath of the 2004 tsunami:

> Let us therefore close with this little exercise in logic:
> No wickedness, no Flood.
> No Flood, no change of earth's environment.
> No change of earth's environment, no geological disasters.
> Thus, no wickedness, no geological disasters.
>
> Now just who is responsible for the trouble on this "planet
>   in rebellion [against God]"?
> The fault for these disasters is not God's. It is humanity's!

The La Brea paleontologists, however, can sometimes sound as if they too are being a little cagey. Reading them with Jackson's (and Noah's) Flood in mind, you have to wonder if maybe they aren't entirely forthcoming. In *Rancho La Brea: Death Trap and Treasure Trove*, the tar pits' curator, John Harris, writes,

> Some of the animals represented in the asphaltic deposits, such as the domestic dog and sheep, evidently accompanied humans into the region. Remains of the tule elk, and some marine snails and clams, are also known from Rancho La Brea only in the context of human artifacts. *The presence of other marine species is more difficult to explain, but perhaps some of the microscopic diatoms and ostracods were transported by onshore winds, and the smaller marine clams and snails could have been brought inland by shore birds.* [my italics]

Harris seems to be hedging here about how those normally oceanic clams and snails got mixed up in the pits; those onshore winds and shore birds sound a little weak as arguments, to me, knowing how far the pits are from the Pacific—at least today. But I wouldn't turn to Scripture to find a more plausible explanation.

Still, I rejoice that catastrophism should find its greatest proof in the tar pits in California, virtually in my backyard, and that La Brea Woman, star of the controversy, should turn out to be the only human in the pits. Why is it, I ask the creationists, that so many wolves were carried to the pits by the Flood, but only one lone human? I search and search for Wayne Jackson's explanation (Jackson has an explanation for everything, based on Scripture), but although I find a mention of "the fractured skull of a young woman," I can discover no clarification concerning this anomaly.

Yet I am convinced that Jackson has an explanation. I myself believe that if you follow the logic of Jackson's Flood argument, La Brea Woman must have ended up in the pits because—even back then—L.A. society found her too old and too ugly to be invited onto any ark. But if you are not a catastrophist, you come up with two possibilities. Either La Brea Woman was the stupidest human around and somehow missed the news that the tar pits were sticky death traps, or—as paleontologists have assumed—she was killed elsewhere and her remains thrown into the pits. If the paleontologists are correct, La Brea Woman is L.A.'s first documented murder victim.

On leaving the tar pits museum, I feel a customary twinge of sadness and regret. Regret, because I am abandoning La Brea Woman there in her file cabinet. I want to give her a name, but what would it be? Emily? Ashley? Samantha? Isabella? Natalie? (These were the five most popular girls' names in California in 2004, some nine thousand years after La Brea Woman was born.) None of those seems right. My heart reaches out to her, nameless and alone in her drawer, so broken, so ancient, so forgotten.

And I feel a twinge of sadness too, because the museum is threadbare and, like California itself—whose prehistory it depicts—underfunded. Because it's done on the cheap and only sporadically updated, the tar pits' cheerful showmanship rings with the innocent sweetness of another era, and that era is not the Late Pleistocene. Everything inside the museum has a worn look. The moving, growling exhibits—mammoth and saber-toothed cat and giant sloth—are mangy and low-rent, even if they do make young children scream. Their stuttering motions and tinny sound have you looking around for a hidden tape player. The mammoth lifts its trunk and you can hear it creak.

It's unnerving too that the museum is—no matter how you try to block the fact—an homage to an oil reserve where millions of creatures died. It has an almost childlike respect for petroleum and petroleum by-products, a wide-eyed appreciation entirely appropriate for an institution that commemorates tar and was built above what can only be described as a mass grave.

As I walk out toward Wilshire, the sharp, dangerous smell of methane intrudes on my wistfulness. You can't ignore methane, and it conjures up involuntary memories because it's so distinctly related to the smell of oil and of gasoline. I see myself as a little girl, pulling on my mother's skirt, trying to get her to stop talking to boring Jerry, the gas station attendant at King High, on High Street in Perth Amboy. I recall the iridescent puddle that spilled gas will make on black asphalt. The tar pits smell like King High, a familiar smell, especially in my L.A. neighborhood, where methane alarms are visible in all the commercial establishments. With the stench of organic fumes in my nostrils, I walk past Pit 9, the museum's display pit, out front on Wilshire.

Poor woolly mammoths of Pit 9, a mother trying vainly to escape the sucking tar and reach her calf: Huge replicas of these animals struggle eternally, their elephantine legs caught in the tarry blackness, their broad backs straining. Pit 9 bubbles and steams, releasing noxious gases from the underworld as if it were a witches' gaping black cauldron. This Boschian tableau of a family going under is L.A.'s idea of what constitutes good publicity for a kids' museum. "They're just playing," I hear a mother tell her small son.

A few days later, I'm locked away in my own file cabinet at Laurie and Larry David's house in Pacific Palisades, though at least I'm able to retain possession of both my femurs. The Davids are hosting a fundraiser for Eliot Spitzer at their enormous rented place. Eliot Spitzer was beginning an early run for governor of New York. He is not a California politician but that doesn't matter because Hollywood is not a California town. It's a nationwide donor. Spitzer so far had no opponents from either party in his bid for the New York governorship, but that didn't matter to the Hollywood givers. Nor did it matter to them that Spitzer has a huge personal fortune to spend on his career. No one even brought any of this up in the public chat with Spitzer, though he freely acknowledged it afterward.

They all liked Spitzer because he's intense, and he's very visible. (They see him in the *New York Times,* which most of them read instead of the *Los Angeles Times,* because they are from New York or the East Coast, and they also think it makes them seem smarter.) He's a star, like them. That is the first and most important assumption. It must promote the givers' image for them to be able to say, "We gave to Eliot Spitzer."

Spitzer's national image is of an embattled doer of good, a man who stands up to evildoers—sort of like Batman. He presents an identity Hollywood can understand, and he's a liberal who can win. They like that. And then, he's a New Yorker, as so many of them are, which Spitzer pointed out to them in a gentle, mocking way. The crowd responds almost joyously, because they are New York snobs; New York means superior, still, to them, even if they would argue, in a very rational, coherent way, that that's not true: Deep down, they still believe it. Deep down, they are unreconstructed.

Lynda and Stewart Resnick were there; they'd been to the predinner dinner. There is always a predinner dinner for the big givers and the celebrities, some of whom fit into both categories. (It must be nice for people from Pennsylvania and New Jersey, like the Resnicks, to be treated by Spitzer, visiting L.A. from Manhattan, as if they were New Yorkers.) I hadn't been invited to the early bit, needless to say. In terms of money, I am as threadbare and mangy as the saber-toothed cats at the tar pits. I'd seen the Davids recently, at another party at Huffington's, another fund-raiser, this one for investors in the progressive, much-beleaguered talk-radio station Air America and its return to the Los Angeles market. At that party, Larry David pledged $100,000. The Davids, like the Resnicks, are assiduous Huffington supporters, boosters, and friends, and good, generous liberals.

At the Air America party, Al Franken, who was emceeing, kept kidding the crowd. "Now, we're not like some groups that seek investments," he said. "We don't want any money that you all absolutely need for food or medicine or rent . . ." At the end of that party, I heard that Air America had raised almost all of the $1.7 million they were trying to get. Leigh Taylor Young was there, smiling as usual. I've never seen her talk to anyone; like Huffington, she is a John-Rogerite, herself an ordained minister of the Movement of Spiritual Inner Awareness, what they call a "wayshower." She has the look of a cultist or a person whose smile has been stretched beyond the limits of the humanly possible.

During the Air America party, Huffington showed me her secret office. Her visible office is like a set for the office of a junior MP in a Masterpiece Theatre production: it's "like" a library—the paneling, the desk, the couch, real books, and a spiral staircase to an open interior balcony that looks down on the office and that is lined with more paneling and bookshelves. All that is missing are two alert hunting dogs to flank the hearth, and a prime minister with his back to the fire, talking about the exchequer and drinking port. But one panel of books on the upper level opens like a door to disclose a real working office. This office, unlike the one below, has real metal file cabinets and bad floors and crowded working conditions. It's as if the camera had pulled back from the set to reveal all the techies rushing around with makeup, clipboards, costumes, props, lights, cables, and so on.

"I have four people working back there," Huffington told me. It's the hub of her operation, and the locus from which she would eventually launch her extraordinarily successful weblog.

Much of the social whirl of Hollywood is spent in fund-raising. The party gossip in *Angeleno* magazine, an oversized monthly shopper that looks like *W* magazine, is a primer on this subject. *Angeleno*'s motto is "Modern Luxury™"; it's one of fourteen magazines sold under that brand. "The company's unique mix of award-winning national and local fashion and celebrity with the buzziest coverage of local trends in culture, home design, travel, society, and food has made the Modern Luxury books the ne plus ultra in the competitive world of high-end lifestyle publishing," says a note at the beginning of *Angeleno*.

Every party item in the magazine has to cover several subjects: the party, the venue, the players, the dress code, and last but not least, "the cause." (I remember when that meant the end of apartheid, or Palestinian statehood, or free elections. Here it often means various children's charities including Make-A-Wish, P.S. Arts, Ride On, the Elizabeth Glaser Pediatric AIDS Foundation, and the Teddy Bear Cancer Foundation.) These causes have been turned by the Hollywood publicity machine into photo-op vehicles, places for stars and has-been stars to be photographed in association with causes that cannot possibly generate controversy but that make it appear as though the star has a real commitment to a caring, giving, meaningful, helping organization. These are the Franklin Mint of causes, "political" events and organizations stripped of politics, like "art" separated from art.

Celebrities associate themselves with certain charities, and when the charity holds a fund-raiser, there's always a photographer there to capture and promote the star's generosity as well as his or her ability to get other stars to come to his or her fund-raiser. Of course, the photographer is also there to provide material for the "Scene in L.A." party pages of *Angeleno,* because if all of this is not witnessed by others, it becomes virtually valueless.

Larry David gets Tom Hanks for the Spitzer party: Hanks wanders in, seemingly from down the street. According to *Angeleno,* Diane Keaton gets Steve Martin, Ellen DeGeneres, Helen Hunt, and Martin Short for the Los Angeles Conservancy. A month later, there's Diane Keaton again (a fixture of these pages) at the book-launch party for a coffee-table photography book, *Looking at L.A.,* co-edited by Ben Stiller. And Ellen DeGeneres, again, at the party for Stand Up for Mentoring, also attended by Laurie and Larry David and Cedric the Entertainer (who makes it into *two* items in one issue), and by Brad Grey, the new head of Paramount Studios. What I like to imagine are the stars and heavy money hitters sitting with their serious faces on, listening for a good long part of the evening to people from the L.A. Conservancy talk about nature and the environment or to people from Stand Up for Mentoring talk about the good you can do having lunch with an underprivileged child.

Sometimes I relish not understanding a single thing in the column; it reinforces my La Brea Woman alienation. Here is another item:

"The Party: Sanrio and Target teamed up to host Hello Kitty's 30th Birthday Bash." Who is Sanrio? I wonder. Target the store? Or is this Target another one-name celebrity, like Cedric? Or maybe a hip-hopper? (It's the store, of course; I can tell now by the double-circle targets in the background of the photos.) And what is this Hello Kitty, which has supposedly been around for thirty years without my noticing? Is it a person? Or a charity that supports homeless girls? But perhaps it's not even a charity; often these parties are for store openings or for new fashion lines. Possibly, it is a fashion house of some kind . . . for teenage girls, maybe? This Hello Kitty thing seems to have a pink motif; the Target targets are pink, for example. (I'm taking in all the hints, all the clues.) . . . Japanese possibly, judging by the style of the large, human-size cat figure in the pictures . . . I do see an older Japanese woman in the pictures. All the ladies seem to be holding small dogs. Maybe it's a pet couturier, or a pet plastic surgeon. (Such things are not unknown in L.A.) For *female* pets, because of the pink? Now I will Google it . . . Ah yes, Japanese maker of babyish trinkets, stationery, bags, and clothing that uses a beady-eyed, featureless, fat-faced white cat as its icon. Of course. Why not?

When I ask a Filipina of my acquaintance to respond to the two words "Hello Kitty," it turns out she knows everything about it, in detail, including the fact that the maker of Hello Kitty is a company called Sanrio, and she's known all this for almost thirty years, since her childhood in the Philippines. *And* the party took place around the block from my house, at Raleigh Studios. Now that I think about it, I believe I have seen some of these Kitty things at . . . Target.

An auction was held at the Hello Kitty party to benefit UNICEF; items guests bid on included a pink baby grand piano and a custom-built Airstream recreational vehicle. (The trick of the charity auction is that a guest pays for an item that has been donated for auction, and all the money goes to the charity in question.) The bigger the moral and material discrepancy between the item sold and the institution benefiting, the more fantastic (to use a favorite word of Schwarzenegger's) the event is, the more appropriate, the more Southern California. I wish Angelyne had gone to the Hello Kitty party: that baby grand would have looked good in her next pink video. And she would have been so proud that by buying it, she was helping all those cute little skinny children all over the world, who (as she said about herself in her campaign video) don't eat very much.

At least at this event, no one had to sit through hours of people being serious about UNICEF or Hello Kitty. Instead, there was a concert, and a pink-lit floor show.

I wanted to see the Resnicks' water bank. The name of it intrigued me. I imagined a sturdy building with columns, made out of water. Or a series of safe-deposit boxes that, when you unlocked them, poured forth a silver waterfall. I was fascinated. After all, the Kern County operations of the Resnicks' agribusiness is a part of the empire that pays for Little Versailles, yet Kern County itself is a great bland rectangle in the southern part of California's Central Valley. It's bigger than New Jersey, and very different from the world of Sunset Boulevard. Kern County is the real California—conservative, white-bread, midwestern, booming in its way, middle-class, unsophisticated: a farmland. Kern has accounted in the past—in agriculture, oil, and gold—for much of California's perpetual prosperity.

The Central Valley, which includes the Sacramento and San Joaquin Valleys, isn't a place Angelenos think of when they want to get away from the urban environment, but for me, it's refreshing in all of its aspects that do not resemble L.A. You thank God for the sowers and sprayers, the wells and pumps, the threshers and harvesters, for the tree shakers and crop dusters, the earthmovers and diggers and Dumpsters, for the center-pivot sprinklers and the irrigation pipes, for the dust and dirt. Better than L.A.'s Maseratis and Bentleys, better than the endless stream of Lexuses rolling on boulevards between long strings of carwash establishments, better than the parking structures, better than the metered freeway entrances, better than Crystal Valet.

Not that there are no cars. On most days, you can barely make out the ridge of mountains that makes the place a valley; it's hidden by smog. Kern County pollution is a new phenomenon, a cloud of exhaust from the growing number of personal vehicles owned by the growing number of residents lured by the low cost of housing made possible by huge developments on former farmland and former desert. The brown blanket of particles lies above the fields and water canals between the 99 and the 5 like another layer of arable earth. Kern County is the only place in California where air pollution is still getting worse.

The Resnicks have two areas of operation here in Kern, all owned by their farming wing, Paramount Farming. One sector of Paramount is called the West Side and Belridge, after the oil family that once owned the land here (as well as Resnicks' Sunset Boulevard house); the other is called the East Side. What they're east and west *of* is the 5, California's, and perhaps the country's, most economically important freeway, because of the path it cuts through the Central Valley's agricultural corridor.

It's in Kern County too that the Resnicks have, essentially, bought up the water. Although I keep thinking that the Kern Water Bank, of which Paramount has a controlling share, must be a cement-walled cavern with a neat little funnel for ingress and a spigot for outflow, that turns out not to be the case. The Kern Water Bank is, for one thing, about 48.5 squares miles in size, not all contiguous, and is one of the largest aquifer storage and recovery projects in the United States. It is land with water seepage beneath it. When I drove over it, I barely noticed. I had to keep crisscrossing the same area to be sure. It looked more like the Sonny Bono National Wildlife Refuge, bare and marshy and overflown by the odd assortment of birds, than it did a bank or a lake.

"Water," says Stewart Resnick, "can in some instances be more valuable than land, or than the crop it's watering." Unlike many farmers and most California city officials, Stewart does not worry about water, because he doesn't have to. "Whenever we bought land," he says, "we bought an adequate water supply, so that we are not dependent on surplus water."

Owning his own water is part of the way Resnick likes to do business in general: he likes to own the whole shebang, to be vertically integrated. He treats farming like an oilman. Edward Doheny was like that too, but instead of just wanting to pump locally, in Los Angeles and in Kern County—which he managed to do thanks to Interior Secretary Fall and the Elk Hills Reserves—he also wanted to own large swaths of Mexico, and he eventually developed hundreds of thousands of acres there and took sides in various violent Mexican political skirmishes. When his oil investments were threatened by political change in Mexico and, later, by the Teapot Dome scandal, Doheny's whole empire was menaced.

Unlike Doheny, Resnick is protected by the diversity of his investments and business interests. The Resnicks are not in Fiji for the Franklin Mint, nor are they raising almonds or pomegranates there. They like Fiji, and they like the idea of a bottled water company in an era when bottled water has an extremely broad market. They want to put it on the high end and make it different. They know that in the end, it's all water, but with Fiji, the Resnicks are giving their marketing ability the purest kind of test. How is Fiji water different? Fiji water is the first tropical water to be brought to the American market: it's water from paradise, rather than from France or Italy. The advertising copy on the website follows this Gauguinian logic:

> Far from pollution. Far from acid rain. Far from industrial waste. There's no question about it: Fiji is far away. But when it comes to drinking water, "remote" happens to be very, very good. Look at it this way. Fiji Water is drawn from an artesian aquifer, located at the very edge of a primitive rainforest, 1,500 miles away from the nearest continent.

Something will pique the interest of one of the Resnicks, and they'll go for it. They are yuppie businessmen, absentee farmers. Stewart even has what could be described as a kind of attention surfeit disorder; he focuses on many things at once, but he *focuses*.

The Resnicks are very much of their era, and their businesses reflect the culture of California today, a boutique culture: water in square bottles; pomegranate juice in curvy bottles with many different, added flavors to choose from; almond slivers of all kinds in little resealable bags (original oven-roasted, as well as ranch-style, honey-roasted, roasted-garlic Caesar, butter-toffee-glazed—they could be in labeled bins in a Willy Wonka factory; "Toss on Taste!" it says on the bags, a fitting admonition from the Resnicks); as well as Teleflora flowers in collectible vases. Everything the Resnicks do has a little flourish. Even their crops are boutique. Nothing their businesses provide is necessary. We are not speaking of oil here, or wheat, or cotton.

If you've noticed that Arnold Schwarzenegger's political ascendancy, such as it is, has been making you nervous, you are not alone. The disturbing idea, or possibility, that the Constitution might be amended specifically to allow Schwarzenegger to run for president—since as a foreign-born person he's constitutionally forbidden to do so—makes most people I know, including me, unhappy. Liberals think they should be worried about Arnold's emergence because he's a conservative; Democrats think they should be worried because he's a Republican; politicians think they should be concerned because he's a movie star. But the real reason you should be worried is that there is—according to the kinds of people who know this kind of thing—a distinct possibility that Arnold Schwarzenegger is the Antichrist.

I admit I'm a little disconcerted. Sure, it sounds unlikely. But then, there's the weight of the incontrovertible evidence. First of all, he announced he was running on August 6. Did anyone else realize that this was the anniversary of the bombing of Hiroshima? Did anyone else realize that this is the approximate date for the dawn rising of the star Sirius? Do you know what this means? In case you don't, here's what Goro Adachi, a well-informed Antichrist watcher, wrote on May 3, 2004:

August 6 . . . happens to be the day of Sirius' heliacal rising . . . as viewed from Giza/Cairo, the astronomical center of ancient Egypt. This is very meaningful. . . . As I noted on the day of the event, Schwarzenegger's dramatic election announcement [on the Jay Leno show] was probably—consciously or subcon-

sciously—meant to coincide with the heliacal rising of the star
Sirius—an event that signaled for the ancient Egyptians the
beginning of the annual life-giving flood of the Nile (signifying
the resurrection of Osiris . . .). Notice the conceptual parallel
here: Sirius *announcing* the coming of the flood/Osirian resurrection and Arnie *announcing* his intention to become governor
of California (the name "Schwarzenegger" being very "black"
resonates with Osiris being the god of death/blackness).

Sounds plausible to me. But perhaps I am not the most objective of
observers in this instance, for it turns out that I too have a connection
to darkness, to all that is dark. I was born—consciously or subcon-
sciously—on the thirty-first anniversary of the Great Kanto Earthquake that destroyed Yokohama and Tokyo in 1923, killing 142,385
people; my birthday also marks the anniversary of the Great Fire of
Constantinople, *and* (significantly, no doubt) is the day the world was
created in 5509 B.C., according to the Byzantine calendar, never mind
all that carbon dating that puts the earliest tar pits remains back some
forty thousand years. I am sure that Goro Adachi could find something
ominous in my connection to all that fire and the very day of creation.

For someone who is the Antichrist, however, Schwarzenegger was
keeping his head down these days, while he let his wife try to patch up
his image for him, in the form of her chipper It Works! tour of California programs for children, and other activities. Maria Shriver also
suddenly became the honorary chairwoman of a statewide disaster
preparedness program that interested me greatly. I am always looking
for tips. This program was called "Be Smart. Be Responsible. Be Prepared. Be Ready!" (BSBRBPBR, for short). The inauguration of
BSBRBPBR was signaled by the sudden appearance in supermarkets
of red backpacks at the cash register, at a cost of twenty-five dollars.
These were preprepared emergency packs like the ones hanging in
my garage, minus the outgrown sweatshirts and the dead, corroded
flashlights. They included a first-aid kit with Band-Aids and further
instructions about what should go into the pack.

Another aspect of BSBRBPBR was the family disaster plan. I

imagined at first, seeing an ad for it on a bus, that this was a plan for family disasters, which even in California are much more common than natural disasters or terrorist attacks—but no. Nothing about what to do when Dad hits Mom. Instead, Shriver's family disaster plan is mostly about a family's not losing one another after some external crisis, which strikes a chord with anyone who was raised on the legends of the displaced families of World War II, the camp survivors, the refugee horde, *and all that kind of stuff.* One, you need out-of-area phone contacts, assuming the phone systems are working. Two, make sure you have a meeting place close to home, and another one farther from home, assuming home might be the epicenter or ground zero.

But Mrs. Antichrist can't fool me, with all her helpful hints and extra-wide smiles. I know that the words "President Arnold Schwarzenegger," when analyzed numerologically, yield the number 666, which you will, of course, recognize as the number of the devil and the Beast of Babylon. According to Phil Maxwell, a reliable Antichrist watcher and encryption expert who writes on the website ScatteredSheep.com,

> My first test (using $A = 1$, $B = 2$ . . .) yielded exactly half the beast number, 333, and led directly to counting the numbers on a case-sensitive 52-point scale ($a = 1$, $A = 2$ . . . $z = 51$, $Z = 52$), which totaled 666. As my investigation had revealed a substantial and very convincing case pointing towards Schwarzenegger and no one else, this was a jaw-dropping moment, like matching winning lottery numbers.

Knowing all I do about Schwarzenegger now, I am longing to meet him. I need to know if that really was his throat lozenge that appeared on eBay. I want to ask him how it feels to be a meme. But most of all, I want to see what it's like to be in the same room, chatting offhandedly with the Antichrist. I'll be safe enough, I'm convinced, because I am too old for groping. My dark Terminator doll is getting dusty; his assault rifle is hanging by one plastic thread. When I press his button, he says, "It is time."

PART THREE

Crashland

CHAPTER SIX

These Things

I THOUGHT THAT THE FELLOW who stopped at my door one morning, chipper and confident and dressed in a businesslike tie and crisp white shirt, was a location scout; he was insistent and focused. But he turned out to be, instead, a process server, bearing a summons concerning an alleged incident with my car more than a year earlier, in Hollywood. It was a sad moment, a turning point in my fortunes, I felt. My commercial director, Martin, and his Ingmar Bergman-like Scandinavian ads about homeownership were a thing of the past, apparently (although film trailers still lined the streets in front of other houses in my neighborhood).

From now on it would be process servers and bail bondsmen and bailiffs, the bleak county courthouse, and a future filled with loss. Still, I was unsurprised; it's hard for catastrophe to ambush me—although I'm sure it will, one day. This now would just be a new way to lose my house: not to earthquake or to fire, but to a stranger who just happened to enter my life, and to the slow, inexorable wheels of justice.

I had to get away and I knew just where to go.

That's one thing about California: it smashes you down like an unlucky dung beetle, but then there are places where you can rise up again.

I fled up the Pacific coast to Esalen.

The basis of the Esalen Institute at Big Sur is the human potential movement, and with a lawsuit on my hands, I was feeling a need to tap into whatever little remaining human potential I might possess, and possibly then some. In normal times, I am not an Esalen type: I'm not floaty or sweet; I'm not nice to my fellow human beings simply because they are also human; I'm shy and self-conscious and excessively verbal. I am the very essence of the untouchy, the unfeely.

But I like the remove of Big Sur, where Esalen is located, up along the coast just below the Monterey Peninsula. It is almost far enough away from Los Angeles. The institute itself hangs halfway up a cliff overlooking the Pacific, with redwoods behind, and its grounds are crowded with sunflowers, monarch butterflies, and hummingbirds. Sometimes you look up and you can barely see the sky through the fluttering of butterfly wings. Someone has made a giant, curving mandala of pine needles around the big tree stump on the great lawn. Near the dining-room door, in front of a bulletin board plastered over with flyers about fund-raising, a young man and woman are kissing passionately, intimately—and they are not beginning to back off as others approach for dinner; instead, if anything, they are *going deeper.* Down a path in the distance, a tiny girl leads a goat named Mama by a string.

I'm glad for the unreal quality of life up here, for the closeness of nature and the distance of lawsuits.

"Come on, Mama," I hear the little girl call to the recalcitrant goat in a high voice. "Mama, come on."

My process server, not unlike me, would be nervous here at Esalen because someone might hug him or kiss him or ask him what kind of *place* he was in, or simply drag him lovingly down to the nude baths and convince him to take off that button-down shirt and tie, etc. My process server, also not unlike me, would probably be slightly uncomfortable opening up to strangers. He seemed direct and businesslike, but not someone who was about to . . . connect. The usual guest at Esalen, on the other hand, enjoys nothing more than a profoundly intimate chat with an utter stranger. I don't think my process server would be ready to leap into a discussion of what I hope are his bad feelings about his work or about what I assume must be his failed marriages and dysfunctional family. Whereas Esalen guests are normally ready, at the drop of pants and the lift of a shirt, to talk frankly and in the nude about their alcoholism; or the car accident that almost decapitated them; or the Jews they rescued from Auschwitz; or the condom that fell off in the middle of *lovemaking* and stayed "up there"; or the children they fathered at age seventeen; or the massage therapist who bit their shoulder, stuck his finger in their ear, kissed the top of their head; or their great-grandfather, the slave killer.

Those are among the topics I discussed at Esalen this time, with various believers, nurse-practitioners, dirt eaters, womb worshippers, massage professionals, yoga instructors, preachers, storytellers, shamans, witches, businessmen, secretaries, tech writers, executives, wives of gurus, actresses, playwrights, an old-fashioned Marxist, and one self-described homeless person (though after some questioning it appeared that, in fact, Esalen had been his home for the past three decades).

Here are the titles of some books in the Little House, a dormitory and meeting place at Esalen:

> *Analyse transactionelle de Bio-énergie*
> *The Interpersonal Underworld*
> *Nerve, Muscle, and Synapse*
> *My Little Flowers: Gifts of the Moment*
> *The Darkness of God: Theology after Hiroshima*
> *Le Rolfing: Bâtissez-vous un nouveau corps*
> *The Mind Race: Understanding and Using Psychic Abilities*
> *Let's Get Well*
> *The Third Chimpanzee* (by Jared Diamond)
> *The Solar System* (by Lieutenant Colonel Arthur E. Powell,
> Theosophical Publishing House, London, 1930)
> *Sri Caitanya-Caritamrta: The One-Volume Edition*
> *The True Story of Chinese Acupuncture*

And not least, *Exploring the Secrets of Treating Deaf-Mutes*, published by the Foreign Language Press in Peking, whose opening sentence runs as follows: "Deaf-mutism, a fairly common disorder among the working masses, was once pronounced in China as 'incurable' by 'noted' bourgeois doctors and 'authorities.'" This last book includes a wonderful, joy-filled photograph with the caption, "Chao Pu-yu sings *The East is Red* with former deaf-mutes."

Like the volumes on its bookshelves, Esalen is idiosyncratic and unpredictable, and occasionally very silly. But silly is the order of the day here, and right now I find silly and dopey better than traffic jams and billboards featuring Schwarzenegger and movie afterparties with live bungee jumping, and the general closed-circuit life of Los Angeles, turning in circles of traffic, with mudslides closing down the 5 and everyone freaked about the Pakistani school-hour earthquake and the governor, who's been rattling on about some hugely expensive special election he plans to hold. Can't the guy do anything that's not special, anything just ordinary? Maybe he thinks an election is like a Hollywood party: it has to be special and it has to cost a lot. Being up in Big Sur is a release from all that: the air is clean and the surf unrelenting and there's an impulse toward cooperation and self-expression in the air. Sometimes you find yourself talking too much, like a former deaf-mute.

Esalen reached its zenith in a long, Marxist-related, hallucinogen-fueled alternative cultural rebellion against the corporate system of the 1950s, a rebellion that lasted here in a profound and significant way from 1962 until sometime in the early 1970s, when its powers began to dwindle and dissolve. Esalen's founders, Michael Murphy (whose family owned and still owns the original grounds) and Richard Price, both Stanford graduates, wanted the institute they created here on the fog-crowned coast to give voice to everything that represented freedom from what was believed to be the straitlaced, corporatized national norm. The two young men hoped by these means also to rescue themselves from becoming cogs in the corporate machine, as so many of their peers were becoming. Having stumbled upon Hinduism and having taken it seriously, Murphy was trying to cultivate the spiritual side of his existence. Price too, a natural-born seeker after *something*, was fascinated by humanity's deeper potential. They also had the benefit of the idiosyncratic and charismatic Alan Watts, author (at the age of twenty-one) of *The Spirit of Zen,* and a self-styled "philosophical entertainer." Watts led seminars at Esalen in the early 1960s about such topics as Buddhism, Hinduism, theosophy, and "the religion of nonreligion." He called the subjects on which he based his wide-ranging seminars "these things," according to *The Upstart Spring,* a vivid account of Esalen's early years by Walter Truett Anderson.

Here by the vast, pounding sea, under the stars, there would be sprawling discussions of "these things"; there would be nudity; free love too; naked volleyball; radical thought; an occasional Marxist high table in the dining room; Gestalt and primal therapy in the Big Yurt; nude bathing in hot sulfur springs; deep, and even nude, yoga practice in the Dance Dome and on the lawn; and in the long afternoons, lectures on the mind-body conundrum and after-death experiences and other philosophical problems, often given by people of high repute among those who thought about such eccentric areas of metaphysics. Esalen seminarians took drugs of all kinds—especially hallucinogens like LSD and peyote and mushrooms. The goal was always in every way to achieve a higher or at least an altered consciousness, to find a new and better self. Murphy and Price's spiritual and intellectual quest is reflected at Esalen even now, although in most cases without the purity and intensity of the original seekers. Esalen is where the word "alternative" became an adjective with a positive connotation. This is one of the places where the idea of "lifestyle" was invented. It's where the word "energy" stopped being about physics and calorics and started to be about "aura," as in "I really like your *energy.*"

Before the 1960s took Esalen by storm (and vice versa), it was a generous spread of family-owned land with an inn on it called Slate's Hot Springs. On the site were also a couple of shacks, some old homes, and medicinal, skin-softening baths that were fed by hot sulfur springs gushing from the palisades. According to Anderson, the baths were frequented by boisterously cavorting groups of gay men from pre-safe-sex San Francisco, whose wild carousing the proper proprietress ignored whenever possible. To understand how things proceeded at Slate's, and how Esalen became what it was, it's important to keep in mind that the head of security at the compound was, for much longer than should have been permitted, the young, reckless, explosive Hunter S. Thompson. On one night, Anderson recounts, Thompson, who later became the originator of gonzo journalism, wanted to go to the baths with his girlfriend, and feeling emboldened by the presence of a couple of soldiers from nearby Fort Ord whom he'd picked up hitchhiking, he made his way down the path to the springs. The boys in the baths were lying in wait for him, however. (There was a system in place of secret warning lights.) The soldiers fled, the girlfriend disappeared, and Thompson was roundly beaten. Bloodied but by nature unbowed, he crawled back to the Big House and—Anderson writes—spent the next day in his room "firing gunshots through the window; he did not bother to open it first."

Who passed through Esalen? In its earliest days, Linus Pauling, Gregory Bateson, Aldous Huxley, Henry Miller, the very young Joan Baez; a little later on, Anaïs Nin, Bishop James Pike, Timothy Leary, George Harrison, Ravi Shankar, Bob Dylan, Boris Yeltsin, John Cleese, R. D. Laing, and hundreds of other writers, artists, performers, and thinkers. In concert with other, similar movements, institutions, and spiritual leaders, Esalen's human potential movement has been responsible for much of what are considered the slightly loopy cultural changes that California pioneered in the late 1960s and 1970s: the self-help craze, twelve-step programs, sensitivity training in management, the still-cresting yoga fad, the wave of massage therapies now available, crystals, and astrology, and for everything New Age, for the beginnings of America's fascination with Buddhism and other Eastern religions, for our continuing belief in contact with other worlds and with the dead, for the idea of channeling, and for the popularity of sex therapy, couples therapy, Gestalt therapy, and group therapy, as well as alchemy, meditation, and biofeedback.

The way we live now is in some important measure owing to the changes wrought by Esalen's freethinkers, nutty though they may have seemed, stringing beads and weaving baskets and dreaming in the sulfur baths and imagining and hallucinating freely at the country's physical edge. There was also a dark side to this dreamy place that fed the 1960s' youth lust for all experience, good or bad: there was indiscriminate sex (known by its euphemism, free love) to the point of psychic emptiness and meaninglessness; there were gurus forcing unwanted and difficult psychological revelations on naïve, unready participants; and there were distraught, unsupervised, neglected Esalenites, a few of whom ended up committing suicide in the baths or in the cabins; one woman killed herself with her boyfriend's rifle in his Volkswagen camper, according to Anderson.

I never imagined that Esalen would constitute a stop on my unintended Charles Manson tour of California, but of course, it made a certain kind of 1960s sense when I discovered that three days before the Tate killings, Manson had stopped in Big Sur, bought gas with a stolen credit card (would he have ever had any other kind?) at a tiny town called Lucia (I'd bought gas there too), and then popped into the dining room at Esalen late one evening when a few people were still hanging around, and offered an impromptu and unsolicited concert.

Anderson cites the book *Helter Skelter* for Manson's account of the Esalen crowd's reaction to his music: "Some people pretended that they were asleep," Manson apparently told a friend, "and other people were saying, 'This is too heavy for me,' and 'I'm not ready for that,' and others were saying, 'Well, I don't understand it,' and some just got up and walked out." I wonder whether he sang the original version of that song the Beach Boys covered: "Cease to exist, just come and say you love me / Give up your world . . ." It does speak well of the Esalen crowd that even then, at the height of the national hallucinogenic insanity, Manson was too much for them. Manson, it turns out, was not the only person involved in the murders who had visited Esalen. Abigail Folger, the coffee heiress who was killed along with Sharon Tate and the others, had also spent time at seminars there.

Naturally, however, Esalen is not what it once was. First of all, the generation who created the place and the buzz in their midtwenties are, as is Manson, now in their sixties or seventies, those who are still alive. Nude volleyball is not really what they are into these days, although they talk nostalgically about it, and they'd probably play it too, if it was available. Today, Esalen is more of a workshop center, less of an encounter group, though encounter still fuels the philosophy. Some seminars from 2005 included Singing Gestalt; Deep Contact: Social Dance as a Spiritual Path; Qigong and Bodymind Healing: The Self-Healing Path; Healing with Humor: An Introduction to Spinal Awareness; Couples Massage Weekend; The Inner Work of Work; Visionseeker 3: Shamanic Cosmology; and Fanning the Embers of the Higher Self.

Seymour Carter was at Esalen at the beginning. He's in his late sixties, tall and straight as a rake, with serious glasses, gray hair pulled back in a ponytail. He flits from table to table in the dining room, but he prefers to settle down to eat outside, no matter how low the temperature goes. Carter comes to Esalen four days a week and lives in Berkeley the rest of the time. He's a disciple of Charlotte Selver, a German emigré who invented and propounded the philosophy of Sensory Awareness until her death at age 102 in 2003. Carter, who also does workshops in Gestalt therapy, is unwifty, however. He's clever and intense; he's exactly what the words "Berkeley intellectual" conjure up—influenced by both Marx and Esalen, and very comfortable with the lingo of the 1960s. For Carter, Esalen is a story of disappointment. What I see as a taming, a making palatable, he sees as a tragedy.

"For me, Esalen collapsed in 1971," Carter says, sitting at a table outside the early-morning coffee dispensary next to the dining room. "It was no longer a group of fifty or sixty exciting people. From 1965 to 1971, it was the center of the so-called youthquake, representing the best of new thinking in the social sciences, in psychodynamics, in systems theories. But then it changed enormously, began to get corrupted and corporatized. Last week, I was listening to a radio spot about the 1960s, Dylan, the demos, the Days of Rage, and I was aghast. I realized I'm living in a fucking nightmare; we are experiencing exactly what we were afraid of in the sixties: a fascist takeover of democracy, oligarchic control of the state. We've become pacified, infantilized. There's no serious intellectual life; no one has any education. There's no more piercing Marxist critique, just spin, spin, spin. Esalen's become the standard-bearer for the worst of the sixties, people who believe it's wrong to do critical thinking; it's all New Age blather. The eighties trimmed off the excesses of the sixties, destroyed the body/self thing. Now we're back to a body and mind separation. And we've lost the audience of young students and professors here. Look around!" Carter gestures to the mostly middle-aged, paunchy, balding, or sagging ex-hippies who populate Esalen, wearing dumpy yoga clothes or Indian-made robes and skirts and longhis. "No one who's in his twenties comes here anymore; it's no *fun*. And it's too expensive. Esalen has priced itself out of the youth market."

In the 1960s and into the 1970s, people argued about the value of Esalen and of the human potential movement in general. Many felt that the movement diverted attention from real, pressing political issues like civil rights, the Vietnam War, poverty in America, and U.S. foreign policy, and focused it on liberating and perfecting and satisfying the individual. Tom Wolfe, the writer, attacked Esalen as a cornerstone of what he called the me generation, the navel-gazing post-1960s consumer kids. (Of course, Tom Wolfe never met a generation he liked.) One could easily argue, as well, that the ideology of the human potential movement made it possible, later on, to interpret greed as altruism, one of the more ridiculous theories to arise and be taken seriously during what business pages like to refer to as "the go-go 1990s." At Esalen today there is nothing to remind seminarians and workshop students and staffers that, say, the United States is at war in Iraq, or that major corporate interests are trying to exploit the environment in spectacular ways, or that another generation of Americans is growing up in poverty. Simply put, Esalen has no overt politics, even though it could be seen as a latte-sipping, liberal kind of place.

What's especially tragic to Seymour Carter is how the Esalen alternative has become just another part of the culture: he seems horrified by what others would interpret as success, very much a revolutionary who wants to keep the revolution forever new, unlike others who think overturning the old order and instituting the new is enough. He's irritated by what he calls the "Marin Country, cliché-mongering idiots" who, he says, worship at the altar of what he considers to be a nonexistent New Age.

The sad thing is that Esalen, which was always to some extent a parody of itself, has become even more so, its catalogue something people pick up and leaf through for an easy laugh, partly because its New Age proponents have triumphed noisily while its economists and scientists and social activist types have faded or died. Thus the 2005 fund-raising session offered the following program topics, each one ending with a sorry attempt to spin self-help into the broader political realm, as if Esalen is aware that it is time for a realism correction (my italics):

Utilizing ancient and contemporary mind/body techniques to better understand the path to total health and well-being for oneself *and for society;*

Envisioning the role of the new leader—a "social artist"—capable of applying the skills, dedication, and wisdom of the fine artist to the noble canvas that is *the human world itself;*

Collectively crafting a blueprint for a new paradigm for optimizing mind/body/individual/*global* potentialities. Together participants *will 're-story' the world;*

The annual (and outrageous) 'What's the Value of Anything' Auction;

Morning movement programs;

Fabulous Esalen meals and entertainment.

In a way, I think of myself as a "social artist," applying my "skills, dedication, and wisdom" to my canvas, which is the whole "human world." For example, by turning right out of the Mobil station on Argyle near Franklin in Hollywood at around noon on a September day—and by doing so in a way inimical to the apparently fragile psyche of a man named Angel, a pedestrian who proceeded to bang on the back of my car—I managed to *connect*, as the Esalen people might call it, with someone I did not know, and whom I would never have otherwise known. Turning to the right up Argyle in my beat-up Honda minivan, I had unwittingly—though no doubt in some pre-ordained fashion—reached across a gaping social divide to make contact with Angel, to make him a part of my life.

I think one can clearly call this social art—especially if one has spent time at Esalen.

It's also why I'd received that visit from my process server.

Angel had entered my consciousness as a dim figure in my passenger-side mirror, when I glanced briefly at this angry, mustachioed seeming wild man who was hitting my car. Like any sane New Yorker, I did not immediately jump out and say, as a good Esalen encounter veteran might, "Oh, what's wrong? What's bothering you? Did I harsh your buzz?" Instead, I assumed the man was a maniac, and I continued about my business. (New Yorkers are like that: we're still getting used to the idea that the guy on a street corner who is talking out loud to no one in particular is not insane. He's on the cell phone.)

Although Esalen might call my vehicular encounter social art, Angel apparently did not feel the same about it. Which is not to say that he was not also eager to make that human connection. He seemed to feel that my minivan and I had bruised him in body and soul and should be held, or at least *could* be held, liable for the damages. First, he tried to have me charged with hit-and-run vehicular assault. He failed.

But not before my attorney, a matter-of-fact Korean-American woman, let me know that I could end up in jail and that she'd heard of such endings in such cases. I was suddenly faced with the real world of Los Angeles, which of course can only be brought home to a person like me in an incident involving a motor vehicle, because the city is constructed so that there are virtually no random encounters between economic classes. Such encounters are by necessity only accidental, in the most literal sense.

Once the criminal charges were dumped, Angel and his lawyer began their civil case, and that is why the other morning, the process server had come to my door—bringing the real world of Los Angeles *home* to me. That's why I had to get away somewhere: to Esalen. I thought I'd take a seminar that was being offered, called The Way of Story. Perhaps like the fund-raisers for Esalen, I could learn to "re-story" the world. In my re-story, perhaps I would not have gone for gas at that particular gas station. Or, in my re-story, perhaps Angel would not have been there. Or perhaps I would have met him at a party; he would be a different Angel, perhaps a gaffer on a movie that someone was making or a staff person in the governor's press-relations office, someone I could call up to put pressure on Rob Stutzman, the governor's spokesman, to let me in for an interview with Schwarzenegger. In a re-story, anything is possible.

In Los Angeles, less so.

I was learning the way of story or, more correctly, The Way of Story. This Esalen workshop was taught by Cathrine Ann Jones, an energetic seminar leader who writes professionally for television and the movies and who knows about things like "the inciting incident." I am always looking for an inciting incident, because, as all writers know, plot is the thing that makes the story go, or *go,* as Cathrine would say. A baby is kidnapped, a body is found, a car crashes, a princess is swept from the castle by a man in a mask, a movie star is elected governor, and, as Cathrine likes to say "the ride has begun."

The seminar included people from all corners of the earth including Greece, Spain, and New Jersey, but really we were all *now* from California—with the exception of the woman from Spain, who was British. One woman was a medical writer from Menlo Park; another ran a bed-and-breakfast; Richard was a retired city planner, living in Rancho Santa Margarita, one of the cities he'd helped plan; another seminarian sold real estate in San Rafael; one Irish girl had been a staff person at Esalen for more than a year; the Greek man wore a funny hat and was a World War II veteran now living in Modesto; there was a James Dean double who came to class and just drifted there, lying on his pillows (he was a lost soul living in Desert Hot Springs); another man, Bill, was the self-described homeless fellow who used to run the Esalen kitchen and now simply continued on here, doing odds and ends. His address was a post office box in Big Sur. Bill was famous, in a limited way, for his Esalen chocolate chip cookies. Karla was a tall blond woman from Scotts Valley who was getting her life back together after a divorce. She was dating a man down there who ran a hairdressing salon. Even though we all lived in the same state, California, we were very much strangers from everywhere, with little in common.

At dinner one night, Jennifer the banking heiress was chatting: "I ran off with my guru when I was seventeen, and my parents tried to kidnap me back. The night my son was conceived, I had my first orgasm in my third eye. It was amazing." Though Jennifer might sound to the average New Yorker as if she were from Palo Alto or the Haight, in fact she was from New York City, from a very straitlaced family, and had attended Spence, an elite girls' high school that is a Manhattan society institution. A friend of mine from Southern California alleges that only people who are *not from* California but who now *live in* California have the typically Californian spacey, gullible, New Age bent. She thinks that perhaps such people end up coming to California because it's newer and freer. "They are ineluctably drawn," she alleges. As Stewart Resnick says, you can do things in California that you would never be able to do on the East Coast.

While we ate, Jennifer continued her personal narrative (father paying detectives to locate her, while also paying bodyguards to keep those same detectives *away* from her). As he passed me to sit down with his tray at our table, Richard, the retired city planner from Rancho Santa Margarita, touched my leg.

"That was an accident," he said, leaning toward me. "Touching your leg like that. But it felt sensual to me, and totally natural."

"I'm glad," I said.

I had long ago given in to the course of conversation at Esalen.

———

Cathrine tried to make us *dig* into our own lives and memories for material for our work. (She had also been an actress.) I had to stand up with Karla and we pushed on each other's hands as hard as we could while I talked through a pretty hokey monologue I'd written about an alcoholic man who is angry at his children. Cathrine wanted me to find the emotion in the story. What I found was that Karla was taller and stronger than I was. The Greek man, in a similar Cathrine-induced situation, located his emotion in a repeated retching noise, accompanied by violent forward motion. Incredibly, his hat, a sort of Swiss yodeling doohickey with a feather in it, did not come off in the process.

At the end of our week together, the students from my seminar reconnoitered in the dark at our classroom, flashlights in hand, before heading off to the fire ceremony Cathrine had planned. Everyone wondered whether the James Dean clone would show up with his guitar, as promised. At Cathrine's request, I'd written down the lyrics of "Blowin' in the Wind" from memory, starting with all that I could at first remember: the end rhyme of each stanza—"died," "see," "banned"—and working backward. James Dean had been glimpsed at dinner, and someone else had just spotted him crawling into the dark baths. All the other seminarians were headed down toward the fire pit at the Art Barn, even the Greek veteran with his hat and bad knee. Each brought an offering for the fire. And then—fresh from the baths—the James Dean double showed up, but it turned out his guitar playing was not so great, and he soon peeled off to the Dance Yurt with a swaying, wandering girl.

It all seemed odd to me. We were in arguably the most advanced state in the most advanced country in the world; we should have been having a virtual ceremony on our iPods. The last nighttime ceremony I'd been invited to was in the countryside in Haiti, in a slip of a village called Duverger, a place you could not call an advanced anything. There was fire there too, but only an occasional blast set off with rum poured on the ground to smooth the gods' way down to earth. Here at the Art Barn in the most advanced state in the most advanced country in the world, the seminarians threw corn and tobacco on the fire, in honor of the great female and the great male. Why were these modern, mostly secular Christian aspiring writers honoring the great yin and yang—and this, with offerings from Native American tradition? I couldn't fathom it. It was multicultural meaninglessness, another doomed attempt to get *grounded*, like Huffington's quest to find God in the person of John-Roger, or the red wristbands of the Resnicks. As with so much in my new state, the desire for authenticity was present at this ceremony, but there was nothing authentic about it.

All the writers brought offerings. If I could have put an appropriate gift into the fire, what would it have been? My court summons? No, that might have been illegal, plus it would be cheating: I'd be burning it simply to get rid of it; instead, the offering had to be something that would conjure up protection or success. My friend Karla put in a piece of eucalyptus bark with flowers and bay leaves, and hoped it would help her set aside time for writing. Maybe I would have tossed in my Terminator doll, if only I'd had him with me. That was a good idea. He would have said, "Don't do that"—one of his four phrases. My wish would have been to be granted an interview. Rob Stutzman was still mulling over my request. His latest e-mail—a laconic response to my eloquent pleas—had said, "will be easier to figure out after nov. 8," the date of the governor's special initiatives election.

Then, as the Terminator's ashes wafted through the night air, we writers would hold hands and sing "Blowin' in the Wind."

The ride has begun.

In his tough-minded way, Esalen's Seymour Carter is nostalgic for an old-fashioned life, one lived in nudity. "Nudity is a political statement, you know," he says. "My childhood was spent with nudists; my grandfather was a nudist in 1906 in Spokane, Washington. Esalen was started by people who believed in nudity; it's a re-creation of German romanticism, of the existentialism and the natural-body world of late-nineteenth-century German, Austrian, and Swiss culture. There was a center in Switzerland in the 1880s that was a prototype for Esalen, with an eclectic mix of anarcho-socialists, Jungians, body-movement people, Freudians, and theosophists who worshipped the nude body in the sun and developed alternative practices within what was a very repressive society; I mean, it all started when the women took off their corsets."

I'm thinking, as he talks, about how the fashion industry has colonized the minds and bodies of L.A. and of America: about how powerful *dressing* is in my town—how important to young girls which designer they wear, who *has* what, who *wears* what. It is decidedly not just about looking good. How the girls giggle as they walk down the street with the word JUICY printed in large letters across the material that stretches over their buttocks, a ready-to-wear designer label, how shopping for clothes is their *admitted* favorite leisure activity. Carter is advocating for nudity in a culture that publishes and subscribes to magazines like *Entertainment Weekly* and *US Weekly*, with their spreads of movie stars wearing couture dresses—a different costly gown each week—and this is what Americans want to see. Traipsing around nude is antithetical to the current gestalt of L.A. and the country. It's not just the problem of propriety anymore, not stern Aunt Pollys and bustling Auntie Ems and Marmees who will not permit Any Such Thing. Being clothed is not about Puritan sexual anxiety today; it's become a materialist obsession instead. The clothing obsession is bad in New York, but at least on the East Coast, you have to wear a coat for four months. Here in L.A., your wardrobe is on display year-round.

Though he used to get as naked as possible, grease down, and parade himself around in front of audiences *as a profession*, the governor of California is now a self-described "major shoe queen." He participates in the fashion obsession; he loves to talk about how he loves to shop for clothes, and about how much he enjoys not only the possession but the purchase of his full-knuckle-sized heavy rings and big gold watches. One problem of nudity for the society we live in here in Southern California, other than a general WASP reluctance to reveal the possibly unappetizing naked body, is that when you are nude, you have no clothing ready at hand to testify to your financial status. Those people at the celebrity parties that are chronicled in *Angeleno* magazine would not have much to do or to say or to think about if they were naked from morning till night.

In all fairness, I must reveal that my husband's grandfather was Hugo Beigel, a Viennese sexologist who believed in nudism. In our house we have a book he owned called *Among the Nudists*, which I try to keep hidden from my children. (He also published several books, including a monograph on coital positions.) *Among the Nudists* has a lot of photos of bearded Viennese thinkers in the buff. Whenever the children find it, they cackle as they page through. Also for the record, I am personally a failure at the fashion game, a serious failure who feels herself to be one. A friend of mine who worked at a woman's magazine once asked me to write a piece about pointy-headed girls and what they wear. In the end she rejected it: "It's funny, but we *did* think you would have a more extensive wardrobe . . ."

Nudism, though, is a concept peculiarly suited to California. In Germany and Austria, nudism was, as Carter points out, a reaction to a profoundly repressive culture. Here in California, I feel that it might be a response to repression, sure, but more likely, it simply works with the good weather. You can't really be nude year-round in Perth Amboy, New Jersey. During the snows of December, you can hardly bear to be naked in Boston, even under a hot shower. From the pictures in *Among the Nudists*, I gather that the Germans practiced nudism mostly in the summer months, at their country homes.

Here's another proposal for a short film to be directed by Rob Minkoff, the Disney animator and director, this one a capsule fantasy of American history and fashion: it opens with settlers wearing coonskin hats and furs and skins and high leather boots in the East, and then, as they make their way west across the country, casting off more and more of their garments as their clothes become ragged and shredded, like Mrs. Brier's in Death Valley. As the weather gets warmer and warmer, jackets, buckskins, waistcoats, muffs, bustles, crinolines, hoops, and chaps fly toward the camera in a sort of macédoine of Wild West fashion. Finally, with a last gasp of rushing breath, these hardy American pioneers arrive at the sunny coast at Big Sur and, in a burst

of oneness with a now benevolent Nature, throw off their woven remnants and merge with the ocean spray, the mountains, the majestic
coast—all of them, man, woman, and child, reborn.

I'm back from Esalen, sitting in the pool house, thinking about the
Pacific. The thought does cross my mind: Should a writer have a pool
house? A pool? A deck? Isn't a shivering garret a more appropriate
dwelling? These are questions one asks oneself, if one lived through
the 1960s. It's like the old question of President Aristide in Haiti:
should the president of Haiti, about which it is a cliché to say that it is
the poorest nation in the hemisphere, have a swimming pool? Should
he build a dream house? There are the stories of writers in Los Angeles, of course. George S. Kaufman, Robert Benchley, John O'Hara,
F. Scott Fitzgerald, Ernest Hemingway—they all had a pool in L.A.,
because they all lived, at one time or another, at the sprawling, Span-
ish-style Garden of Allah hotel complex on the Sunset Strip, where
there was a central, kidney-shaped pool.

So that's having a pool, isn't it? I decided that the Garden of Allah
pool was a lofty precedent for writers with pools, although a hotel
pool—shared by other literary figures and movie stars and directors—
has more glamour than a Hancock Park pool near the tar pits, shared
with your dog and your children and the neighbor's kids' Wiffle balls.

Anyway, I needed a structure of some sort to store my inflatable
boat in, and the pool-house closet was a step up from the late garage.
The blue bucket with boat inside was now on its own personal shelf,
easily reachable. I could convince myself that the whole pool house,
and thus the pool too, had been built to accommodate a shelf for the
boat. After all, the pool was the only place where I was even remotely
likely to use that boat, if it were ever to be inflated. We could use it as
a swimming tube or a raft to float along in—although it was a big
inflatable boat, and a very small pool.

I'd dreamed of sailing away when I was up in Big Sur, the coastline
such an obvious escape route. I thought about joining the merchant
marine, maybe, sailing away across the sea to the South Pacific or to

Thailand, someplace hedonistic and slow; someplace that was like what California was supposed to be. Maybe I'd debark in Fiji and meet the Resnicks for some pineapples and a big bottle of water or a bowl full of yaqona, the Fijian national narcotic. I could use a narcotic. Maybe I'll take a swim, empty my head of Los Angeles and fill it with Pacific waves.

Fitzgerald's Garden of Allah, where he too sat around a pool, no doubt daydreaming of the landlocked city of St. Paul as he thought up scenarios for *The Last Tycoon* and other sparkling stories, is now a mini-mall, with a Pollo Loco as its anchor.

Up in Coldwater Canyon there is a birthday party that is being given by Carrie Fisher for Carrie Fisher, among others. I'm invited because a father from my son's school happens to be a screenwriter who is an old friend of Fisher's. Upon arriving, I feel I've been thrown back to the 1960s, to the era of Esalen and Sharon Tate. This is a birthday, but it is also Hollywood, so none of the normal rules apply. Just as when I went to Arianna Huffington's "barbecue," there was nothing about it that was like a barbecue, here, at this "birthday party," the only thing like a birthday is the cake. First of all, it's a birthday party for four people. Second of all, as far as I can ascertain, not one of them was born on the day of the party. Third of all, no presents; fourth of all, each guest might know one of the birthday boys and girls, but very few guests know all of them. There are about 250 guests.

Fifth of all, the party is being thrown a few nights before Halloween, so all the guests are enjoined to wear a costume. A follow-up e-mail to the invitation reads:

> We have been contacted by the office of Parks & Recreation:
>   Pursuant to Section 5150 of the California Health & Welfare Code, all GUESTS in attendance of a public gathering must be in some gesture of COSTUME (glitter in hair, clown nose, carnation in lapel, etc.), if the following conditions exist:
>   A: Four or more birthdays are being celebrated.

B: If said public gathering occurs within 72 hours of All
Hallow's Eve.

C: If your nose is in the middle of your face.

The only way to know that there is a house up the driveway here on
Coldwater is that Crystal Valet has a cohort of about twenty parkers in
white suits and lavender neckties standing waiting for the guests.
Otherwise the house is too far up from the street to be seen. Just down
Coldwater, about five feet from the valet station, there's another clue
that something's going on. Three paparazzi in scruffy black outfits
with huge old-fashioned cameras with flashes hanging around their
necks are standing together watchfully. Some parties—usually corporate parties or fund-raisers—hire a gossip photographer, who gets to
come inside. Otherwise the uninvited photographers hang around
outside. In any case, if celebrities might be present, so are the
paparazzi. I sometimes think there must be a quiet financial relationship between Crystal Valet and the paparazzi.

As my husband and I pull up, the paparazzi do not jump to attention. Alongside the driveway, on a low ridge above it, is a long, narrow
outbuilding like a motel almost, with many entries to many rooms. My
friends tell me that this is where "Carrie's friends" crash when they
need a place to stay. From a tree that overhangs the driveway, someone has strung and wired an elaborate crystal chandelier. I wonder, Is
it always there? I have acceded reluctantly to the Halloween instructions to the extent that I am wearing a silver hat and I have a plastic
rat, one that squeaks when squeezed, peering out of my pocket.
Because these are Hollywood people, though, it's not always easy to
determine who is in costume and who isn't. If I were one of them, I
could turn out to be the kind of person who wears a rat in my pocket
every night. It could turn out to be my trademark.

We walked in the main door of the house, past the piano (where
dozens of pictures of Fisher and her famous friends and family were
lined up like a validating army) and through the living room. Other
people from our son's school were standing like hobbits against walls

and in clumps; there were only a few of these out-of-place guests, and it was as if the lights, which were bright in this room, were somehow dimmer where the hobbits lurked. I felt a solidarity with the other hobbits, though none of them was so misguided as to carry a rat.

We continued on past a knot of guests, a big couch, and a side table (on which there was a 1950s-era issue of *Photoplay* magazine, laid out carefully for show, with a picture on the cover of Fisher as a girl, and her mother, the actress Debbie Reynolds), and then we were suddenly out in a wide courtyard filled with guests, caterers, bartenders, and waiters. A cowboy was standing at the bar; a woman in an extreme feather boa tripped on her high heels, another had cat ears that blinked with lights, and our serious screenwriter friend smiled at me, unembarrassed, beneath his red clown nose.

All sorts of teenagers wandered around in various states of décolletage and coolness. In some rooms the teenagers sat on the floor. In the courtyard, they gathered more people at their tables than could possibly fit, and yet they fit. On the big white bed in a back bedroom through which lackadaisical guests nonetheless filed, a collection of girls were gossiping and channel surfing at the same time, as if the party were a sleepover. Sean Lennon, a musician and the son of John Lennon and Yoko Ono, passed by in a top hat and a corduroy jacket. His birthday was among those being celebrated. A little girl came up to him and introduced herself and he bowed and kissed her hand. This was enough to turn the 2000s into the 1960s, for me. Lennon's resemblance to his father was uncanny; I wondered if *that* was his costume.

Near the birthday cake, the actress Meg Ryan was having a heated discussion with her teenaged son, carried on in a polite but intense undertone. He had a skateboard under his arm. Daryl Hannah, another actress, sat on a sofa in the courtyard next to a man who needed two assistants in order to stand up. She talked to him, looking at him intently, as if he were an alien being she was trying to understand. Hannah was dressed as if for a *Vogue* shoot entitled "Adventure in the Himalayas." White and beige fur and skins, shearling boots past the knee, feathers, perhaps. I was not convinced it was a costume.

When her friend's assistants lifted him, she stood too. She looked as if she were ready to go off to shoot polar bears. She's very tall. At the other end of the couch sat the actress Kirstie Alley.

The reason it feels like the 1960s here, besides the costumes, is that it's Carrie Fisher's house. Carrie Fisher, whose father was the singer Eddie Fisher, is very much a child of that era. Her parents split up in 1959, when she was around three years old, in a very public divorce, back when divorce was still a scandal, and soon after, her father married Elizabeth Taylor, with whom he'd been having a well-known affair. Fisher was brought up among some of the most hedonistic figures in Hollywood during the hedonistic decade that followed, and as an adult has run—at various times—a mythically decadent, generous, and welcoming household. She's a successful novelist, a script doctor, and an actress who played Princess Leia in three *Star Wars* movies. Tonight, in a sort of good-spirited metacommentary on herself, she's dressed as Princess Leia; it's weirdly disorienting. Out of context, the braided buns Leia wears on either side of her head make Fisher look like an aging Heidi.

Her personal story is one of serious addiction and serial rehabilitations. Right now she's well, according to my friends who are her friends, but to an outsider's eye she looks frail and spent. Just eight months before tonight's birthday party, Robert Stevens, a Republican media adviser and Hollywood party boy, was found dead at the age of forty-two of an overdose of cocaine and oxycodone in one of the guest rooms of this house. Nothing more 1960s Hollywood than a public overdose at a movie star's house. If you remembered the 1960s, Stevens's death seemed almost art-directed.

Carrie Fisher is a writer with a pool. You take a long path from the courtyard up the canyon, past a bungalow, and there it is, steaming under lights. It's as if pools have a secret life here in Hollywood, like wild animals. When they are not right outside the living-room window at such houses, they're off in the distance, usually up a long, winding stairway, almost hidden in the hills among the trees. They seem to be waiting, breathing. Standing at the edge of Fisher's pool, I think of the pool where the unfortunate screenwriter ends up, floating face down, in Billy Wilder's *Sunset Boulevard,* with the paparazzi rushing to shoot him after he's been shot. I think also of *The Anniversary Party,* the 2001 film about actors' lives in the Hollywood Hills, where the pool is frighteningly near, and menacing, always waiting for the party's guests to dive in—guests who assume it's just there for their amusement. The pool is an element of suspense in that movie, and that's how Fisher's pool looks to me. Having a pool, especially one that is heated in the cold months, is a sign of success in Hollywood, as elsewhere, but here in Hollywood the pool is also symbolically the instrument of downfall.

I'm meeting Warren Beatty for lunch in a strip mall. Note: It is a fancy strip mall, up on Mulholland Drive. Its parking lot is filled with Mercedes-Benzes and Lexus SUVs, and even one Rolls-Royce two-seater. Still, it's a strip mall with a dry cleaners, etc. On the phone Beatty said, "Let's meet at the little Italian place in the corner; you'll find it." As if I had any idea where the strip mall was, much less the little Italian place in the corner. On the day we're supposed to meet, I call him to confirm. I have figured out where we are meeting, because fortuitously, when I mention a strip mall on Mulholland, a friend of mine who spends a lot of time on the west side of town knows exactly which strip mall that is and knows exactly that restaurant. "The Starbucks there is filled with celebrities," she says. Beatty also has one of his array of assistants call me to give me directions.

It's hard to describe what it's like to talk to Beatty on the phone. He's a phone addict. He will go on. In our first conversation—to set up lunch—he tells me about his daughter's speech to the family at Thanksgiving; about an incident involving his daughter, a barstool, and her boyfriend; about a death in his wife's family; about his early days on Franklin Avenue at the Montecito, which was then a fancy residential hotel; and he tells me many other things. He's charming and funny, in a roundabout way, but it's plain that there are very few people in his life who are willing to cut him off, and I am not going to be the first.

Not that I want to.

Beatty was a cultural originator and an embodiment of the 1960s. Like Jane Fonda, he was a Hollywood icon who represented free love, and practiced it. He was also at the center of what was exciting and original during one of the most creative periods in American movies, and for more than a decade—from *Bonnie and Clyde* in 1967 through *Shampoo* in 1975, and then on to *Reds* in 1981. He wasn't just a movie star. As a young screen idol, he brought the idea for *Bonnie and Clyde* to the director Arthur Penn, and solo-produced it. He was a writer on *Shampoo*, as well as its star. And he directed and wrote *Reds*, as well as directing, writing, producing, and starring in *Bulworth* in 1998. At the time of *Bonnie and Clyde*'s release, in August 1967, he was a very bad boy, a well-known Lothario, a young rebel, and a big success in Hollywood. He was thirty.

I'm late to our lunch, but like any self-respecting celebrity or just plain movie actor, Beatty's later. ("He's been delayed," the maitre d' informs me. It does not seem to be a new phrase for him.) The maitre d' shows me to a back table in a corner. When Beatty arrives, he and I have the distinct L.A. pleasure of discussing traffic conditions before he even sits down. He's wearing jeans and a black crewneck shirt and a sports jacket. The overall impression is of someone who is well groomed, well cared for.

First we order. He does that thing with the waitress that he did in *Bonnie and Clyde* when he first sees Faye Dunaway. He gives her a penetrating look, but saucy at the same time. The waitress seems to like it, to be familiar with it. She takes him in stride. He wants his pizza crust very thin.

"I mean *thin*," he says, making a thin gesture with his thumb and forefinger.

She gets it.

"And barely any cheese at all," he says. She nods; she has been here before, as we say here in L.A. It's beginning to remind me of the scene in *Five Easy Pieces* where Jack Nicholson orders the toast from the waitress. A chicken sandwich on toast, hold the mayo, hold the chicken.

"The crust is bad for you," Beatty says to me. "But the cheese is even worse."

Celebrities are always picky, especially at restaurants where they are regulars. They have to be demanding in these situations, almost as if to justify the extra attention they get. It's as if it's their right to order the chef around and have things that are off the menu—sometimes seriously off the menu. When I interviewed Roseanne Barr about a decade ago in L.A., she took me to her favorite place, an elegant Italian restaurant in Beverly Hills, and then had her assistant run out and grab her a low-fat muffin from down the street. The maitre d' there did not even blink.

I want to talk to Beatty about coming to California; it's a shared experience we have (and there are not many a normal person can share with him). I ask him what it was like; originally he was from Richmond, Virginia.

"Oh, well, I was already famous when I got here, so it's not that illuminating," he says, dismissively. "I've never had a normal life."

He is the first celebrity I've heard of who does not immediately want to do the we-are-just-like-you thing.

"Actually," he says, "someone once said to me that I've been famous longer than most people have been alive." He laughs. "But it's true, really.

"Also, I'm a rich man, and have been forever," he says. "It's funny, my parents never really understood. They stayed in Richmond; they were teachers. My mother, I used to visit her, and of course, I could get her anything she wanted. She did not want much; it was so hard even to get them to visit here. But really, if I'd said to her, Mama, I am moving the *entire* city of Cleveland down to Virginia, she would have said, 'Oh, that's nice, dear,' and not blinked, because she thought anything was possible in my world."

But *is* anything possible? It is said that one of Beatty's dreams is to be governor: it may be an eternally idle dream with him, something he fantasizes about and toys with. It's hard to tell, with Beatty, the difference between what's idle, speculative, or theoretical, and what's real, in part because his reality is so attenuated and so far off the charts, in part because he has a glancing way of coming at things; his conversation has to be distilled afterward because it's *unreal,* as we used to say in the 1960s when we meant bizarrely fascinating. But what's true is that while his name is still frequently mentioned in stories about the next gubernatorial election, he has never put his name forward as a candidate.

The pizza arrives, and he regards it. Beatty can't help his theatricality; he's not *regarding* the pizza in order for me to notice his intelligent, judgmental assessment; it's just the way he looks at things, head to the side, slightly, a little quizzical.

"Why do I do this?" he asks. He's not talking about coming here and eating pizza: he means politics.

He ruminates as he finishes his first slice of the tiny, very flat, very *thin,* but still—in his opinion, with which he decides not to torment the waitress—too-cheesy pizza.

"You find yourself at a certain point in your life," he says, referring to himself in the second person. "It's like asking why are you social, to ask why are you politically active. If you are famous enough and can put five or six words together, and you're moderate in your delivery, then you can lead and you can help. Something that has only 49 percent behind it, you can maybe boost it to 51 percent, and be of service. To not do it—to be silent—is to be complicit.

"I don't know if it's that important to *run* for office," he says. "So many of the people you see in politics, they're just involved in their own personal ambitions, and that's what pushes them to achieve public office. There's no higher motivation for them.

"Now, don't get me wrong," he goes on, just in case I hadn't realized to whom he's now referring. "I always liked Arnold. We aren't close friends, but we used to see each other occasionally. He's very good-natured, and we never talk seriously about politics; he's a kidder. He kids around, he always sort of teased me, and obviously we differ. I'm a Kennedy Democrat. Also he makes movies that make a *lot* more money than mine do. But I make *good* movies."

Like many celebrities, Beatty is both narcissistic and mistrustful.

"Do you know that Google has a record of every search that's ever been made on it?" he asks me, raising his eyebrows and sitting forward. His pose of relaxed, laid-back raconteur is dropped for a second. "Do you realize the implications of that? If they have your name, they can trace your history; millions and millions of searches!" He doesn't like to use e-mail; he fears the new media and worries that anything a celebrity does with it will come back to haunt him or her. He's nervous about Google in a way that reminds me of people who were spied on and victimized by J. Edgar Hoover, the mad, politically motivated head of the FBI, in the 1960s.

"Anyway, people hate celebrities," he says. This is news to me. Why am I reading *Angeleno* magazine, then? Why is it filled with celebrities? Why does America read *Entertainment Weekly* and watch *ET*? Why are there movie stars on the covers of fashion magazines now, instead of the anonymous models who used to pose for fashion covers? Why has the *L.A. Times* started an Internet service called The Envelope, which is largely about celebrities and the Academy Awards? I ask Beatty, but he skirts the question.

"There has been a demonization of celebrities on the part of the far right," he says. I realize he's talking about attacks on Barbra Streisand as a lefty liberal Clinton groupie, and on the whole Arianna Huffington Hollywood salon phenomenon in general. "Latte-sipping" is the adjective of choice when right-wingers describe liberal celebrities.

"I never made a single speech during the recall," Beatty says. "I was afraid it would do more harm than good. Look, Bruce Springsteen went out in Ohio for Kerry and they even made *him* look bad, and Springsteen is a saint." But during the campaign for the special election that Schwarzenegger called for November 2005, Beatty overcame his reluctance and, fittingly somehow, hit the trail on behalf of California's nurses, whose working conditions were threatened by one of Schwarzenegger's initiatives. He was received by the nurses' crowds with wild enthusiasm, and he seems to feel that his appearances on their behalf made a difference in eroding Schwarzenegger's popularity with a wider constituency. Beatty was testing the political waters.

During the week of *Bonnie and Clyde's* British release, the movie critic Roger Ebert interviewed Beatty in his London hotel:

> "A lot of people out there just kind of dismiss me as an irresponsible kid," [Beatty] said. "All of Hollywood is old, old, old, for that matter. There are as many good young actors and directors in America as there are in Europe, but Hollywood shuts them out. Hollywood is afraid of young blood. It's a ghost town."

With his ethos of youth, Beatty would have been right at home at the Esalen Institute of Seymour Carter. "I've been married for fifteen years now," Beatty says. He raises his eyebrows. "But back then, I just believed in doing everything, experiencing everything, spending what I had—money, sex, all of it. Is that bad? Life is short, isn't it?" Today, even though he's part of the Hollywood that's "old, old, old," Beatty would still enjoy himself at the institute, among the people in the baths who love to talk about themselves and the world they're confronting.

He did represent a 1960s sensibility, after all, even though—in an effort to be contemporary—he used Ice Cube in *Bulworth* and did a good job being a white, middle-aged, rapping politician in that movie. Beatty tried courageously to keep up with the times, but it was a particular 1960s quality of mind that stopped him from being of the *now*. He wasn't a new-century man, he was more fin de siècle. Under all the fame, the cavalier charm, the self-love, and the habitual movie-star behavior lay the triple killers: empathy, doubt, and self-consciousness. Beatty could see that others might not consider him to be the world's best candidate ("People hate celebrities"), and he wondered if he could win. He was also always capable of getting outside himself and seeing himself as ridiculous. None of these qualities was palpable in the character of Schwarzenegger, and their lack—which is not normal—provided the governor with much of the untouchable power and otherness that served him so well as he pursued his unique career.

———

As I said, I was always on the lookout for an inciting incident. One day I was driving down Highland near the Franklin intersection in Hollywood, not far from the scene of my encounter with Angel, and not far, also, from an entrance to the Hollywood Freeway. The intersection includes a corner in front of a mini-mall where a few homeless regulars hang out and often solicit funds from passing motorists stopped at the very long red light. I'm used to the old bearded guy who rants at the traffic; I'm used to the fashionably dressed young woman who doesn't seem homeless, but whose clothes, upon closer inspection, haven't been cleaned in a long time; I'm used to the handsome young *dude* whose sign says "I am homeless Will marry rich woman"; I'm used to the guy with the mustache who hangs out with the old bearded man. It's not my usual time of day to pass through. Morning rush hour is over, and the customary gathering at the mini-mall corner has dispersed, along with the traffic jam that feeds it. It's around noon. No old man, no young woman, no handsome guy. Only the mustachioed fellow. Today, for the first time, he has a sign: "Lost job because of hit and run."

CHAPTER SEVEN

Instant Cities

T HINGS WERE COMING TO A CLOSE. Angel asked for a $40,000 settlement, and my insurance company was deliberating. In another life, discouraged, I might have left off driving. But not in L.A. One morning in the fall of 2005, I was driving down the Hollywood Freeway, and as I approached the NBC Universal building, I felt something was not right. There had been a change in the landscape, a palpable change but I couldn't pinpoint it. It's not easy to notice much when you're driving on a freeway in L.A., other than how closely Californians follow each other, and at what high speeds. I am always dropping back and allowing space in front of me, which someone always switches lanes to fill. Sometimes on the freeways I feel as if I'm in reverse.

But then, seconds later, I did realize what had changed, because today a little patch of the freeway's southern bank was different, denuded: the *T3* billboard had disappeared. I was alone out here in the traffic now. Big Brother was no longer watching, through his sunglasses. In his place was a plain olive green wall, three stories high, a wall that was the back of the Davis*Glick Entertainment building. On the top left-hand corner, where stars, smoke, and explosions had previously reigned, the name Davis*Glick now appeared.

It was as if our Fearless Leader had been deposed in the dead of night, and history was erasing him. I wondered how this could have happened. It was not a good time for the governor to disappear like that, like a magic trick. Right now Schwarzenegger needed all the help he could get. He needed a boost from his alter ego. Where was that Terminator when you needed him? That had always been my anxiety: would he be there for me? And now he was gone.

And in reality, it was true. Schwarzenegger, my unconquerable, unassailable, triumphant new emperor—the man who never questioned himself—was floundering in the polls. As governor, he'd made an astounding series of political miscalculations, culminating in a special election filled with initiatives he'd supported that were then soundly rejected by the voters. When I got home from my freeway shock later that day, I went to my Terminator doll for support; it's still standing next to my desk, even though the *T3* billboard was gone. I looked at it appraisingly: can it have shrunk? It looks smaller, thinner, somehow. Maybe it's my perspective that's changing, along with California's. I wonder what my doll would look like in bathing trunks. (A recent photo of Schwarzenegger had him standing on the sand somewhere in front of palm trees—it may have been taken during his 2003 Hawaii vacation—looking not too buff in his tiny Speedo swimsuit.) After some pulling and tugging, however, I discover that my doll's black leather outfit is unfortunately not removable. This is no Barbie, with a change of clothing for every mood. Here, the costume is the doll. That may be part of Schwarzenegger's problem.

It's almost as if Schwarzenegger's hypermasculinity—his head-to-toe black leather suit—has defeated him, his greatest qualities perhaps abetting a downfall, like that of a true tragic figure, only it's Schwarzenegger we're talking about here, a man who, as his former agent Lou Pitt observed in Laurence Leamer's biography, "went from being an icon to a life force . . . because of his fitness program, his presence in that world, Hummer, his dress, the Hawaiian shirts, smoking cigars." This is not Martin Luther King, Jr., or—a different kind of great man, more Schwarzenegger's type—Teddy Roosevelt. This is an actor smoking a cigar, wearing too much jewelry, cowboy boots, and a loud shirt, and driving a great big car, I remind myself. Can such a man have a tragic fall? These days, Schwarzenegger has been reminding me of those blow-up men that women drivers used to put in the passenger seat in the crime-ridden 1980s to make it look as if they were escorted, protected. When you went right up to him and squeezed those biceps, they deflated. I was saddened, dejected; if Arnold couldn't stand firm, what hero was going to be big enough, steadfast enough, to pull me from my predicament? What hero was going to be sturdy and strong enough to bolster the state, my state?

Gone were my elaborate fantasies of Arnold's hosting dignitaries in the Oval Office, his arms spread, humidor open, extended, at the ready. You could even have argued that Schwarzenegger would be doing well simply to keep Sacramento, because no one much liked Arnold anymore. Maybe the problem was the hubris, the cigars in the AstroTurfed smoking tent he built for himself just outside the capitol in Sacramento, the tent with its ceiling fan and its stereo system, and the strong-arming, the extragovernmental tactics, and that maddening self-assurance that so few of us felt. There were policy decisions, too, that added to his drop in popularity.

A minor one, though remarkable for what it revealed, was his 2004 veto of a bill that would have regulated substances deemed dangerous for high school athletes, a list that would have included steroids and some dietary supplements. In a story that ran a year after that veto, the *Los Angeles Times* reported that two days before Schwarzenegger was inaugurated, he accepted an $8 million contract to "further the business objectives" of American Media, a company that publishes bodybuilding magazines. Under the arrangement, Schwarzenegger was to receive one percent of the publications' advertising revenues, according to the *Times*. The main advertisers in *Muscle & Fitness* and *Flex*, American Media's muscle magazines, are manufacturers and distributors of those same nutritional supplements that the governor's veto saved from regulation in California, which is of course a major market for those products. (The two muscle magazines had been sold to American Media by Joe Weider, an early bodybuilding friend, mentor, and promoter of Schwarzenegger's.)

American Media is also the parent corporation of both the *National Enquirer* and the *Star*, two surprisingly influential nationally distributed supermarket gossip and reporting rags. According to Leamer, in the 2002 California gubernatorial election, Schwarzenegger decided *not* to run against Gray Davis for governor in part because of a series of scandalous *National Enquirer* stories, especially those concerning his long-term, on-again-off-again relationship with a "former television actress" improbably named Gigi Goyette. But later, when the recall election became a possibility, American Media saw an opening for a negotiation. According to a press release from Learner,

> [In] July, 2003, as Schwarzenegger was actively contemplating entering the recall election, he met with [David] Pecker [head of American Media] in the star's Santa Monica office. "There was no discussion about the *National Enquirer*," Schwarzenegger [said]. "There were all sorts of people sitting there. It would have been inappropriate. Nor did I want to be on the record that I'm hassling him about another agenda." Arnold did not have to say anything. "I think it's common sense," he observed. "Do you want to work with someone who you are attacking? You don't have to say anything. You don't have to be sleazy and make deals. It's human nature."

The point of Schwarzenegger's comment appears to be that the sleazy deal was already understood: "You don't have to say anything." After the arrangement was finally made public two years later, Schwarzenegger moved quickly to annul the contract, though he kept whatever monies he had already received from the deal, an amount he refused to disclose. "You don't have to say anything": in some ways, this could have been the motto of his governorship.

Still, it had been shocking to see that blank zip past, and after contemplating my Terminator doll, I called up Davis*Glick Entertainment. (If John-Roger can have his hyphen, then Davis*Glick can have its asterisk.) I thought that a public-relations person there would tell me that the contract for the *T3* billboard had simply lapsed. How naïve I am, still, after all this time in noirland. There's always a subtext.

Robbie Davis, president and founder of Davis*Glick, called me back.

"We package the wall together with other things we do, usually," Davis said. "When it was the Jurassic dinosaur, we had a permit from the city for a supermural. It's a term they use in outdoor advertising." Before that, Davis's agreement with the city had been for an "artistic mural."

"The dinosaur came down because after a while, they wanted to change the creative," Davis told me. "We ended up canceling the relationship." Business people in Hollywood resort to a lexicon of clichés: "The creative." "The relationship."

"So anyway," Davis continued, "at that point when we amicably parted company, I turned it over to Viacom, who we work with. I told them, 'I'm not the billboard guy, work it out.' Next thing I knew, they had sold it to Warner Home Video for the release of *T3*." The billboard went up about a week before the recall election, Davis remembers. A lot was happening in those weeks before the recall election.

"So the Democrats in the city government assume that I'm some kind of Republican, and that the *T3* billboard was a complete ruse to get votes out for Schwarzenegger. The city came at me with a vengeance." Los Angeles filed criminal charges against Davis. "And it's ridiculous, really," Davis said. "I'm not a Schwarzenegger fan per se. I couldn't care less about politics; I'm an independent. What I am is supercapitalistic: I make money. I've got a wall, I've got a permit. I put them together and make money. So anyway, Viacom hired lawyers and we maintained that our 1997 permit gave us every right to go from the Jurassic dinosaur to *T3*."

Davis said that the criminal charges locked him into the *T3* supermural ("If I took it down, the city would win"), and that that was how a billboard that was contracted for sixty days and was supposed to advertise a DVD release ended up staying there for more than two years, as if it were a governmental symbol. When the city offered a settlement in mid-2005, Davis finally was able to take the Terminator down.

Was *this* earthquake weather, I wondered as I drove down Vermont Avenue to my appointment at USC, through the Latino neighborhoods. The sky was greenish, and the atmosphere seemed to be hanging suspended over the region. It reminded me of tornado weather in other places, but I recalled, my courage building, that Carey McWilliams argued in his book that there is no such thing as earthquake weather. "The persistent failure of the press to report the findings of modern seismologists has resulted in an immense amount of folklore about earthquakes in Southern California," he writes in *Southern California: An Island on the Land*. "Most Southern California residents are thoroughly convinced that earthquakes are invariably preceded by a period of what is called 'earthquake weather.'" All my friends used this term. McWilliams goes on: "In the sense in which most residents understand the expression, 'earthquake weather' refers to a close, stifling, sunless, muggy day. . . ." My friends also believe that earthquakes happen more during the solstices, when the sun exerts a greater gravitational pull on the earth's tectonic plates. This too, as McWilliams might have said, is hogwash.

Don Waldie was waiting in the sun for me to pick him up at the USC driveway on Exposition Boulevard. In an e-mail he had said, "Look for the patient-looking, bespectacled man." But he and I knew each other already; he was just pointing out the obvious. Our relationship had been facilitated by Steve Wasserman, of the *L.A. Times Book Review*. Waldie and I had talked together at many a Wasserman-inspired get-together. Wasserman facilitated a lot in L.A. before he left town: the *Book Review*, which he ran as his own personal intellectual fiefdom; the *L.A. Times* Festival of Books, a huge springtime event that he founded; and of course the L.A. Institute for the Humanities—the Geniuses.

Wasserman was a California-born boy, but one might not have guessed it because Wasserman was also an intellectual snob, with a predilection for Europe, for bespoke suits, for long sentences filled with improbable vocabulary and eloquent, old-fashioned rhetorical flourishes and Johnsonian periods. He ran the *Book Review* for the sole purpose, I had always thought, of impressing Susan Sontag, who had been a friend and mentor of his for a long time. The extremely dapper Wasserman, who'd moved to New York to become a literary agent, left behind a long and complicated legacy in the West. One important part of that legacy was Waldie. Wasserman was the very last person you'd expect to understand Waldie, and certainly vice versa.

But according to the patient-looking, bespectacled man, Wasserman created Waldie. "He is personally responsible for my career," Waldie told me, "and for everything interesting that I've been able to do." And Waldie's has been a very special career; he is the Walt Whitman and the Edmund Wilson of the American subdevelopment. In part because Wasserman promoted it, Waldie's work on the tract-house community of Lakewood in Southern California has been celebrated by people like Didion (another unimpeachable intellectual snob) and Dave Eggers, the Northern California writer and publisher. Waldie, whose writing under the name D. J. Waldie is detached, elegant, and filled with repressed emotion, is also the Lakewood town public information officer. In 2004, in this guise (and as *Donald Waldie*), he wrote a 211-page, fully illustrated coffee-table paperback called *The Lakewood Story: History, Traditions, Values,* in honor of the fiftieth anniversary of the establishment of the town. The cover of the book is a close-up of the regular slats of a picket fence, on a background of blue sky and green lawn, with just enough shadow behind it to create a sense of depth, if not of dread.

I never imagined I could worship this kind of man, so seemingly bland, brush-cut, his face as empty as a map of Montana, awkward, inward, provincial, peculiar; the words "awkward" and "peculiar" were invented for Don Waldie. But whenever I see him, my heart melts, and he means it to. He's not unaware of his effect; he has the kind of grace peculiar to an awkward man. And yet I know—knowing him, reading him, watching him crouch and lumber, and listening to him, to his fascinating talk—that his own heart is eternally broken. He has an intensity of regard that is like Beatty's. (I'm certain this is the first time Waldie has been compared to Warren Beatty.) I've just picked him up from a meeting of the Geniuses. He's one.

I'm not.

Don Waldie doesn't drive, and why should he? First of all, Geniuses don't need to drive, they can always get Morons to drive for them. And for another thing, Waldie is legally blind, according to him. Of course he is, and why does this not surprise me? Also, he's rather gawky and he makes you think he'd be a menace on the road, blind or sighted. And then he likes to be contradictory, and his muse is the freeway and the subdevelopment, so it's almost mandatory that he *not* drive. Plus— an aside but it must be mentioned—he's the whitest man, none whiter. I couldn't have found a man to admire who was less Haitian, less East Coast, even less New Jersey. He's palely suburban, a flatlander; he could be an Illinois homesteader or a missionary to the Amazon, or anything else that requires whiteness and American backbone, matter-of-factness, independence, and stalwartness, and pale, pale passion— but passion nonetheless. He loves lawns.

And indeed, you feel—because he is so secretive, personally, and so private, the kind of writer who writes in the chipper first person until the story becomes obviously about himself, and then switches to the distancing "he"—you feel that Waldie very well might have a few brutalized bodies buried under the neat, postage-stamp lawn in front of the small, neat Lakewood house he has (always) lived in; he is a con-tained man who is powerfully attractive because of his valiant but failed attempt to repel. He's too intense to be normal, too offputting, and he has worked too hard to perfect himself as a character. He's a writer: what can I say? The way I feel about books in L.A., I also feel about writers, and I don't mean screenwriters, although they too are tragic figures in this culture.

On the Lakewood tour with Waldie, I almost feel like laughing. It's odd to wander the streets of Lakewood with a cultural guide. I've been on a tour of Paris with a field marshal of a French teacher, and seen the Pyramids and the Taj Mahal and Big Ben and Marrakesh and Tikal in Guatemala and Haiti's La Citadelle castle on a remote mountaintop *and all that kind of stuff,* but never have I bothered to do an actual tour of an American development, or really of an American anything. If I were going to tour an American place, it might be Boston or Gettysburg or Yosemite, but not Lakewood. And yet here I am with my blind guide.

We're walking down a block. There are single-family homes on both sides of the street. There's a sidewalk, cars, driveways. There are little bushes next to the houses. Some residents have planted flower beds. Each neat little house is very like the next neat little house. There is hardly any room for idiosyncrasy, though some have managed it. One fellow has enclosed his yard and turned his garden into a marine landscape, with palms and banana trees and anchors, shells and buoys. (His yard, situated as it is in straitlaced Lakewood, is like a beatnik in the 1950s—unallowable but there, nonetheless.) This man's eccentric but well-kept garden has upset his more conformist neighbors. Waldie, in his capacity as public information officer for the town of Lakewood, has received many an irate call on the subject, but for now, the marine yardscape remains.

Waldie points out for me what is regular about the town (the hundred-foot setbacks, for example; the footprint of the houses; the regulation height of the trees, which are cut down by the town when they grow so big as to be out of proportion to the trim houses below; the pattern of driveway and lawn, driveway and lawn). What fascinates Waldie about Lakewood is the artistry of the development, the planning of a human universe that works. Its newness and its ready-madeness. When he talks about the three men who developed the place, you don't think to yourself, the developers. You think, The Developers, like majestic architectural gods from an Ayn Rand novel, even though they were really just three average men.

Writing about his grammar school assignment to build a miniature replica of a Spanish mission, Waldie says, "Assembling one of these models, when you were eight or nine years old, made California history seem mostly about building materials." Which in a sense it is: a story made first of rock, skins, tar, grass, and mud (during the time of La Brea Woman), and moving on to brick, stucco, and clapboard, and then, not that long afterward, to steel, plasterboard, Sheetrock, plywood, plastics, composites, sheet metal, and lightweight concrete. Everything in California is telescoped because history is so much shorter here. You feel a not-so-long leap between the long houses and the missions and Frank Gehry's Disney Hall, downtown.

———

Lakewood I want to run from, almost as fast as I want to run from the Resnicks' house on Sunset, possibly faster, since there is not one single restaurant in Lakewood that is not a fast-food chain, and the Resnicks have a very good chef. I desire flight not because I question the love that Waldie has for Lakewood or the Resnicks for their house. The two possible ends of the spectrum are alienating to me: one too ready-made, too much a part of a system, the other too eccentric, too entitled. Even my ramshackle town in New Jersey was not anything like what I'm seeing here in Lakewood. We did not have that mass-produced look. We were not "an instant city," as Lakewood was called. Like so many East Coast towns, especially the ones founded during Colonial days, Perth Amboy did not have design or repetition, it was not an assembly-line churn-out. Its streets meandered, sometimes grid, sometimes circle, sometimes star, sometimes maze. Nor was it egalitarian in any way: the rich people had big houses on great lawns, and the poor huddled together in their neighborhoods, depending on race, ethnicity, and the decade during which their particular wave of immigrants had arrived. In Perth Amboy, we could not say that we represented this era or that era, the way Lakewood *represents* the 1950s. We were not made full-blown and then sold all at once. We were never born, really, we just came into being little by little in our corner on the Raritan Bay, like moss or lichen or barnacles, a slow spread. Our houses may have leaned one way or another, and the paint was chipped, perhaps—a cellar flooded, a porch banister broken and unrepaired, garbage cans visible, wood waterlogged, a toolshed here, a garage there, the sidewalks broken up by tree roots in places, potholes in the alleyways.

But here was Waldie walking over driveway after driveway, white cement paths laid out flat on the ground, block after block, like neatly spaced lines of a giant grid from which the residents could not escape. He was almost counting the plain regularity, the *beat*, of square footage and setbacks, and reveling in it, as if it were his own personal patchwork design, the pattern of his life, the map of his mind. He felt this way in spite of the suffering Lakewood endured, economically and psychologically, when the aerospace industry fell apart in the

1980s and the town's reason for being evaporated. You love what you've decided to call home, even if it's a planned community in Southern California. For Waldie, not only does Lakewood express deep truths about himself, his family, his personal history (he still lives in the house his parents bought there in 1946; he was born two years later), but it's also a manifestation of something profoundly American, deeply Californian. As he writes in *Holy Land,* "I live where a majority of Americans live: a tract house on a block of other tract houses in a neighborhood of even more." In so many ways, Lakewood is not L.A. or New York, or even Perth Amboy. Lakewood is a place that admits what it is, that longs for nothing more, that lives up to small, reachable expectations.

Whereas L.A. . . .

"Los Angeles," Waldie tells me, in his office in Lakewood City Hall, "is a city of disappointments." This is Waldie; this is his talk, not his writing:

Its glowing billboard is never matched by reality. Or of course, there's the dystopian story too. These are our two default narratives, but they don't work anymore. The booster billboard drew people, but it didn't offer any way to solve real problems. It has caused people to make terrible decisions about how we live with each other. For example, in L.A. there are only thirty thousand acres of parkland, most of it located far from those who need it. But this is based on a booster theory that you don't need parkland because L.A. is a paradise everywhere.

On the other hand, the dystopian story also led to failed public policy choices: if it's so lethal and ready to off us, what can we do about it, really? So you have civic fatalism. It means giving up and arming to the teeth. You have the paramilitary behavior of the LAPD, out of the conviction that something bad will happen *right now.* The dystopian narrative also encourages a kind of cocooning of certain components of L.A. society: the wall of television security cameras, immediate armed response signs . . . there's nothing left of you to engage in the public sphere. What perpetuates itself instead is the inability to see through these master narratives to the real issues of place. The city evaporates from your vision. Instead, you're left with the consoling illusion that you live in a place where all the benefits are unearned.

When I told Richard Reese, the man whom I'd met in my Way of Story seminar at Esalen, that I'd visited Lakewood, he looked puzzled. He said, "Well, there's nothing there." Reese helped develop Rancho Santa Margarita, which he calls an "enhanced lifestyle community." It's a new community of about forty-nine thousand people, established in 1989 in Orange County, out past most civilization there, on the old Rancho Santa Margarita de las Flores, a Mexican land grant in the foothills of the Santa Ana Mountains. Reese, a tall, slightly stooped, white-haired man of retiring disposition and strange obsessions, has retired to Rancho Santa Margarita—and why not? It should suit him, since he helped invent it; he lives in a trim house with a tiled terrace that overlooks the man-made lake.

In the days of the old Mexican rancho, the lake was a barley pasture for cattle. In more recent times but before the Rancho Santa Margarita development began, the place was one of the biggest cattle ranches in the West, and a major McDonald's supplier. Now, from Reese's terrace in the heart of the former cattle ranch, you can see mothers walking their babies around on the running path that encircles the lake. "The path," Reese says, "is ten feet wide, wide enough for three mothers with three babies in strollers to walk side by side; it's wide enough for companionable conversation." Reese, who was the Rancho Santa Margarita project's senior vice president in charge of planning and entitlements, believes that RSM, as he calls the town, is closer to perfection than any other recently developed community. As he tells it,

We have an amphitheater that seats five hundred, a beach club with a swimming hole and a real sand beach. It's modeled on

Pop's Willow Lake resort in Glendale [a town adjacent to Los Angeles], where I used to swim as a boy. It's forty dollars a year for a family membership, which entitles you to access to any of the recreational facilities throughout the town. We have a higher percentage than almost any planned community of attached housing for sale and for rent, which has resulted in the presence of a broad cross-section of economic classes and origins. And we wanted it that way. We planned it that way. We wanted it to be a cross-cultural, multiethnic, economically diverse community.

Every gathering place in RSM had to have a bell tower; they're modeled on the campanile of Bruges, Belgium, where I once awoke to the bells. We have preserved two of the original pepper trees from the cattle ranch. You can open up the trees in town by cutting away at the interior branches, but you can't alter the exterior shape of any tree in RSM. We had to teach the landscapers that. Had to literally show them how.

We have all sorts of religious disciplines here too, Catholic, of course, and Zen Buddhist and Episcopal, Christian Scientist and Lutherans, Mormons: most of the churches are at the end of the interior trail, that's where the cheap religious real estate was put. We gave religion a little break; it's all part of our lifestyle system. The preschool is also along that trail.

On the lake, there are boats for rent. And that's the fishing rock you see here at the edge of the lake. The lake, by the way, is only eighteen inches deep for the first six feet in, so that if a child falls in, he can be plucked right out. After that it's eight feet deep. We plant fish in the lake every year. The ducks those kids are feeding come on their own. Geese too. See the arrangement of benches here by the fishing rock? They're placed so the wives can chat and face each other while the husbands fish. It works. Sometimes I come out on a weekend and I see this happening. Or the men are smoking pipes and cigars and talking in a language I've never heard before. Even the placement of benches is important.

By the way, palm trees signify gathering places. In the

architecture too, there is a hint of "Spanish." You might not notice, but it becomes a part of the fabric. The sense of community is measured by the view from the road. We even had a color consultant down from L.A. There are big things and there are little things. These are things that create and perpetuate values and a sense of community.

Reese and I go for a walk. It's not a sunny day; the sky is a flat white, and it's drizzling sporadically. A few desultory ducks look hopeful by the edge of the lake. A boy and his friend, a little girl in a pink snowsuit, are snacking at the water's edge, and from time to time they throw out a spare crumb to the ducks. On the convivial benches under a tree at lakeside, the children's mothers are hobnobbing in an Asian language. A plaque has been placed in front of the tree: "For Lisa Frost," it reads, "12-21-78 to 9-11-01, who died on Flight 175. This tree is dedicated to parents who have children that are with God in heaven." Reese looks at it with me. "We put that up three months after the attack," he says, shaking his head. "Such a waste of human life." Here in Lisa Frost's hometown, a plaque in her honor doesn't seem out of place. It seems like a fitting statement of loss rather than a political manifesto or a paranoid protest—like the tiny twin towers of California City.

Richard Reese seems at first like any city planner: committed to getting the job done well, efficiently, and economically. Like Waldie, he's a genial, happy guide in his hometown. But he's a Californian, and that usually means there's an extra something in a person's character that's not immediately evident. True to form, Reese had a secret weapon in his creative arsenal when he was helping to shape RSM; like many urban planners, he had a philosophy. But not just a design philosophy, such as "Form should follow function," or "No unnecessary decoration." Reese is high-concept, and his concept is something called the enneagram.

I have never heard of enneagrams, so when Reese springs this on me, I am unprepared. In his reedy voice, he says, "You know the enneagram, don't you? I told my planning team about it, and I wanted them to go to some of the meetings, so they would understand, but they laughed and said, 'No, Richard, you go, and then you can explain it to us.' It was fine with them as long as they didn't have to know about it."

I can understand his planning team's reluctance. It's not easy to wrap your mind around an enneagram or even to describe one: the concept is convoluted and Far Eastern-seeming. The enneagram itself seems to be a circle with a nearly complete star of nine points within it, intended to describe in totality the types of human personality. Each triplet of points, or "triad," represents a kind of personality: instinctive, feeling, and thinking. Within the intuitive category are three types of personality: leader, peacemaker, reformer. Within the feeling category: helper, motivator, individualist. Within the thinking group are the loyalist, the enthusiast, and the philosopher.

Reese did not make this up, at least. It was developed in the late 1960s to mid-1970s from a heated concoction of ancient Sufi fortune-telling symbols, Masonic runes, Jesuitical theories, Freudian psychiatric terminology, Jungian ideals—and later, New Age philosophy developed by, among others, a former Jesuit seminarian named Don Riso. When I realized that the enneagram was based on Sufi fortune-telling, I recognized it immediately: it was like the little folded squares—numbered, elaborated, and colored, with thumb and fore-finger stuck inside—that schoolgirls fold and unfold on the play-ground to predict their classmates' love lives. It was equally baroque, equally useless.

Various figures who have delved into and helped refine the enneagram (from the Greek words for "nine lines") have, not surprisingly, been associated over the years with Esalen. The diagram's piebald cast of proponents, who of course believe in it as if it were a holy text, taught it there, so when Reese began jabbering in his kindly way about mystic stars and points, and human personality types, I felt I was *in a place* where I could begin to understand and translate—from the Esalenese. After all, Reese and I were Esalen blood siblings, we had *shared,* and together we had learned the way of story. I felt I understood him well enough: he was another California believer.

And why shouldn't he believe? "Of course the enneagram works in terms of planning," Reese says. "It explains and reflects human character, and what is a city but a broad reflection of that?" What he had helped to make in Rancho Santa Margarita was impressive, in its way. It was pleasing to the eye; in the words of another age, RSM was a fit place for human habitation, with lakes and groves and parkland, and "community gathering places," which in another era would have been called by their proper name: village greens. In Reese's mind, it was different from any other new development; it was built to lofty specs, created with the kinds of human and divine designs on which cathedrals, pyramids, and holy cities had been built in earlier ages, even if to the untrained eye, which mine was, it was almost exactly like Cucamonga or Crestline or Falcon Pointe or any of the other developments I'd visited.

These planned places—Lakewood too, though on a lower budget and quicker construction schedule; California City too, though a failure and a sham—all seemed to be responses to Los Angeles, a place where no one bothered to think hard beforehand, where everything planned was planned after the fact, to meet pressing needs of uncontrolled population growth. But somehow the deliberately conceived places like Lakewood and Rancho Santa Margarita are false and too clean, too neat—somehow not organically human—whereas L.A., as ugly as it is, as boxy and asphalted and pollution-spewing and inauthentic, seems real and alive. It doesn't *look* like London or New York, but like them, it has no single underlying philosophy or plan, nor was it built just so one man or one company or group of corporate developers could make a killing. Still, you couldn't say that L.A. has grown up organically, exactly, or that it has accrued little by little, over a great span of time, like London.

"The history of Los Angeles," Carey McWilliams wrote, "is a history of its booms. . . . One continuous boom punctuated at intervals by major explosions." I like the description of preboom Los Angeles that McWilliams cites: "a town of crooked, ungraded, unpaved streets; low, lean, rickety, adobe houses, with flat asphaltum roofs, and here and there an indolent native, hugging the inside of a blanket." That old L.A. is where I want to live, instead of here, now, although over-all, L.A. today retains an atavistic flat, adobe-and-asphaltum kind of esthetic.

In L.A. it's plain that one developer after another built the city to lure new residents to the town, and that each based his construction on what he believed were the real-estate dreams and fantasies of the rest of the country. This explains the predominant palm trees, which are not native, and the naming of so many streets after glens and groves. It explains the highly irregular, though not always pleasing, residential architecture. Sometimes, surveying Los Angeles, driving, say, through Koreatown—which is modern, unadorned, fenced-in, a stream of new, patched-together construction going up on old emp-tied lots—I feel like the curmudgeonly, old-fashioned Prince of Wales (a self-styled arbiter of architectural ethics and a profoundly conserva-tive city critic); I find myself longing for a return to the old ways of cities. (Note: on his first remarital tour of America in 2005, Prince Charles came with his bride to San Francisco but avoided L.A.) In Koreatown, I miss ivy and alleyways, and anything urban that curves. Almost nothing in Koreatown curves except the dome of the 1929 Wilshire Boulevard Temple, one of the few remaining buildings put up before the 1970s, before the area was Koreatown.

I had to learn to be charmed by new and different things in Korea-town, or K-town, as its residents call it. For example, cars behind bars. These are the secure, password-protected, fluorescent-lit garages of the squat apartment buildings that line Koreatown's back streets—cars in a sprawling zoo, just before dawn, waiting in the blue light for rush hour's liberation. And the lit-up ceiling-to-floor windows of the Aroma Wilshire gym, on the fourth floor, more than halfway up a new Koreatown business building, treadmill after treadmill looking out at Wilshire, just before sunrise, and no one on them. The man from Star-bucks down below is putting out tables and umbrellas in the darkness of early morning as traffic begins to pick up on the boulevard. Later in the day, you can appreciate the regularity of the fences the Korean population puts up around their square gardens (they would be comfortable in Lakewood): the ironwork filigree twists and turns delicately, and the afternoon shadows it casts across the squares of lawn are complicated and lovely. All the signs are in Korean, a boxy script. Along a residential street that extends from Wilshire to the freeway, an astonishing number of day-care centers are advertised on billboards written in Korean, in cheerful primary colors; who knows what they say? A profusion of big, bright plastic toys is scattered across the gardens where the afternoon shadows of those endless fences fall. A new generation of immigrants' children is growing up here. And as dusk comes, the sharp smell of charcoal, salt-fish, and hot pepper from the barbecue shops and restaurants begins to permeate sections of Sixth Street.

Koreatown: this is where I discovered that supermarkets have backs. Before I got to Los Angeles, I'd never seen the back of a supermarket, anywhere. Real urbanites never have that privilege. But the Ralph's in K-town has an entire stretch of back wall, a beautiful and blank high white wall on mysterious, empty Seventh Street. It's blank like a wall surrounding a movie studio lot, or a prison. Ralph's has placed white lights at intervals along this wall, and low bushes too. The wall stretches far into the distance. I expect a watchtower at the end, with a gunner looking out.

Also there are rats in the ficus trees of Koreatown. One dropped down into the radiator of my parked car at dawn one morning and didn't make its presence known until I pulled into my driveway a couple of miles away. Strays like my former dog Freddie seem somehow attracted to me here in L.A. Anyway, there is no other way, really, for an adventurous Koreatown rat to make its way to my neighborhood, since there is no subway tunnel from Koreatown to my area, much less past us to the richer zip codes on the west side of L.A. (Being from New York, I know that the tunnels of subways are the beloved forgathering place of a city's rat population, and the circulatory system through which they fan out in an urban setting.) Subways have been contemplated in Los Angeles, and even funded, but rarely built. The subway from downtown to the west side was mapped out; it was to be excavated more or less directly through the tar pit areas near Fairfax Avenue, where the Grove shopping mall is now located, before changing direction toward North Hollywood. But geothermal forces got in its way; a big methane explosion caused by an undetected concentration of gases rising to the surface demolished a Fairfax discount women's clothing store in early 1985 and gave already reluctant west side officials an easy excuse to halt the politically volatile project.

Peering around from the hood of my car at the manicured lawns on my street, and at the sprinklers showering down, my Koreatown rat could not find the courage to take the plunge down to the ground; perhaps it did not want to make the transition from Koreatown to this place. Maybe with its refined rat sensibilities, it could smell the methane that, in this chilly season, we could not. It hesitated at the precipice of the hood and then began running back and forth distractedly in front of my windshield. I could see its little ears listening intently, and its long bald tail whisking to and fro.

At this moment, I recalled Reynaldo, who looked like an Aztec king but was a rat man in the profession of protecting Los Angeles homes and businesses from rat infestation. A while ago, Reynaldo had screened over openings in our exterior walls and closed up whatever holes there were that seemed to be providing access to the basement and attic for street animals like cats, raccoons, rats, squirrels, and opossums. The house was ostensibly secure now, and I had an agreement with Reynaldo: for a year, he would come back whenever I needed him. Still, even though I knew I could call on Reynaldo, the thought of carpooling a rat from Koreatown direct to my house seemed foolish—the phrase "asking for it" popped into my mind—so I pulled back out of my driveway and parked my car a few blocks away, hoping my rodent stowaway, my illegal alien, would disembark there. It was still dark as I walked stealthily back to my house. I never saw my rat again, but surely by now he is living in the basement of one of my neighbors' homes.

And he will be pleased to know that if he lives a very, very long rat life (about five times as long as the average rat), one day he may be able to take mass transit back to Koreatown. L.A. has changed a great deal since the 1985 methane explosion. The demographics of the commuters' back-and-forth have altered; for one thing, L.A. County had about 2 million fewer residents back when freeways seemed a logical transit solution. Ethnic fears have also abated. Koreans are staunch members of the middle and upper classes, and Latinos and their employers on the west side are more used to each other now too—economically a little less alienated, less angry, less fearful.

Most important to the changing attitudes, though, is the pressure of traffic congestion. Rush-hour traffic is so terrible all over town that it's become politically thinkable to recommence the subway project, overriding long-held class concerns and geographic distastes. A congressman has interceded. A study of the methane threat has just been completed. As D. J. Waldie wrote in late 2005, "If it's ever built, a subway . . . will carry more than passengers; it will bear our imagination into a city as yet unrealized."

It may also carry one very old and disoriented rat.

Rick Caruso is self-confident, sure of himself. He carries himself with quiet pride, and his thick dark suit, made of heavy, important material, speaks of wealth, power, prominence, command. He has big cufflinks and, like Schwarzenegger, who is a good friend of his, knuckle-sized rings. He's earned a right to his mien of a grandee; he's one of Southern California's biggest and most influential commercial developers, and the Grove—the high-end, open-air shopping mall that sits over an abandoned oil field and tar pits—is his creation. He has built a functional "city" inside a dysfunctional one.

Of course, Los Angeles is a city of malls, in part because its booms have been residential booms, and its residential areas have grown up separately from its commercial zones. (All of this because L.A. is the first major city in the United States to grow up during and after the advent of the automobile; it's built around car capabilities. By 1970, according to the urban theorist and social critic Mike Davis, "more than one-third of the surface area of the Los Angeles region was dedicated to the car: freeways, streets, parking lots, and driveways. What generations of tourists and migrants had once admired as a real-life Garden of Eden was now buried under an estimated three billion tons of concrete, or 250 tons per inhabitant.")

The Grove is different from other malls, or at any rate, it looks different. It's retro, an attempt to go back to some idealized version of what "city" might mean. You can walk around it under the open sky; it feels like a pedestrian mall in a midsized European city, like Copenhagen or Florence or Lyon. Yet pedestrian malls in those places have been created by municipal councils declaring historic commercial areas of town off-limits to cars. The spot where the Grove was built never was a downtown until Caruso made it one. The Grove looks like a pedestrian mall in a European city, but what it really is is a Los Angeles shopping mall—minus the roof.

Caruso is pleased with himself. He radiates pride mixed with self-satisfaction; he's another brash character to whom doubt is foreign. He doesn't waste time letting you know he's a friend of Schwarzenegger's, but he doesn't brag. Such things have come to him, he seems to feel, as a matter of course. He is every inch a self-made man.

As the Grove was taking shape, Caruso moved his offices and staff from Santa Monica, overlooking the Pacific, to the new site.

"Everyone was horrified. The east side—it was like they'd never been east of Doheny before," he says, laughing. "But I felt this was the center of the business, and that we really had to be on site. And now . . . they *love* it at every level from intern to executive. It's like being on a movie lot. They can go down for lunch, shop, people-watch, whatever. It's very comfortable here."

And it *is* comfortable. Caruso's offices are located on a side street of the Grove near a chocolatier and a fancy soap and toiletries store. On the ground floor of Caruso Affiliated, a doorman sits behind a dark mahogany stand, as if in the lobby of an office building in Manhattan. You have to check in. The stairway up to the offices, if you don't take the elevator, is majestic, open and semicircular, like the *grand escalier* of a Renaissance-era hotel in Paris or Florence. There is a reason Caruso seems like a doge, sitting up here with a view of his city below. He's an Italophile and travels to Italy—to Florence—on a regular basis; much of the Grove is based on ideas about the interplay of commerce and humanity that he's learned from that city, although, as he points out, the mall was also "patterned after Charleston."

Like developments and malls and everything else in Southern California, the Grove is built on the land of what used to be a Mexican rancho (actually on parcels of land from two adjoining ranchos), because before the creation of the state, the Mexican government had divided most of Southern California into huge land grants for favored citizens and members of the elite. The Grove's ranchos were purchased by Arthur Fremont Gilmore and a partner in 1870, after Gilmore moved to Los Angeles from Illinois, seeking his fortune. Gilmore could not have imagined at the time of the purchase that, already, the fortune he was seeking had been found. He and his partner eventually dissolved their relationship and split the land, Gilmore taking some 260 acres, on which he built up a successful dairy farm. Often the farm would run low on water for the animals, and it was thus that Gilmore, near the turn of the twentieth century, found himself drilling a well on site, from which to water the herd. Instead of coming up with water, however, his pump pulled up something black and viscous: oil. It turned out that the rancho was sitting on top of a productive oil field, an extension of the tar pits. By 1905, the Gilmore Oil Company was well established (after 1921, it became the largest independent oil producer in the West), and the land on which the Grove now sits was dotted with pump jacks and oil towers. (Today, the stores at the Grove—like other establishments in the area—have methane-warning plaques and methane alarms.)

By the mid-1930s, a new generation of the Gilmore family was expanding the business. A farmers' market grew up on the property's periphery (farmers could rent space and put up stalls for fifty cents a day), and a racetrack for midget cars—the Gilmore Midget Racetrack at Gilmore Stadium—was established; a drive-in movie theater was built. Eventually, Gilmore Stadium became a venue for athletics, as well. Los Angeles's first professional football team, the Bulldogs, played there. Gilmore Field, nearby, accommodated a new minor league baseball team, the Hollywood Stars, owned at the time by Barbara Stanwyck, Bing Crosby, and Cecil B. DeMille.

Throughout all this development, change, and financial success, the Gilmore family never let go of their land, and today they still own the land on which the Grove sits, much of which used to be a parking lot for the farmers' market and the drive-in. Caruso has a ninety-year lease.

"The benefit of the arrangement for them," Caruso says, "is that we were going to build something that would help the farmers' market. For us, it was that we would be in an established and beloved Los Angeles commercial neighborhood."

Whenever I come to the Grove, I feel more at home than I usually do in Los Angeles. More at home because once you drive there and park your car, you can walk around it, go shopping, go to a restaurant afterward, then see a movie, without getting in your car—*as if* it were a real city. You can have drinks and then go sit in front of the fountain (if you don't mind hearing Sinatra while the fountain is flowing to a computer program that syncs its water's flow to the song's rhythms). You can see other people, strangers, and they are not behind their steering wheels but out and ambulatory. You might even run into people you know. It's sort of like real urban life. But then, it's sort of not: everything about the buildings is slightly false, and many of the visitors are tourists coming to see the Grove. They stand in front of the fountain while their friends snap their picture.

The place elicits the same dreamlike, disoriented response— Where am I? What is this place? Who are these people?—that walking through the sets at Warner Brothers or any other major studio does. At Warner Brothers, I walked through an Old West town square, a typical American neighborhood from the 1940s, and then a New York City block or two. Caruso is right that the Grove is like a movie lot, only more seamless: it's all one project. Norman Klein, the urban historian, calls it "a scripted space." Now that so many movies are filmed abroad, perhaps it would be a wise business decision on the part of the studios to take a page from Caruso, and turn their Los Angeles lots into malls.

The Grove is a multicultural place: the people who come here are from everywhere. Sitting near the fountain at Christmastime, I watched the crowd passing by the hundred-foot tree, a rival to the seventy-four-foot one at Rockefeller Center in New York—passing by, also, the two holiday teddy-bear topiary trees guarding the fountain, each with a red ribbon around his neck, one holding a saxophone, and the other, a drum.

The ethnicity of the crowd is visible: Latino, Asian, Russian, Iranian, foreigners of all stripes. Just for my own amusement, I begin counting African Americans, because in my first fifteen minutes, I haven't seen one. During the next twenty-five minutes at the Grove, fourteen African Americans pass by my sight lines, most of them in couples, going to the movie theater. Here they are: A fellow in a sport jacket with a briefcase moving at a fast clip across a little bridge that passes over a tiny pond; a middle-aged man, wearing an Eisenhower jacket and a baseball cap, walking down the main thoroughfare with his wife, who's carrying a shopping bag. The trolley passes by, its bell ringing. Then there's a guy with a shaved head and an earring striding by in the opposite direction; a young, long-haired woman with an older white man heading into the movie theater. Two young men wearing baseball caps; an old lady with long, straightened hair; an older woman in a tailored brown pantsuit; a young man with long cornrows; two more men in their twenties, not together; and finally, a curvaceous young fellow with clipped blond hair, wearing a pink shirt and hip-hugger jeans, and pushing a stroller occupied by a small African American girl. All this, as hundreds of people of non-African origins pass by.

Everyone likes to talk about how diverse L.A. is and how it is becoming a brown town, the different ethnicities melding into a pan-American breed, but African Americans have been left out of this supposed fabulous melting pot. "They are not our minority," one friend of mine said. It's a historical irony, since African Americans were present at the founding of Los Angeles. In 1792, according to various historians, nearly 40 percent of the Los Angeles population was partly of African origins, because the settlers who came north from New Spain were already racially intermixed. Continuing intermarriage meant that the *californios* encountered by white settlers to the West were not simply Hispanic and Indian but also, in many cases, part African, including the last Mexican governor of California, Pio Pico. As white settlers flowed into the area by the hundreds of thousands, the concentration of people of African origins dissipated. In spite of the city's early history, racism was entrenched among the newer white population. In the mid-1800s, whites tried to exclude blacks from the state; a California law against intermarriage was still in force as late as 1948, accompanied by all sorts of customary racial discrimination.

Today, the African American population of Los Angeles—most of them great-grandchildren of a more recent flow of black settlers to the area—is no longer really welcomed or integrated into the larger society, even though, of course, there are many exceptions to this generalization. For the most part—left out of the instant cities and the dream developments—the African American community is off in its own territory, in Compton, in Leimert Park, in Hawthorne, Inglewood, Watts, and other pocket neighborhoods. In terms of the African American population, the great brown town still has an apartheid geography.

I was returning from a trip to Lakewood. Lakewood is not a mystical place, nor do freeways in Southern California generally offer themselves up as places of spiritual fulfillment. Most of the time, freeways rush in the sun past one huge car dealership or another, or past refineries and amusement parks, or past vineyards and wide fields of wheat and corn, or, even more commonly, past the high sound barriers of enormous rancho developments. ("This was once a barley field"—how often that phrase comes up when you're looking at Southern California's suburban sprawl.) Occasionally, as you zip through the geography, you'll have a slight feeling that you're in Old California, something about the configuration of the hills. On the Hollywood Freeway, for example, you can—if you're in a dreamy mood—sense the Cahuenga Pass of old, between the San Fernando Valley and Hollywood, as the freeway winds between hills on either side. As you look at the cypress-covered landscape, you can even imagine horses, those icons of the West, especially if it's foggy, if a marine layer happens to be obscuring the houses scattered at the foot of the canyons. But soon the exit sign for the Hollywood Bowl or for Cahuenga itself (now a street in Hollywood) appears, and the feeling is lost.

Returning from Lakewood, I'm on the 105. We're on a floodplain, Waldie once told me, as we traveled in the other direction on this road. The highways in Southern California are basically flood outlets. In a hundred-year flood, Waldie pointed out, this highway along which we were flowing so nicely with the traffic—while he who does not drive directed me in detail, from lane to lane—would be a rushing river within an hour, providing an outlet for the waters and thereby sparing the surrounding communities. For most people this would be hard to imagine, but for me, the idea of a hundred-year flood comes naturally. It sounds biblical, like so much of the weather here.

I'm imagining the crashing flash flood as I drive along, but it's rush hour and nothing on this road is traveling fast. A light commuter train travels above the freeway at one point—one of those few, sporadic attempts by Southern California planners to make the area livable and workable. It's almost sunset. Silhouettes of commuters—carrying briefcases and holding newspapers, magazines, cups of coffee—seem to hang in the air above me. They're waiting for their train on a platform up above the freeway in the late afternoon. Just above their heads, a filigree of black electrical wires for the trains hangs in the air, as if waiting for music to be written on it. The sky is a saturated pink, and a Santa Ana wind is rising out of the desert. Above the walls that protect the developments from the noise of our cars on the freeway, palms are waving their feathery heads like crazy birds in a Dr. Seuss reverie. All along the way beside us—from Lakewood up to L.A.— march the electrical towers, Erector-set giants all in a row, carrying power from one part of the grid to another. Here and there, a tall tower festively decorated with satellite dishes stands like a listening post at the end of the world; they've put cell phone transponders on fake palm trees too. And then the sun starts to sink down as we all turn northward.

I'm on the 110 by now. Why are license plates always speaking to me? Vanity plates are the worst. A red Ford pickup crosses in front of me; its license plate reads VITL NRG. But then another car—without even meaning to—posits the contrary: numbers with letters LZY in the middle, put there randomly by the state of California, but still bearing an inscrutable message. An *Eyewitness News* communications van keeps me company to my left for a few seconds and then passes me by, while a freeway-maintenance pickup truck pulls in front of me, orange highway safety cones and unimaginable ducts and pumps and mowers and rakes askew in its open trunk. And then I pass the Dosan Ahn Chang Ho Memorial Interchange—named for a Korean immigrant leader from the earliest days of the 1900s—and get off at the 10. Skid marks like exclamation points—dark ends of past crashes and scrapes—punctuate the guard wall that stops motorists from simply going over the edge. And then the city of Los Angeles is standing there, directly ahead of me, faint gray rectangles indicating skyscrapers in the light of dusk. The Friday evening sports blimp—for some reason logoless and decorated in psychedelic swirls—is already high in the sky over the stadium, the sinking sun below it. I exit the 10 at Crenshaw, and at the corner there's a man by himself, bringing life back down from freeway to human scale. He's selling red roses from a supermarket cart.

CHAPTER EIGHT

The Game of Celebrity

I N MY NEIGHBORHOOD, a couple of miles down Third Street from the Grove, Michelangelo's nineteen Davids are wearing Santa hats. So is the petite Venus de Milo who stands among them. A few years ago, the Davids also wore festive red jock straps, but that element of holiday haberdashery has been abandoned. It's December 2005. The house in front of which the Davids and Venus stand throughout the year (minus the Santa hats) is considered a local eyesore and an infringement on its neighbors' property values, but I've come to admire its outlandishness, its over-the-top tastelessness, its bad-boy nose-thumbing in my neighborhood of goody-goodies. Still, I'm glad the Davids are not my next-door neighbors.

In this season, fake snow blankets their yard; on the roof of the well-kept white-brick house are the white letters *FHP*, as tall as a man, with the exhortation "Feed His People" written on them in smaller type. In front of these three letters, an African American Santa—a plump mannequin—is balancing on the eaves, a golden saxophone at his lips. The numbers 2006, in glittering, lightbulb-encrusted white, stand on the white lawn, each digit five feet high. In a corner of the garden, visible from busy Third Street, two African American life-sized dummies of Santa and Mrs. Claus sit companionably on a love seat, wearing gilt-rimmed sunglasses.

It's one way to welcome the New Year. At night the scene is professionally lit, and every once in a while, as I drive by, I'll see a family of tourists standing in front of the white cast-iron fence, having a picture taken.

———————

Like the redwood forests and the Santa Monica shoreline (protected by shorefront property owners like David Geffen, the record and film producer, from untoward intrusion by the public), front lawns have become a political and philosophical battlefield here in California, where the small-scale topography by now reflects all the ills of development: the suburban sprawl, the decimated forests, the dry rivers, the tangle of freeways. What is natural has been all but covered up, except for protected places like the Desert Tortoise Natural Area and those spots where it's just not feasible to build: the steep, unstable, and noninfrastructured canyons where I hike, for example.

Even what is natural here is unnatural. A tour of Cook's Meadow on the Merced River in Yosemite Valley is available now for amateur photographers and tourists who want to stand where Ansel Adams once stood and see the exact view that he put in his famous pictures. They can even try to take pictures of what was in his pictures. On the Ansel Adams Gallery Tours (nine to eleven a.m., Tuesdays, Thursdays, and Saturdays), you can take the photograph Ansel Adams took; this is a profoundly mediated way of approaching both art and nature. In fact, it's a celebrity-sighting approach to nature, the equivalent of wanting to go meet the David of those Davids, shake his hand, or meet the model for the *Mona Lisa*, tell her a joke. ("Yeah, I met them," you could say after.) As if that were the value of the photograph or the painting.

There is enough falseness in nature itself here; you don't need a gallery and an artist to see that. The alien palm tree again comes to mind, long a symbol of California's sybaritic, generous warmth but not indigenous (like so many Californians—the governor being a prime example). Palms are beloved here, in spite of their alien origins, but the tamarisk, a Eurasian original that arrived in the New World in the 1800s and now grows in rich clumps and thickets in desert and dry areas, is loathed. Environmentalists put on gloves and goggles and saw down the trees, fanning out over riverbeds and into canyons, and then, quickly, they apply herbicide to the wound before the plant can

begin to heal itself. (In one report in *Sierra* magazine, excited environmentalists are depicted shouting "Kill Tammys!" as they rush about
with their saws.) Tamarisks are not only an eyesore that conceals and
crushes the variety of native plants, but they also contribute to an
increase in fires. According to *Sierra* magazine, American tamarisks
use up three times more water per year than all the households in
L.A. (In California, the crusade for botanical purity has uncomfortable
racial and ethnic overtones.)

An ongoing—and solemn—controversy in Los Angeles exists in
the matter of ground covers for your front or backyard. Mine and most
others look like the East Coast, with grass growing peaceably, and
sprinklers shooting up into the air every morning around sunrise, or
in the late afternoons, as if choreographed. But my neighbors a block
away have devoted themselves with painstaking attention to a backyard that is entirely native (that is to say, native to California, although
of course they had to bring the plants and seeds and trees by car and
truck to their sweep of suburban ground). Half the time their garden
looks—to me, the unenlightened—like one of those neighborhood
gardens in abandoned lots in Manhattan: scrubby, brown, overgrown,
unwatered. The question is whether it's right to grow grass lawns like
mine, alien water gobblers, or whether it's more morally and socially
correct and responsible to have a cactus, rock/sand, tumbleweed-style
garden that is more appropriate to a desert setting.

An American's yard is a place of dreams and ideas, and that's
what's going on in California's horticultural debate: it's a discussion
about American identity; about who we are versus who we'd like to
be. Perversely, the whole argument disregards the fact that millions of
acre-feet of water have been moved (many of them by the Project
Operations Center of the State Water Project up in Sacramento) precisely so that lawns *can* be watered, cars washed, and industry and
agriculture and workers supplied in a place where previously a very
limited amount of water was available. It ignores the fact that Southern California is no longer a desert. It ignores, or dismisses, what
passes for progress.

The Californian quest for botanical authenticity is the desire to

reject what we've become and to return to an earlier, wilder state, a state of greater innocence, really. Those who seek plant purity call into question the kind of development and infrastructure that has permitted the creation of places like the San Fernando Valley, as well as my neighborhood, and also my neighbors' native, cactus-strewn, desert brush garden. They seem to be trying to return to a state that no longer exists. Like so many American political conversations these days, their talk about gardening and planting is preoccupied with innocence, optimism, and moral correctness. It's a romantic movement. On the East Coast, people who talk about such things will muse about what kinds of annuals to put in and what shrubs might enhance the edges of their yard in the back. Here in Southern California, the chat soon becomes an agonizing debate about your lawn's political correctness.

There's a reason for all this enthusiasm and zealousness, and that is the purity and majesty of California's original landscape, which remains etched across America's mind. The sight of the Pacific coastline at Big Sur is enough, still, to make the human imagination reel with a sense of the infinite, the eternal, the perfect. (When asked what his religion was, an early California landscape painter thought for a moment and replied, "California.") By the time California became a part of the country, so much of nature in America was already under human command that the settlers could appreciate the new state's rare natural beauty as a lover might, instead of as the conquerors they were. "Nowhere on the continent," wrote Wallace Stegner, "did Americans find a more diverse nature, a land of more impressive forms and more powerful contrasts, than in California."

The manglings and cruelties subsequently inflicted on that almost mythical environment have left a terrible scar on the soul of the people of California. (There's good reason why the environmental movement is so strong here, why this is the place where billionaire movie stars insist on driving hybrid cars, the place where tree protectors protest development and lumbering by sitting in high branches for years at a time.) As Kevin Starr writes in the most recent of his California history series, *Coast of Dreams:* "Was there not a point . . . at which society had

the right to question the right of any individual . . . to cut down two-thousand-year-old redwood trees to make patio furniture and pay off junk bonds? . . . A tree, many Californians were recognizing, was not just a tree. . . . A tree was a living entity with a life of its own. As such, trees had standing before the law and in the minds and moral imagination of the people sharing the planet with them."

This captures the desperation of the committed environmentalists. And yet when I stood among the redwoods in Big Sur, I did feel that they were far greater beings than, say, me or Angel or the habitués of the Huffington salon, and deserving of some protection.

Anyway, the small questions—grass or brush, hedgerow or cactus, loam or sand—seem less important when you take into consideration the undeniable fact that each lawn, as well as each house, as well as each skyscraper, has been set down on ground that is extremely susceptible to earthquake and liquefaction. My gardener, a Japanese-born man of great age and deep resignation, has simply decided that if he can keep the grass alive, it's an achievement. He'd also like to get rid of the Chinese elm that dominates the backyard, and not because it's nonnative, but because it is deciduous. "Make a mess," he says. "Cut it down." And I have to admit, it's hard to care too much about an elm that some forward-looking homeowner planted in a backyard in L.A. sixty years ago; it's no redwood. Still, so far, I have been able to keep the tree standing in spite of the gardener's occasional emotional outbursts. I've also had to make what have seemed momentous decisions about grasses and sods: Saint Augustine or Bermuda, fescue or ryegrass or zoysia? But since the whole edifice on which we're growing our verdant squares is such a vulnerable and evanescent human construct, why worry about your sod? I'm a victim of Waldie's dystopian fatalism.

I signed a location agreement with *The Family Stone* a while ago. In a tough negotiating session that took place over a lengthy fifteen minutes in my living room, I managed to convince Steve, the scout for Fox, to raise our shooting fee from the high three figures into the low fours. I now felt among the *professionals*—no more insects parading around my kitchen, no more insect trainers, no more Scandinavians in the backyard. We would have real actors, real directors, instead. Our house was to be "a quaint little bed-and-breakfast in New England," Steve told me.

The Family Stone had big plans for us. "Do you mind if we put up that wallpaper in the bedroom?" Steve asked. "You know, the one with *scenes* on it? British thing . . . *toile*, that's it. Would you mind? If you mind, we could tear it down after we're through and repaint . . ." They were also going to put a camera dolly on the flat roof outside the stairway landing. "We'll probably have to reinforce your roof," Steve said. Starring in the movie were Diane Keaton and Sarah Jessica Parker. Sarah Jessica Parker was going to run excitedly down our stairs and into our living room, where the production crew planned to have a lively fire burning in the hearth. This was a way to indicate, Steve told me, that the character played by Sarah Jessica Parker was happy and in love. I agreed to everything. I signed on the dotted line, expecting Steve to sign on his and return a copy of the agreement to us.

There was just one little hitch, however. *The Family Stone* needed that fire. However, although we had a fireplace, we couldn't have a fire in it. When we bought the house, we thought we were getting a working fireplace, since the realtor's photograph of the living room showed a fire blazing cozily in the grate. Upon closer inspection, however, we discovered that our house was one of the houses with a chimney broken by earthquake. The future Governor Schwarzenegger and his mortar-and-brick companions had not canvassed my neighborhood during their riotous adventures of chimney knockdowns and chimney repairs. The realtor's photo, our realtor explained, had been computer-enhanced. The chimney was still unusable. The exterior had been fixed but the inside was a wreck.

Sadly, it seemed that that fire burning passionately in the grate was a make-or-break element for the director, and of course by now, I was desperate: I could taste *The Family Stone*. I wanted to be there when Sarah Jessica Parker ran excitedly down our front stairs, and then I wanted, also, to see Sarah Jessica Parker run excitedly down our front stairs in the movie. I felt that this would be far superior to coming across what I took to be my son's orthodontist's Beverly Hills office in *School of Rock.* I felt it would validate my Los Angeles experience. To have my house in a movie. That was coming to California, wasn't it? So I told Steve we would forgo all fees if Fox would repair the chimney to make it usable for the film. If they would only take my offer, everyone would end up happy.

Instead, Steve told me a month after I'd signed the agreement that Fox had found a house on the East Coast and another in Altadena, north of Pasadena, not far from L.A., a place filled with historic Victorian and craftsman houses. I felt a familiar pang of disappointment. So it was never to be. After all, why would someone from Perth Amboy, a laughably old, forgotten, and unimportant part of the world, have a house anywhere that would end up in a movie? I realized that my repeated rejection by these flighty, unpredictable location people had left me feeling provincial and out of it. I had to steel myself to a fact: I was not joining the stream of cool in my new location. I was not the things that were valued in Los Angeles. Not a tall, thin, blond California Girl, not a bubbly person, not a rich person, not a hip-hop artist, not down with anything or anyone. The models of behavior I'd found here I could not duplicate for myself. After all this time, I still felt that my best California model, the example I could most closely follow, was La Brea Woman.

Half the time, I even drove a beat-up minivan (the height of uncool in Los Angeles, where the kind of car you drive is a statement of *you*, understandably). I kept imagining myself in different vehicles. A Mini Cooper meant a mother trying to remain young. A Prius meant a politically correct person, probably a yuppie (although the rock singer Sheryl Crow once claimed that "nothing screams 'rock star' like a Prius"). A Cadillac Escalade signified drug or record business, very cool, but a polluter. A "vintage" car meant a person trying to make it in the movies. A Bentley meant someone who had already made it in the movies. A secondhand Toyota Corolla means a recent immigrant.

An auto-industry poll taker once called me and asked me this: "If your car were a magazine, which magazine would it be?" I loved this question, because it meant that pollsters were now thinking *synesthetically*, like Proust. *The New Yorker* was a choice the pollster offered; *Cosmopolitan* was a choice; *Playboy* was on the list, *Esquire* also . . . but the magazine my car most resembles was not among the choices I was given. The magazine my minivan most resembles is *Parade*, the magazine that comes stuffed into many of the country's Sunday newspapers. It's friendly, it's useful, it's popular, it's family-oriented, and it's not too smart and not too beautiful.

I've grown tired of my minivan, though, because—to a degree—I've bought into the L.A. esthetic. I have intelligent friends here who say things like "I can't drive a minivan, it's sexless." Or, "If I drove a minivan, my life would be over." Others who have minivans won't park them with valet parking, because it's too embarrassing. And it's true, the valets will look down on a minivan. Crystal Valet valets may even snicker, but then, they are the crème de la crème and probably have their own Aston Martins at home. At the Grove, the valets park the best cars out in public—the Hummers, the Ferraris, the BMWs—and the rest are whisked away down Caruso Place into a dark anonymity. So yes, I'm a little tired of my old minivan, a little embarrassed by it; it has a very old dent on the rear driver's bumper from a tree in a parking lot in Martha's Vineyard, and another more recent concavity from the wall of the parking structure at the Einstein exhibit. A piece of red plastic from the passenger taillight is mysteriously gone. In truth, the car looks as if it needs a wheelchair to get around. I'd love to unload it. Trade it in.

But unfortunately, it's a piece of evidence in a lawsuit, and I feel I must keep it until Angel has had his day in court.

I was still trying to see the governor. He'd been very busy, according to Rob Stutzman, his spokesman. And I knew it was true. First, Schwarzenegger lost the special election; this was what he might call a "major bust." Rick Caruso and Schwarzenegger's close adviser, former governor Pete Wilson (a driving force behind the proposed initiatives that were voted on in the special election), were with the governor on the night when every last one of those proposals went down to defeat. "You know," says Caruso, "the governor wasn't depressed at all. This guy's one hell of an optimist. He was cheering everyone else up. He'll survive it."

Others weren't so sure. The governor had yet to stop his long but steady slide in the polls. And his special election had hurt him at every step along the way. Californians first of all did not want another special election. Perhaps they were just growing tired of the idea that everything about them was special. Maybe it was the tens of millions of dollars the state was spending on the thing. It also wasn't a brilliant idea on the part of Schwarzenegger and Wilson to build their campaign for what they called a "fiscally responsible" California on initiatives that threatened firemen, teachers, policemen, and public service employees. It was as if Schwarzenegger were consciously setting himself up in opposition to every character in a Norman Rockwell painting, every stereotype of American wholesomeness. As he did in the recall campaign, Schwarzenegger tried to paint his opponents as "special interests."

One of Schwarzenegger's biggest problems in terms of public perception at this moment was that he had originally portrayed himself as above the usual petty corruption of politics: he was so wealthy, he said, that he couldn't be bought. And yet the rate of contributions to the permanent Schwarzenegger campaign fund was staggering. According to ArnoldWatch.org and other sources, political action groups established by the governor had raised between $72,000 and $80,000 a day, much of this going to pay for his travel (the private jet that takes him from L.A. to Sacramento and back each week), housing ($7,000 a month for his suite at the Hyatt in Sacramento: he still refused to commit to a Sacramento residence), entourage, extra security, and the Hollywood-caliber catering services and sound and light crews that advanced him at many events. Among the types of business that were funding Schwarzenegger's political agenda (in descending order of contributions) were real-estate developers (who had donated $6.6 million as of March 2005), financial institutions, entertainment, high tech, health care, agriculture, insurance, and car dealerships (who were the smallest donors at this level, with recorded gifts of $1.2 million), according to the Foundation for Taxpayer and Consumer Rights. This was not the kind of list that tended to reassure the voter that his own small interests were being protected. As Schwarzenegger said during the recall campaign, "Any of those kinds of real big, powerful special interests, if you take money from them, you owe them something." (Laurence Leamer writes in his biography that this was "a man who came to Sacramento saying he was different, that he wasn't beholden to the special interests. It turned out that *he* was the special interest.")

On top of this came the news of how extravagantly expensive the special election was going to be. In the end, the election cost the state as much as $80 million, just to set it up and run it. This does not include the money spent opposing and supporting the ballot initiatives by the special interests concerned—including labor unions and pharmaceutical companies—which may well have exceeded $300 million.

It was also possible that Schwarzenegger was sinking in public esteem because, while spending profligately on his special election, he'd continued to allow the state to borrow and was trying to fix all that now by cutting back on funding for education and other services. It was also possible that Latino immigrants, who had supported him overwhelmingly in the recall, did not like the fact that he had appointed only one Latino to his cabinet, even after Los Angeles had overwhelmingly elected a Latino mayor, Antonio Villaraigosa. Or that they resented his explicit support of the bizarre, gun-club-like vigilante militias that had set themselves up to patrol the border with Mexico. "I think they've done a terrific job," the governor told a radio interviewer; he later refused to characterize the remark as a "mistake" (although he did finally admit that it had been "a learning experience" to have said he was going to kick the nurses' butts).

By June 2005, two years into his administration, only 37 percent of registered voters approved of his job performance, according to a Field Poll. He was far less popular than Gray Davis just before the recall movement began.

Still Schwarzenegger soldiered on, sticking with his plan for the unpopular special election. He didn't often let up. It's his signature, this perseverance and focus. In spite of his political and ethical failings, he still seemed to be the perfect governor for California because he appeared so well equipped to wield the special tools of California governance (initiative, referendum, recall) to his benefit. Direct democracy seemed to suit him because he was so famous that it was believed—and he believed—that he could manipulate the electorate with his celebrity; he was so well liked as a film persona, such a comforting presence, such a masculine protector, such a well-spread meme. He *had* won the recall vote convincingly, which was an achievement.

Now as the summer of 2005 wore on, Schwarzenegger was trying to use California's initiative system to go directly to the voters again and circumvent political opposition in the legislature, trying to use his enormous celebrity clout to persuade voters directly, when he had failed to persuade their elected representatives in Sacramento.

Schwarzenegger was doing what he wanted to do. (He once said about a political controversy, "Of course I can do it. I'm Arnold," as if he too had bought into the myth of his invincibility.) Everything he did was evidence of a certain kind of will and even of having become spoiled, as actors will become in Hollywood. That was why, as governor, he still lived in L.A. three or four days a week and stayed in the suite at the Hyatt when in Sacramento, as if he were visiting. As if he were on location. That was why he could go to Hawaii for extended and expensive vacations while the sad-sack legislature was still sitting in Sacramento, doing its dull job.

Schwarzenegger thought he was beyond the legislators' grasp; he knew that taking him down would demand extraordinary force and circumstance, strength he believed the Democratic legislators lacked utterly, those girlie men. Although they were in the majority in the legislature, they were also all term-limited guys with circumscribed lives, anonymous bureaucrats to whom the great movie star might grant an occasional fat cigar or a photo op, but not high livers like him. They weren't *Arnold.* Schwarzenegger seemed to believe this—and others believed it, including many of the legislators themselves—not only because of his fame but because of his character. ("In the first six months," said one legislator from Southern California, "even Democrats were running around the capitol trying to get a picture with Schwarzenegger. Normally, we would not be *seen* with a Republican governor.")

In the event, it would take an act of almost classical hubris, a tragic flaw, to unman Schwarzenegger—if anything about Schwarzenegger could be considered tragic, when the public personality he has developed is essentially and profoundly comic. That prideful act was the decision to hold the special election.

"I said that if the legislature did not act on reforms this year," Schwarzenegger said, finger-waggingly, "the people of California *would.*" He was setting up, as was his wont, a rivalry, even an enmity, between the voter and elected officials, as if it hadn't been the voters who put the elected officials into office in the first place. Schwarzenegger's biggest political weapon had always been his popularity, and he was ready to put the public's esteem for him to the test by bypassing the legislature and going to the ballot box. What this meant was that he had failed in the political game of persuading the legislature to vote his way.

The recall had clearly solidified Schwarzenegger's conservative, pro-business backers' view that in the era of mass communication, the initiative, referendum, and recall were highly amenable to a well-funded corporate agenda, even in a state as Democratic as California, and especially with an extraordinarily popular governor at the helm.

In the summer and fall of 2005, however, Schwarzenegger's celebrity appeal didn't seem to be working. There was a difference, the governor was discovering, between using your celebrity to win a recall election that was one of the purest popularity contests ever—almost completely devoid of the consideration of real issues—and using it to win a vote that was wedded to the particular content of specific policy concerns and powerful interest groups.

In the 2005 special election, the initiative mechanism was used to try to push into law measures that were too complicated for the average voter to understand in the average amount of time an average voter was willing to put into such things. Schwarzenegger as much as acknowledged this fact: "People don't really, uh, you know, know that much about it," he told *California Connected,* a PBS television news show, in the days just before the special election in the fall of 2005, referring to his redistricting proposition.

The official voter information guide for the special election was seventy-seven pages long (on letter-size paper, with the proposed laws printed in tiny, ten-pica print). It was a cheaply made, two-color affair, printed on newsprint paper, with a close-up of the state seal on the cover. Inside were arguments for and against each of the propositions. On the other hand, the *Governor Arnold Schwarzenegger Ballot Proposition Guide,* which also came free to the door of every registered household, was printed in full color on glossy paper, with a photo of Schwarzenegger on the cover, along with the California governor's shield, and was eight pages long, with simplistic, one-sided analyses of each initiative. Depending on the proposition, a notation near the top of each page said, "Arnold Says Vote Yes" or "Arnold Says Vote No." A pocket voter's guide was included to bring along to the polling place. It was like a children's game.

This *Ballot Proposition Guide* was a cheat sheet for voters who weren't expected to think about the propositions or didn't want to (and who would?). It was easier to obey the commander, instead. A measure's many sections and complicated potential effects on society require the kind of study and evaluation that legislators are elected to do, even if it bores them witless, even if they don't always do it. But in California, and in an increasingly large number of states, you can try to railroad such reforms in by direct vote after pounding the public with upbeat television advertising that dumbs the measures down; you can publicly debarb the real measures and make them palatable, even if all your ads are filled with half-truths at best. As Ethan Rarick of the Berkeley Institute of Governmental Studies wrote in the *Los Angeles Times,* "Of all the sly tactics commanded by the backroom bosses in initiative campaigns—elicit fear, evoke compassion, pander to greed—one of the simplest is this: sow confusion." And both sides can play this game with such vigor that it makes the voter's head spin like a roulette wheel. In the 1950s, for example, a Republican secretary of state in California gave a Democratic Party proposition the number thirteen, and a Republican proposal the lucky number seven, according to Rarick—no doubt in an effort to express the party's deep, abiding respect for the voter's political discernment. Later on, however, thirteen was to prove a lucky proposition number.

You can, in effect, make someone vote against his own interests, and not for reasons of altruism or idealism, but because he doesn't even know it, either because there is no opponent there with pockets deep enough to fund a television countercampaign that is really pro-citizen, or because the interests involved are so powerful and so *interested* that they've made it impossible to distinguish truth from lies (the worst problem in American politics today). So the voter ends up relying on whomever he trusts (if he trusts anyone) in order to make up his mind, or he doesn't vote at all, because he trusts no one, and besides, it's all too confusing. "People don't really, uh, know that much about it . . ."

Such methods are not always successful, however; you have to choose your rivals wisely. Coming well into Schwarzenegger's foreshortened term (only a three-year stint, because he was serving out the remainder of Davis's abortive term), it seemed a surprising mistake of political judgment when Schwarzenegger put under fire groups who were able to respond briskly, strongly, and professionally. Teachers and public service employees had huge organizations and full coffers behind them; the public service employees' disability and death pensions, as well as their ability to extract and use discretionary union funds to support political causes, were threatened by the governor's plans.

Marley Klaus, then the executive producer of public television's *California Connected*, analyzed the reasons behind the special election and its shockingly partisan tone:

> The problem was that Schwarzenegger had two main camps inside his administration . . . the Pete Wilson folks and the more mainstream people. . . . He himself added to the mess by making a decision not to repay two billion dollars the state owed to

the teachers. That was a *huge* mistake. He's got a debate-team argument about why he doesn't owe the money, but on his own website he ballyhooed his promise to give it back to them.

In my opinion, that decision uncorked the union's fear and anger, and . . . resulted in the Democrats in the legislature hunkering down and ceasing to deal, leaving Arnold with no one to talk to but his Wilson folks, who could now say, "See? We told you so. Take 'em down. You can do it."

Out of this rancor grew Proposition 74, a proposal to extend the time required before teachers may be given tenure; Schwarzenegger wanted to extend the current two years' probation to five years. But this quick road to job security, according to the teachers' union, is one of the few positives in a career offering little support to its practitioners in California. The state's public education system was ranked forty-third in the country in 2005. Teacher tenure is not the real reason for the poor quality of California's schools. The real reason for the drop in California's quality of education is another proposition— Proposition 13, the property-tax rollback of 1978, which cut off billions of dollars in monies for the state's education system. In the 1970s, California was among the top five states in terms of quality of education. Since 1978, it has experienced a steady decline, and for the past two decades, California has consistently been down there among the bottom ten, along with traditionally poor, underfunded states such as Alabama, Mississippi, Louisiana, Nevada, and New Mexico.

Schwarzenegger's teacher tenure proposition was not a creative solution to this severe statewide problem; it looked more like a propaganda attempt to divert the blame for poor state education away from Proposition 13 and onto the state's teachers. Thus the "Wilson folks" sought to avoid further funding for education while also avoiding a reexamination of Prop 13 and the political maelstrom that that would engender. Unfortunately for the school system, in a state where there is a shortage of applicants for teaching positions, extending probation time was likely to act as a disincentive to prospective candidates.

Most of the propositions in Schwarzenegger's special election were so pro-Republican and so pro-business that they made you blink. Even in his short time in public service, this was not the Arnold we'd come to know. When Schwarzenegger came to Sacramento, he made many nominations that were progressive, intelligent, and inventive. His judicial appointments were respectable and even creative (and 40 percent were Democrats). On the environment, he'd been more protective than expected. He'd managed to work with the Democrat-controlled legislature to reform California's unwieldy and insanely generous workers' compensation laws. He had even brokered a deal with the teachers' union. He had been a centrist, with a progressive bent.

Klaus, of *California Connected*, went on,

> Arnold is not a blind, knee-jerk Republican. What he wanted to do *and did* when he came in was to be a much-needed correction to what had become a one-party state with all the problems that brings. The Democrats had gotten so cocky and truly out of control that they *were* spending money without regard to where it was coming from or the future consequences of their gifts to unions in the form of pensions. More than his talk, his initial *actions* showed real promise for a creative, bipartisan, problem-solving government. There were *many* Democrats who had been against him who really felt positive—even excited—about his first months.

But now, because of the new intransigence of the Democrats and the new retrenchment of the Wilson Republicans, Schwarzenegger was trying to put a new spin on California's political history. He was thinking about the same issues I'd been thinking about in the state's political history. He was attempting to reverse Governor Johnson's progressive agenda.

Anyway, that's how I chose to imagine the situation, because otherwise, it looked simply like an attack on just the people a rescuer should be saving—widows, orphans, teachers (little ladies with buns and spectacles), nurses (pert candy stripers in white shoes)—and the people a rescuer should be working alongside, namely firefighters and the police (although it's hard to work up a lot of sentiment on behalf of the police force if you live in Los Angeles).

There *was* one small bit of satisfaction in the special election campaign. The governor was forced to rethink his position on public service employees' pensions when it was found that that measure unfairly affected widows of public service employees. This is what Schwarzenegger said at the time to a group of public safety officers: "Mawning. I'm pleased to be choined here diday by owa great leadiss from local govamint and public safety. To me dare is nothing maw impawdint than public safety. Being a son of a balice officer, I falya the gontributions made by Caleefawnyah's balice, firefighters, and bublic safety officials."

Arnold was backing down. It was an impawdint moment in the life of the Schwarzenegger meme, because it conflicted with the universally understood meaning of "Arnold Schwarzenegger." And that was good.

After all of his initiatives were defeated on November 8, Schwarzenegger clearly did some rethinking. He must have looked at the results, scratched his head, and said, "Gee, this state is more liberal than I thought." Three weeks later, he appointed Susan Kennedy, a longtime Democratic activist and party operative, to be his new chief of staff. Kennedy, a forty-five-year-old lesbian who has taken marital-style vows with her partner, had been deputy chief of staff to Gray Davis, as well as running his gubernatorial campaign and the Clinton/Gore presidential campaign in California. She was also a former adviser to the liberal Democratic senator Dianne Feinstein, and a former director of the California Abortion Rights Action League.

"This makes Schwarzenegger a man without a country," Dave Gilliard, a Republican strategist who advised Schwarzenegger during the recall election, told the Associated Press. The right wing of the state's Republican Party went crazy. There is now a website called StopSusanKennedy.com that is illuminating for the profound sense of betrayal it reveals.

Many liberals hoped that the Kennedy appointment meant that Schwarzenegger was in a new frame of mind, and maybe he was.

Unlike the governor, Kennedy had a long political record to stand on, one that could not easily be shrugged off, although she did claim—as her new job was being announced—that she had supported *all* of the governor's losing initiatives in the special election.

One thing Schwarzenegger doesn't relish is wallowing in defeat. Conservatives were worried that in the wake of their governor's stunning losses in the special election, this protean character, who had reinvented himself so many times professionally, might try to reinvent himself politically. In any case, it had never been quite clear where he stood on the political spectrum: the most one could say was that he tended to be a fiscal conservative and a social liberal, but even these broad brushstrokes were inaccurate in many specific cases. This political impenetrability was one of the things that kept him interesting. However, it was not necessarily a deliberate stance. As Lloyd Levine, a Democratic assemblyman from the San Fernando Valley, says, "Arnold has a chip in the back of his head, and it's always telling him to be popular. That's his main drive." Levine laughs. "Not too uncommon in a politician."

"Sometimes," another legislator told me, "you go in for a meeting with Arnold, and you're sitting in the tent and you've come with your staff people and you present your case. He has a couple of his people there, and after you're done, he'll turn to them and say, 'That sounds like a good idea, doesn't it? What's wrong with that?' As if he has no idea about the thing on his own and needs his people to tell him what to really think. And because his staff was in conflict, it was a case of whomever he spoke to last; he had no political expertise, and everyone with him was trying to mold him to their values. When things are hard, he focuses on what he *can* do rather than on what he *should* do."

For better or for worse, Schwarzenegger made a splash by appointing a very liberal Democrat as his chief of staff: he confounded his liberal critics and astounded his conservative backers. But during his autumn of pain in 2005, a year before he was to face reelection as governor, he had another hard decision to make: would he grant clemency to the convicted four-time murderer Stanley "Tookie" Williams, founder of the Crips, a famously brutal L.A. gang? Just after Schwarzenegger's defeat in the special elections, many liberals and those who oppose capital punishment thought that the governor would try to recoup by pardoning Williams. But I couldn't see it. That analysis didn't comport with Schwarzenegger's character.

One: he would never give in to what he must have seen as wimpy, feminine sentimentality—as if the life of a cold-blooded murderer were somehow the same as the life of an innocent child, simply because it was a life. "Pussy stuff," he might call such arguments. Two: he had always supported the death penalty. Now he had a convicted murderer on his hands, all of whose appeals had failed, some with very liberal courts. In order to spare Tookie Williams, Schwarzenegger would have had to have had a change of heart on capital punishment, and that was unlikely. I didn't see him coming before the people of California, hat in hand, to discuss his newfound beliefs, as if he were Jimmy Carter or Bill Clinton. So no matter how weak he was feeling politically after losing to the liberal-minded voters of California, I didn't believe that he would let that weakness dictate something like this: a stand-firm moment, a be-a-man decision. And twelve hours after Schwarzenegger refused his appeal, Williams was executed, at midnight on December 13.

But that was not the end of the Tookie Williams story. All around the world, many people and political parties were disgusted by the execution; not only did it reconfirm America's contemporary reputation as a bully state, but it went against the grain of the European nations that have rejected capital punishment, including Schwarzenegger's homeland, Austria. In Austria, there was an uproar. The native son had committed a sin. The elders of the city of Graz, who had so cheerfully awarded Schwarzenegger the city's ring six years earlier, were now pulling on their respectable beards and considering the Williams execution. Not only did Schwarzenegger have that ring in his possession in Brentwood; in 1997, in a moment of delirious satisfaction with its favorite son, the town of Graz had put his name up on its athletic stadium, which had been known ever since as Arnold Schwarzenegger Stadion Graz-Liebenau. Ever since, when Schwarzenegger did something considered controversial, someone somewhere in Austria would threaten to have his name taken off the stadium. During the Tookie Williams case, the threats arose again, only the hubbub was louder, both because the case had received more international attention and because it was the first time Schwarzenegger had had a clemency issue before him.

Schwarzenegger was sick of the whole thing, sick of the Tookie Williams case, which was *over*, and especially irritated with the elders of Graz, whom he felt he had always supported in spirit and economically as well—with the use of his name and person. In a characteristically pointed move—but revealing a part of his character that had been pretty much hidden during the course of his governorship—Schwarzenegger composed a bitter but controlled letter in German to the mayor of Graz, Siegfried Nagl. He pointed out that he had heard that the city council was contemplating removing his name from the stadium because of his rejection of Williams's clemency bid:

> In all likelihood, during my term as governor I will have to make similar and equally difficult decisions. In order to spare the responsible politicians of Graz further concern, I withdraw from them as of this day the right to use my name in association with the Liebenauer Stadium. You will receive related correspondence from my legal counsel shortly. I expect the lettering to be removed by the end of 2005, and in the future, the use of my name to advertise or promote the city of Graz in any way is no longer allowed.
>
> I have also learned that a proposal has been proffered to rescind from me the city's ring of honor. It was a beautiful day in 1999 when I received the ring at City Hall and I assumed at the time that it would be a token of sincere friendship between my hometown and me. Since, however, the official Graz appears to no longer accept me as one of their own, this ring has lost its meaning and value to me. It is already in the mail.

Schwarzenegger was breaking up with his hometown, and you could hear the hurt feelings right through the formal language of the letter, published in the *L.A. Times*. Leaving things behind was not easy to do, I knew, as a freshly minted Californian. You're somewhere else, perhaps. Your back may even be turned, or you're not thinking about home. But it still can strike at your heart. It's not easy to give up those reminders of who you were, even if what you've become is an internationally famous bodybuilder, a shockingly rich actor, and a powerful politician. You want the ones at home to continue caring. Once upon a time, Schwarzenegger had been a young villager, an outsider making his name in Graz, having fun in Graz, looking up at the high walls of that stadium in the night, never dreaming, etc. (or, knowing him, maybe dreaming, etc.).

The ring "is already in the mail." Tough, very tough. But was he the kind of fellow with whom there is no recourse? Or did he want the elders of Graz to come crawling on their knees before him and beg him to relent? Tookie Williams could argue—if he were still alive—that relenting was not habitual behavior with Schwarzenegger.

Meanwhile, Rob Stutzman, my useless conduit to the governor, was moved out of his job as press coordinator. Had Susan Kennedy gotten rid of him? That was the word. I wondered now if I would ever get to be in the presence of the Schwarzenegger meme. I wanted to be near him, to talk to him, and yet I didn't want to. When Stutzman was moved out, I didn't feel bad. I noticed that I wasn't freaked or worried. I was relieved. No one I knew who'd interviewed the governor made me feel it would be fun, or pleasant, or normal in any way. Not like talking to Beatty, who at least had accessible emotions. Still, after having watched Schwarzenegger close up for so long during the recall election, I would have liked to see him now, see the change, if there were a change. I was still hoping: someday.

After Hurricane Katrina hit New Orleans in the last days of August 2005, the citizens of Los Angeles were shaken from their complacency. There hadn't been a big earthquake here since Northridge in

1994, and we're supposed to have one every decade or so. We're also always waiting for what is known—irritatingly—as the Big One. The damage done to New Orleans shocked people everywhere, but here, in this disaster-prone place, it seemed to take on special significance. Once again, Angelenos began filling their gas tanks religiously in case of evacuation. (The abandoned cars on the highways leaving New Orleans, and the empty gas stations, were a reminder of how bad things could get.) Once again, everyone was buying water and updating emergency supplies, checking flashlights. My son's school—located in classrooms rented from a church—sent out a new sheet vouching for the school's architectural soundness, even though all its rooms lie within easy reach of a tumbling steeple. "The church buildings," the memo read, "have been called 'the safest buildings in Hollywood'; they are built on bedrock and forecast to withstand the mightiest of earthquakes." This was the state of mind in L.A. a month *before* the catastrophic Pakistani earthquake.

Malibu was also thinking about catastrophe, but Malibu is a beach community, so its thinking is not always like the rest of the world's. Indeed, to call it "thinking" might be a stretch. Almost a year after the tsunami that destroyed a large swath of Southeast Asia, Malibu City Hall began distributing a brochure offering advice to its residents concerning earthquakes and tsunamis.

"Never go to the beach to watch for, or to surf, a tsunami wave!" the brochure advised. I was thinking about the tsunami video footage taken from the beach hotels in Phuket, where the floodwater pours in stunningly, and within a minute, the palm trees are covered with water up to their necks and debris is floating up near the ceiling of a restaurant that was dry only a few seconds before. Tsunamis, the Malibu brochure continues, "are not like regular waves, they are impossible to surf. They are much faster, higher, and can come onshore filled with debris."

When questioned about the necessity for such a warning, the emergency preparedness director for Malibu, Brad Davis, told the *Los Angeles Times* that "you can't overestimate the intelligence of people out there. Some people still might see it as a gigantic wave and think, 'This is going to be the ride of my life.'" Another reason not to surf a tsunami, as far as I could tell from watching the wave come ashore in Phuket, is that there's nothing to surf: this is not a wave that curls. But in the land of the Beach Boys, such details might escape you.

In California I'm constantly provided with spiritual awakenings, in all sorts of places: in yoga class, for example, where the teacher reads from the thirteenth-century poet Rumi and says things like "open yourself outward," or along the freeway, when a flock of birds rises suddenly, even if I happen to know they are either crows or pigeons. But the last place from which I expect enlightenment is the automated ticket issuer at the entrance to a parking structure, yet this is what it's come to in Car Land. One afternoon, I'm bringing my son to the orthodontist's office (the office I thought I saw in *School of Rock*). I turn the car off Roxbury in Beverly Hills into the AMPCO System Parking structure, and there is my inspirational quote of the day, in a special plastic cover hanging from the automated ticket giver: "When we have done our best, we should wait the result in peace.—J. Lubbock." I looked at this quote as the machine gave me my ticket. It did not seem a particularly profound piece of advice. I thought to myself that perhaps this J. Lubbock was a member of Huffington's salon, or perhaps a contributor to her weblog. Did he call himself "Jay" in Beverly Hills circles? Was he much quoted at the ends of yoga classes, before *namaste?*

I looked up J. Lubbock when I got home. Hardly a Huffingtonian, Sir John Lubbock, born in 1834, was a banker as well as the first baron of Avebury. He may never even have heard of yoga, although judging by his wide reading and learned output, he may well have. He was the author of *The Origin of Civilisation and the Primitive Condition of Man* (1870) and of *Pre-historic Times, as Illustrated by Ancient Remains and the Manners and Customs of Modern Savages*, perhaps the most important archeological book of the 1800s. He is said to have coined the words "paleolithic" and "neolithic." But the real reason he's on the ticket machine at AMPCO System Parking is that someone has put two quotes from him onto different much-visited Internet quotation sites. One is the quote I saw that day. The other turned up at AMPCO a month or so later, on another visit. (This parking structure is a hub for the medical profession in Beverly Hills—which means that even if Sir John is not one of Huffington's guests, he's probably been read by many of her invitees.) "Rest is not idleness," goes the other Internet-popularized quote from the baron of Avebury, "and to lie sometimes on the grass under trees on a summer's day listening to the murmur of water, or watching the clouds float across the sky, is by no means a waste of time."

These are the kinds of quotes that appeal to people out here. Although Sir John was a man of varied interests who shared the great Victorian curiosity of his age, the quotes he is memorialized for at AMPCO are the ones that advocate resting and waiting. People from back east are always being advised here to slow down, take it easy, shrug it off, lie back, relax, lighten up, look inside yourself, calm the inner you, go with the flow, stop *thinking*. The other day at rush hour, we were getting onto the 5 from the 110. My husband looked at the traffic. In the left lane—the one designated for exiting to the 5—the traffic was almost at a standstill. In the lane next to it, the traffic moved a bit, but not much: it was a secondarily designated 5-exit lane. In the lane next to that one, the traffic was moving nicely.

We took the nicely moving lane, even though we were planning to exit onto the 5 very soon, and my husband explained: In the left-most exit lane were the Californians, waiting obediently in a motionless line to exit as they'd been taught. In the next lane over were people who'd lived in California a long time but were not originally from here. In the third lane, cutting across the other two at the last minute to exit onto the 5 ahead of all those who'd waited, were the people from back east, the new arrivals.

I thought, He's probably right. We easterners were not the type to "lie watching the clouds float across the sky." We rushed to the head of the exit lane, we were *in* that lane, we were *across* it, we were already on the 5 and on our way to our destination by the time that first little cloud got a quarter of the way across the great big sky. This was because the people from back east, even if they were not from cities, were urban beings in some way that was more truly urbanized than Californians. Even if they'd grown up in L.A.—which in terms of population is a denser metropolis than New York City—Southern Californians, at least, retained something of the Iowa countryside in their spirit, something of the middle of America: something slow, something that might chew on a piece of straw or skip a stone. We backeasters didn't have that. After three years in California, I was still trying to wake up to that kind of experience here. Still trying to stifle inner laughter during the "Oms."

My thirteen-year-old son had a soccer game in Santa Monica, and I went to meet him and my husband at the Ivy restaurant near the beach. They were a few minutes late, and I waited near the door. Ever since yoga with Nicole, I have been on the alert for new celebrity sightings, and it struck me that this would be the perfect time and the perfect venue: a late weekend lunch at the Ivy in Santa Monica on a cold, clear, blustery winter day. But I saw no one I recognized. Mostly the crowd consisted of young and not-so-young well-dressed parents with small babies. There was a tall, blond Asian girl. There were two Mediterranean-style women having lunch together. Some tourists. Then my husband and son arrived and we were seated.

As I looked at the menu, my son elbowed me. In very low tones, he said, "See that woman in the corner?"

I looked. It was a redhead who seemed to be deeply Botoxed.

"She's famous," my son hissed.

"She *is?*" I said. I certainly had never seen her before. But she looked as if she could be in front of a camera, and she had that celebrity self-consciousness that seems to say, Everyone is secretly looking at me. Which I was.

"Yes," my son said. "She definitely is."

"Well, who is she?" I asked.

"I don't know," he said, "but I know she's famous. I've seen her before."

I took his word for it and gazed at her occasionally as she did things to make people gaze at her. Her actions were stylized, and she was physically impressive, tall, bony, white-skinned, very redheaded. She was with two girlfriends, both blond, tall, bony, white-skinned.

That night I was sitting on the sofa in my living room. My husband had given me an iPod video for the holidays. I am not the kind of person who normally has such an advanced piece of technology, but it replaced a music-playing one I had had for five years that had been broken for a long time. It was a transplendent machine, I thought. I was using it to discover television, since we do not have TiVo and I haven't managed to figure out when things are on or how to fit my schedule to the broadcast schedule, or which shows are good. But by now, I'd watched two episodes of *The Office* and downloaded one of *Desperate Housewives* and one of *Monk*.

My son was playing the piano in the same room when he heard me shout. For there on my tiny, tiny screen, walking across a living room that could almost have been ours (if ours had been bigger), was the single scariest redhead I'd ever seen, and it was my son's redhead. I pointed madly at the tiny screen and paused it. My son came over to look, and he nodded. He was very proud, but we still did not know her name.

After I finished watching the show, I went to Google and searched "desperate housewives redhead." Here are the first six sites that came up: "slut wives getting fucked! housewife whores and nude house wives"; "housewives in nylons! sexy redhead wife and adult wives uk"; "wife swapping! Great wife swapping and housewives with fantastic . . ."; "amateur slut wives! Amateur housewives and hot housewives"; "French sexy wives! Stories slut wives and british housewives"; "Nude wife! Outrageous fuck my wife and housewife with incredible . . ." It went on like that.

So I reentered my search as "desperate housewives redhead -slut -fuck -sexy."

That worked, and now we have a name for our latest celebrity: Marcia Cross.

Back when I visited California City, I suspected that the desert tortoise, that much put-upon creature—so elderly, so stalwart, so slow and indefatigable—had certain emotions. The one I saw moving like tar from shadow to shadow back in the Desert Tortoise Natural Area had feelings, I knew it. It wasn't as if I had to ask myself, Does he feel things? I knew he wanted things; he felt desire, for shade, for water. He felt fear, of cars, of ravens, of me. But I did not pause by the side of that thirsty road to argue with myself about whether he felt these things by instinct or otherwise. Now a few biologists are debating this concept, with the desert tortoise, possibly *my* desert tortoise, at the center of an important biological controversy. Do animals have emotions? Or is it all instinct?

Ask your dog.

At the heart of the whole discussion here in California is Desert Tortoise Number 29. I believe this must be my tortoise, the one I saw when I stopped on the side of the highway on my way to California City. U.S. Geological Survey biologist Kristin Berry believes that Number 29 Tortoise is a true individual—just as, say, Larry David is a true individual. "[All desert tortoises] are not the same inside their shells," she told a reporter for the *L.A. Times*. "They are individuals interacting in complex communities. . . . There may be behavior occurring in ways we haven't yet learned to observe, or interpret. How does a tortoise exhibit joy, or play, or express frustration?"

These are good questions. Certainly what little I saw of the fellow I'd like to believe was Number 29 did not lead me to expect expressions of joy from him. Joy seemed out of his range. And perhaps I am right, at least about Number 29. What Berry, the biologist, says about him is that he is a "cad," and a "fearless kingpin." That would explain why he dared to show himself in broad daylight, with me watching.

The tortoises, who have had quite enough problems in recent years, including the slow expansion of California City and other nearby towns in the Mojave, the advent of off-road racing, as well as the appeal of their remote native habitat to methamphetamine manufacturers, are now about to encounter a new enemy: the U.S. Army. It is entirely possible that Number 29 and his extended family may end

up as casualties of the war in Iraq. Fort Irwin, a Mojave site designated for army training in current engagements, is also a natural habitat for the desert tortoise. In order to avoid destroying tortoises as it
expands its mock Iraq training grounds and increases the firepower of
its weaponry, the military plans to relocate about fifteen hundred of
the animals to safer grounds, beginning in 2006. If the desert tortoise
were not protected by special state and federal laws, it's doubtful that
the military would show such tenderness. Their concerns are man-
dated, but still, Number 29 must move.

I have to admit here that it is unlikely that Berry's Number 29
could really be my tortoise, although the animals do range widely. The
tortoises of Fort Irwin live about fifty miles from the Desert Tortoise
Natural Area, much to their detriment. Still, I cherish a hope that the
tortoise I encountered was Number 29. He was an intrepid soul, after
all. However, no matter how wily, how brave, how caddish Number 29
is, his gnarled, hundred-year-old self may not be prepared for what's
coming, which is "a new generation of weapons and tactics," as the
L.A. Times put it.

A friend of mine who has seen the war games up at Fort Irwin says
even a wise old tortoise might be fooled by the simulations into thinking it had been transported into a war zone. When nothing is happening, my friend says, the people who have been hired by military
contractors to help prospective soldiers understand and respond to
the Iraqi environment are hanging out, drinking soda out of swamp
coolers. Most are Kurdish and Iraqi immigrants who live down in El
Cajon near San Diego. At first, you think you've been plunked down
among a bunch of sandy shipping containers and cardboard minarets
in the desert. It looks tacky and unreal. The women are sitting around
tables playing cards and chatting in English.

But when the war scenario starts to play out, suddenly this guy you
were talking to about the Lakers has a limp and a glare and is splutter-
ing in Arabic, and the women are ululating and sobbing, and shouting
slogans against the United States. Four Humvees move into the town.
It looks like the television news, and worse, my friend says. You think
it's over, when suddenly a sniper appears on a rooftop, an improvised

explosive device goes off a block away, and all around you, people are falling to the ground, bloodied, and it's all confusing, muddled, hard to tell who's who, who's on your side, what's what, where to run.

It's Iraq in California, and it would unsettle the most entrenched of desert tortoises. These people, preparing themselves for the worst kinds of things with these war games, are also tearing up paths and tunnels that the tortoises may have built centuries ago and have used for hundreds of years. For the desert tortoise, it's as if someone had come and blithely torn up the 5 or the 101. Our freeways are not as old as the tortoises' desert paths. It is entirely possible that Number 29 was born as long ago as the Coolidge administration, and others of his clan are probably old enough to have been born even longer ago— under Harding, Wilson, Taft, or Teddy Roosevelt.

Let's play a game. It's called celebrity. Celebrity: you take a few sheets of paper and rip them into small strips. On each strip you write the name of a different celebrity. You play in pairs. Once, my friends and I played the game of celebrity with a celebrity, making the game of a celebrity a celebrity game. It was "meta," like a joke if the joke were told by the French deconstructionist philosopher Jacques Derrida. My friends in Los Angeles love parlor games.

In the game of celebrity, everyone writes names of celebrities on paper strips and then all the names go into a central pile. The pile is then shuffled and the strips distributed equally to pairs of players. One partner looks at names scribbled on the paper strips, one after another, and—in a certain number of seconds; we used an egg timer—gives clues to his or her partner about who the celebrity is. The partner must guess the name. The pair who guesses the highest number of celebrities in a given period wins.

The celebrity can be T. S. Eliot. For him your hints might be American, but like British; poetry; initials . . . Usually by then, your partner has guessed him. Or the celebrity can be Schwarzenegger, but he's too easy. You try to put difficult celebrities into the pile, but when I'm playing, they have to go pretty light on the movie stars and television personalities, because I don't know who they are. For example, until a week ago, if the strip had said "Marcia Cross," I would have had no idea. (In those cases, you try to act out the name itself, as in charades. "Cross" wouldn't be too hard.)

My friend the celebrity is, not surprisingly, very good at celebrity. His knowledge of the famous is wide and deep, ranging from fabled cinematographers and inventors of the 1800s to lowly soap opera actors to John Milton and the contemporaries of Charles Dickens. I personally am stronger on Dickens's contemporaries. The bad thing is to be my friend's partner, particularly if you are me. My friend the celebrity, who is usually generous and somewhat forbearing, is genuinely intolerant in this one area. If his partner can't guess a name, it's because his partner is thick. If my friend the celebrity can't guess a name, it's because his partner's clues are stupid.

No matter how thick his partner, however, my friend wins.

Soon it will be the New Year, another new year in California, for me. To mark this moment, I'm signing up for CERT training. CERT stands for Community Emergency Response Team; it's a seventeen-and-a-half-hour course. I like the sound of CERT training; it sounds like a sure thing. By the end of my training I will know how to do the following:

> Manage utilities and put out small fires.
> Treat the three medical killers by opening airways, controlling bleeding, and treating for shock.
> Provide basic medical aid.
> Search for and rescue victims safely.
> Organize [ourselves] and spontaneous volunteers to be effective.
> Collect disaster intelligence to support first-responder efforts.

The history of CERT in Los Angeles is instructive. The city trains volunteers in part because of lessons learned in Mexico in the 1985 Mexico City earthquake. That earthquake registered 8.1 on the Richter scale and killed ten thousand people. After it struck, Mexicans with no training went out into the streets and together rescued about eight hundred victims from wreckage, rubble, and fire. Or, as the CERT-LA website says, "large groups of volunteers organized themselves and performed light search and rescue operations." Although the volunteers rescued so many, however, about a hundred of the volunteers themselves died during the fifteen-day effort.

I was wondering whether my backpack of supplies in the pool house would be of any use during my CERT training. I do have a wrench for turning off the gas—which I assume is what they mean when they say "manage utilities." However, I've forgotten where the gas valve is.

Tens of thousands of crows fly into L.A. every day, like commuters. They come from a few roosts a long way off, one of them at the intersection of the 60 and the 605, near Whittier Narrows, and they fly all the long way into L.A.—maybe fifteen miles—to infest the trees around my neighborhood and caw until the dogs here nearly split their sides barking at them. One morning I got up at four and met a friend to go see the crows begin their early-morning commute.

I passed through the Second Street tunnel downtown, where a homeless musician was sleeping next to his cello and his two violins. Farther south, the streets of Skid Row were lined at that hour with sleepers on cardboard beds, or inside cardboard boxes, like the streets of Bombay and Calcutta. Almost one out of every hundred people in L.A. County is homeless, which accounts for the density of the cardboard domiciles here where the homeless congregate. They also have tents and quilts, and garbage bins for lighting fires, and supermarket shopping carts for their possessions. There are eighty-eight hundred homeless children in L.A. County. Some sleeping spots that morning looked more like Bedouin encampments, with sheets draped down over clusters of boxes, and several carts parked nearby. On the corners at such an early, chilly hour, men were chatting in cold groups, their breath condensing in clouds. I met my friend Sue, a bird-watcher among other things, on an empty corner: I left my car and climbed into hers. Street people watched with little interest.

It was an eerie place we traveled on to, from that eerie place. Our destination was an intersection of two freeways. It should have been urban, and indeed it looked like a wasteland. But inside the crook of the two highways, you were lost: you never saw the highways from within. It was a nature preserve—a swamp with grasses rising from the sandy dunelands and rivers crossing it. We parked at an equestrian ring. The horses were exhaling steam as we got out of the car and began our trek. We tramped through what seemed like an endless wilderness, always alert for the lifting of the birds, their awakening. That morning before the sun was truly up, we saw kestrels, woodpeckers, owls, hawks, cardinals, finches, cormorants, ospreys, egrets, and crows. The dawn turned pink above us, when suddenly I saw it: a crowd of black crows lifting off from a stand of trees in the distance.

"But it's nothing like what it used to be," Sue told me, in a voice filled with disappointment. "Before West Nile, you should have seen it. The sky was black with the birds. Now they say so many of them are dead." Still, to me, it was impressive, the way the birds seem to rise up out of the trees between the highways all at once, as if by magic. The flapping of their wings, like breath over our heads, and the place we were in, not like any place I could imagine as an avian paradise. The last time I watched birds, it was in a cloud forest in Panama, with very little sign of humanity nearby. Now I'm between highways, with electric stanchions all around us, always visible. And we're never far from the sound of rush hour.

And yet nature endures; the birds are there. The sand of the Los Angeles flood plain surrounds us. A lone bowling ball sits near a riverbed, pushed there by last year's floods. And the sky the crows fly through is pink and orange at dawn—all evidence of nature's sheer will to continue on here, regardless of man's depredations.

Well, I know a New Year is coming, because I just received the Resnicks' 2005 holiday card. It's a masterpiece, of course. As usual.

It's got a blue motif, on a watery background. There is the Resnick family at the center. Five of them are seated upon a boat in this magical sea world. Behind them, a pretty volcano is erupting, its smoke forming the numbers 2006. The little Resnick girls are wearing bathing suits, and Lynda is wearing a more modest batik shift. Lynda's daughter, a grown woman, is a mermaid lounging on a nearby rock. Stewart is a native, standing at the stern of the boat, holding a fish on a line and wearing a native headdress that looks suspiciously like a Christmas wreath. He's also got on what can only be described as a skirt, and a straw necklace around his neck.

What interests me most, however, is the Resnick boat. It is a blue boat, like my old boat that's stuck in its blue bucket up in my poolhouse closet. But when I look at it more closely, I can see it turns out to be a bottle of Fiji water. The greeting card is an *ad*, stupid, like the *Terminator* billboard. And although the family is smiling broadly, there are sharks in the waters the Resnicks are paddling through.

Driving home from Irvine on the 5 one afternoon, after an exhausting stop at Costco (like Irvine, another place I never imagined visiting), I witnessed an accident. We were all going about sixty miles per hour, and everyone was tailgating, as Californians will, even at sixty or seventy miles per hour. Except for me, who kept the usual five Victorian car lengths between herself and the next car, dropping back continually as others edged in to fill the void. I was moving quite nicely, and thoughtlessly, my mind filled with cases of tomato paste, toilet paper, and one really big plastic jar of roasted cashews, when I noticed that ahead of me, a white car seemed to be not moving forward with the traffic but rather crossing perpendicular to the traffic. I noted it but didn't start to understand it, until I saw this same car coming back again across the traffic. By now people were swerving and crashing ahead of me, one blue car was pirouetting. And then, right past my windshield went the white car and through another lane of traffic, and then it sailed right off the highway through the big windbreak of pink and white azalea bushes that separates highway from service road. It left a puff of dust in its wake and was seen no more. Already, I was a thousand feet down the road, and traveling back at sixty again, dialing 911 on my cell phone, the mess of cars farther and farther behind me. I wondered what could possibly be happening on the service road on the other side of the azaleas, but by the time I thought to wonder, I was far away,

They've taken down the Ambassador Hotel. It took five months to do, but now the sweeping old place on Wilshire Boulevard, with its alleys of palm trees and art deco modernistic look, is gone. Only the Cocoanut Grove, its fabled nightclub and ballroom, remains standing. On the site, a $270 million school is to be built, which will use the Cocoanut Grove as an auditorium. Funny to think of that place as an auditorium for students, although Mickey Mouse held his second birthday there in 1930. That same year, the first Oscar statuettes were given out at the Grove—which hosted the Academy Awards through the 1940s. There were coconut palms inside the nightclub, and back-drops of beach scenes behind the dance floor. Many early movie stars used to hang out at the Grove (for which Rick Caruso named the Grove shopping mall): Jean Harlow, Rudolph Valentino, Maureen O'Hara, Douglas Fairbanks, among others. It's said that the actress Joan Crawford won a hundred dance competitions at the Grove. Judy Garland recorded a live album there.

A few months after demolition began, methane gas was discovered under the site, no surprise to those who've visited the tar pits down the street. The discovery might have put an end to plans for the school, but instead, it seems that construction crews will now include an impermeable tarp of some kind to line the ground beneath the new school buildings, as well as pipes for venting the gas, and methane alarms in the classrooms and hallways. No doubt there will be warn-ing plaques from the state of California.

Another stop on the Manson tour: the jury in the case stayed at the Ambassador Hotel during deliberations. In 1971, after nine days, Manson and his associates were found guilty and given the death penalty, but in 1972, California revoked capital punishment, and Manson and more than a hundred other death row prisoners were resentenced. Five years later, California reinstated the death penalty. Today, after the execution of Tookie Williams, there is a bill in the legislature to impose a moratorium on executions, but it is expected that the governor will quash it, in part to counter the new perception on the right that he is moving leftward.

The Cocoanut Grove was not the only structure of interest within the Ambassador Hotel complex. There was also a pantry. This is the room Robert F. Kennedy was walking through, after winning the 1968 California primary, when he was shot and killed by Sirhan B. Sirhan. Anyone alive at the time will recall the startling television footage of the senator lying on the pantry floor after he was wounded, with staff half-kneeling all around him. Out of deference to history—a dainty feeling that does not often touch Los Angeles developers and the demolition crews who work with them—the pantry has been spared.

According to the *L.A. Times*, the pantry is in storage. It awaits a decision by "a panel of experts" on its fate. If only there were still a Franklin Mint Museum, it could go there.

Oliver Stone is building the World Trade Center in Los Angeles, out in Playa Vista near the hangar where Howard Hughes used to house his military folly, the Spruce Goose, a ridiculous, unwieldy, enormous wooden hydroplane that flew little more than one mile during its entire existence; it's now on display at an aviation museum. The huge airplane hangar where the Spruce Goose was built was turned into a soundstage in the 1990s (parts of *Titanic* were filmed there), and that's where Oliver Stone is shooting a movie provisionally titled *World Trade Center*. It's supposed to be a feel-good movie about the attack; I like the concept. It's about rescue. Two Port Authority police officers are buried in the rubble; a former marine who is now an accountant finds them there, and after hours of terrible suspense and arduous work by teams of rescuers, the two men are saved.

It's a weird idea for a movie, but it means that the debris of the buildings had to be rebuilt. There were the end shards of the North and South Towers, ghostly, rising up near the water in Playa Vista near Marina del Rey. It was odd enough that the citizens of California City felt it necessary to reconstruct the Twin Towers on the municipal lawn, but to rebuild the rubble is another kind of memorial entirely. Stone is that kind of director, though, always courting controversy and even straightforward aversion. Many say this will be his attempt to come back into the fold and to show that he too can play the Hollywood game: the heartwarming, PG-13, family-fare game. Also, the game of making a lot of money—the blockbuster game. It's a funny subject to choose in order to play that game.

Standing by the artificial rubble, you can see that the ruin is utterly false; it looks more like stacking crates and pallets than it does like steel and cement construction wreckage. On the surrounding hills are palm trees, grassy lawns, retaining walls, and the roofs of the developments behind them. But if you look at Stone's pile from a middle distance (and block the background from your mind), it's otherworldly, and completely accurate. It's what we all saw on the television news in the days after September 11—an indelible recapturing of that angular, twisted heap. In 2001, a week after the attack, my family and I tried to visit what had already come to be called ground zero, but it was roped off from many blocks away, and all we could do was have the boys give cards and fresh pairs of socks to the firefighters there. I suppose Stone's movie will evoke similar sentiments—of pity, charity, and hope.

For me, Stone's set evokes nausea, a queasy feeling: better to have it over with, be finished with it. No more reconstructing, no more reliving. Walk away. As my California friends say, Shrug it off. Get *over* it. That's what I'm doing here in L.A.: I'm getting over it. We're all trying to take a little pleasure from things. Right? I can find pleasure and amusement here in California—pure sensual, esthetic pleasure. I get it from the black palm trees against the dark blue sky at nightfall, for example. From the domes and towers and flat roofs of the sprawl, outlined against the sunset. From the big sign on Pico that reminds me of my Angel and says CrashLand; they do auto bodies. From the secret, fabulous, romantic alleyways that run behind strip malls and gas stations and warehouses and that give you access to every little building in L.A. From the Cambodian temple in bright yellows and ochers on Beverly as you head toward downtown. From the names of places: Studio City—irresistible. Echo Park, Eagle Rock, Silver Lake, like "cellar door," one of the most beautiful phrases in the English language. El Monte and Alhambra (where Phil Spector lives), Bellflower and Cypress, Seal Beach, and Haggerties and Swamies, the last two beach towns memorialized in the Beach Boys' song "Surfin' U.S.A."

And the nice man who plays the steel drum in what they call the Village near my house—a strip of stores—he's providing everyone with so much pure pleasure that he must be bringing peace, as no doubt the poet Rumi would say if he walked among us still. The teachers up at Esalen would agree: self-delight leads to world delight. The man in the baseball cap with the supermarket cart full of red roses wrapped in cellophane, down by the Crenshaw exit: he's selling, sure; he may just be out making a living, but he's bringing peace too. And the people of Watts: thank you for writing WATTS in that brief snow. Snow should be memorialized here. Everything is beautiful, a rose, a word written in snow, dark buildings at night with interiors lit by fluorescent bulbs. Inside those interiors you see, on a deserted second floor, a metal desk, a black file cabinet, a water cooler, and a column of office machines, lit up blue as if for filming. Piñatas line one full block, in the shape of stars and Santas. *Pupusas* are for sale here, and fish tacos at the Cactus taquería, also empañadas and Guatemalan *pasteles,* all the sweet things: self-delight begets world delight.

Still, I wonder: how it can be that when my friend emerges from her yoga class zonked out and blissed out, floating down the pretty little street on brown moccasins to meet me at Peet's, and the drummer is playing on his metal drum while girls in Sunday trousers and babies in strollers glide by, I wonder how can it be that at almost the very same moment when my friend sits down and smiles, and I bring her a double tall percent latte, and a baby in pink who's passing by pats a dog lying under a table outside the door, how can it be that in Baghdad, a suicide bomber is busy blowing a hundred people up into ashes?

The world is sitting on top of Paramount Studios. There is a great blue globe balancing precariously up on top of the corner of one of the studio buildings, where Melrose meets Gower, near Lucy's El Adobe and just a few long blocks from El Coyote on Beverly, where Sharon Tate and her friends ate dinner before going back up the canyon that last night. On August 8, the anniversary of the murders, tourists go to El Coyote to have dinner there, *just like Sharon.* Over at the corner of Highland and Franklin, red bougainvillea is spilling down the hill behind the Chevrolet billboard. Stands of cypress put quotes around the neighborhoods near Runyon Canyon, in among the houses of Hollywood.

But where are all the people who—in any normal town—would be walking down the streets in these places? It's Sunday, after all. Only my "village" seems peopled. Nathanael West wrote about the vacant-eyed crowds that walk the streets of Hollywood. Where are they? I suppose that everybody's off driving somewhere. Or maybe everybody's gone surfing. Even the Resnicks are waterborne. Arianna Huffington's been seen on *The Nation* magazine's cruise to Mexico. Up at Carrie Fisher's in Coldwater Canyon, *someone's* bound to be in the heated pool. On the side of Paramount, at the North Gower Gate near the studio where Dr. Phil's show shoots, huge whales cavort on an enormous blue backdrop.

We finish our Sunday morning coffee, and I go to my car. The rains are late this year, but they are coming. Clouds are piling up, dusting the canyons with their faint wisps. I can't see the Hollywood sign. The Santa Ana winds have died down; fire season is over. In its Surf & Sea column today, the paper reported strong rip currents in all areas and twelve minutes to sunburn for sensitive people. Right now, a stormy northwesterly swell is bearing down on the coast. The California buoy, 357 nautical miles west of San Francisco, is checking in at 19 feet, with 12-second periods. "Reminder," the surf-watchers warn us: "There is a risk of increased bacteria levels . . . following the end of any measurable rain event." It's partly cloudy and cool now, at 1:20 in the afternoon, and it's beginning to drizzle here in the sunny South-land; it's drizzling in the Inland Empire, drizzling in the Imperial Val-ley. It's a measurable rain event.

I'm using my windshield wipers.

And when the rains come down again, what will they destroy, what will they carry away? I'm waiting.

Acknowledgments

Many acknowledgments are owed to those friends and colleagues who offered advice, counsel, and the benefit of their years in California. Among them are Sue Horton, Gregory Rodriguez, Marley Klaus, J. Michael Kennedy, Margot Roosevelt, Jim Muller, Rick Wartzman, Lisa Gross, Steve Wasserman, Allan Mayer, Scott Kaufer, Kit Rachlis, Jacob Epstein, Susie Norris, Bob and Natacha Leighton, Laurie Goodman, Don Spetner, and Michael Finnegan.

Others whose friendship was invaluable include Chuck Weinstock and Martine Singer, Michael and Jamie Lynton, Michelle Slatalla, and Catherine Maternowska (and Al), as well as Marjorie Miller, Marjorie Neilsen, and Margery Simkin. Loida Adriano also provided invaluable assistance. Swati Pandey helped ensure that the facts in the book are accurate; for any mistakes, I must, therefore, take responsibility. Clay Kyle and James Morrison offered enlightenment on a regular basis.

Alison Humes encouraged me in my darkest moments of alienation. Marisa Silver gave her priceless support through multiple early readings of the manuscript. Kate Manning read the book in an intermediate stage and gave many wise suggestions, as well as important psychological sessions by telephone from New York. Klara Glowczewska at *Condé Nast Traveler* sent me to Esalen when I expressed interest. And of course, I owe an incalculable debt to Victor Navasky, who has bestowed his intangible, invaluable support throughout my life as a writer.

Without Kevin Starr's historic guidebooks to the long and complicated history of California, I would often have lost my way. Joan Didion's great writings provided a crisp corrective to romantic views of the state. I consider the California books of the late Carey McWilliams to be the best, the most profound, and the most evocative starting point for any new observer. George Skelton's "Capitol Journal" column in the *L.A. Times* deepened my understanding of Schwarzenegger's political maneuverings and predicaments.

My brothers, James and Thomas Wilentz, have been my affectionate guides and stalwart backers in this world, helping me to carry on even though we are all three bereft of our mother and father. Emily Scheuer, and Elizabeth Scheuer and her husband, Peter Joseph, offered me shelter on the other coast, and all sorts of sustenance.

David Kuhn's encouragement and enthusiasm have been unflagging since my work on this book began, and as all writers know, the enthusiasm of others is an essential ingredient of production.

Alice Mayhew's faith in my work over the years has helped me continue writing with the belief that writing still matters in an age where that is not entirely self-evident. Her sense of humor and her intense commitment have energized this project. I am deeply grateful to her.

What would I do, where would I be, without the Morons? They know who they are.

My sons, Rafe, Gabe, and Noah Goldberg, have been as patient as is possible with me as I've worked my way through this book, and have even exhibited signs of interest in its content. I have relied throughout these years on their love and forbearance, and they have always come through for me.

My husband, Nick Goldberg, has been characteristically tolerant of and good-natured about my volatile work habits, and has read this book in various stages with a critical yet sympathetic eye. Without his support and love, none of this would matter.

Amy Wilentz
Los Angeles, March 2006

Bibliography

Anderson, Walter Truett. *The Upstart Spring: Esalen and the Human Potential Movement, The First Twenty Years.* Lincoln, Nebr.: iUniverse, Inc.

Avila, Eric, *Popular Culture in the Age of White Flight: Fear and Fantasy in Suburban Los Angeles.* Berkeley and Los Angeles: University of California Press, 2004.

Baldassare, Mark. *A California State of Mind: The Conflicted Voter in a Changing World.* Berkeley and Los Angeles: University of California Press (with the Public Policy Institute of California), 2002.

Banham, Reyner. *Los Angeles: The Architecture of Four Ecologies.* Berkeley and Los Angeles: University of California Press, 1971.

Bean, Walton. *Boss Ruef's San Francisco: The Story of the Union Labor Party, Big Business, and the Graft Prosecution.* Berkeley and Los Angeles: University of California Press, 1952.

Bell, Charles G., and Charles M. Price. *California Government Today: Politics or Reform?* Chicago: The Dorsey Press, 1988.

Bidwell, John. *In California Before the Gold Rush.* Los Angeles: Ward Ritchie Press, 1948.

Blitz, Michael, and Louise Krasniewicz. *Why Arnold Matters: The Rise of a Cultural Icon.* New York: Basic Books, 2004.

Bossard, Carla C., John M. Randall and Marc C. Hoshovsky, eds. *Invasive Plants of California's Wildlands.* Berkeley and Los Angeles: University of California Press, 2000.

Brewer, Chris. *Historic Kern County: An Illustrated History of Bakersfield and Kern County.* San Antonio, Texas: Kern County Museum Foundation and Lammert Publications Historical Publishing Network, 2001.

Broman, Mickey, and Russ Leadabrand. *California Ghost Town Trails.* Baldwin Park, Calif.: Gem Guides Book Co., 1978.

Castener, Rory. *Spaghetti Jack and Other Stories: Tales of Big Sur.* Big Sur: Green Island Press, 2000.

301

Cather, Willa. *Death Comes for the Archbishop.* New York: Alfred A. Knopf, 1927.

Chandler, Raymond. *The Big Sleep.* New York: Alfred A. Knopf, 1939.

———. *Farewell, My Lovely.* New York: Alfred A. Knopf, 1940.

Cleland, Robert Glass. *The Cattle on a Thousand Hills: Southern California, 1850–1870.* San Marino, California: The Huntington Library, 1941.

Crampton, Beecher. *Grasses in California.* Berkeley and Los Angeles: University of California Press, 1974.

Davis, Margaret Leslie. *Dark Side of Fortune: Triumph and Scandal in the Life of Oil Tycoon Edward L. Doheny.* Berkeley and Los Angeles: University of California Press, 1998.

———. *Rivers in the Desert: William Mulholland and the Inventing of Los Angeles.* New York: HarperCollins, 1993.

Davis, Mike. *City of Quartz: Excavating the Future in Los Angeles.* London: Verso, 1990.

———. *Ecology of Fear: Los Angeles and the Imagination of Disaster.* New York: Metropolitan Books, 1998.

DeBuys, William. Photography by Joan Myers. *Salt Dreams: Land & Water in Low-Down California.* Albuquerque: University of New Mexico Press, 1999.

Dickens, Charles. *American Notes: A Journey.* New York: Fromm International Publishing Corp., 1985. First edition, 1842.

Didion, Joan. *Where I Was From.* New York: Alfred A. Knopf, 2003.

———. *The White Album.* New York: Simon & Schuster, 1979.

———. *The Year of Magical Thinking.* New York: Alfred A. Knopf, 2005.

Drannan, Capt. W. F. *Chief of Scouts: Piloting Emigrants Across the Plains of 50 Years Ago.* Chicago: Thos. W. Jackson/Rhodes & McClure Publishing Co., 1910.

Friedrich, Otto. *City of Nets: A Portrait of Hollywood in the 1940s.* New York: Harper & Row, 1986.

Gioia, Dana, Chryss Yost, and Jack Hicks, eds. *California Poetry from the Gold Rush to the Present.* Berkeley: Santa Clara University and Heyday Books, 2004.

Hanson, Victor Davis. *Mexifornia: A State of Becoming.* San Francisco: Encounter Books, 2003.

Harlow, Neal. *California Conquered: The Annexation of a Mexican Province, 1846–1950.* Berkeley and Los Angeles: University of California Press, 1982.

Harte, Bret. *Gold Rush.* Berkeley: Heyday Books, 1997.

Hicks, Jack et al., eds. *The Literature of California: Writings from the Golden State: Volume 1, Native American Beginnings to 1945.* Berkeley and Los Angeles: University of California Press, 2000.

Hinds, Norman E. A. *Evolution of the California Landscape: Bulletin 158.* San Francisco: Department of Natural Resources, Bureau of Mines, 1952.

Hise, Greg, and William Deverell. *Eden by Design: The 1930 Olmsted-Bartholomew Plan for the Los Angeles Region.* Berkeley and Los Angeles: University of California Press, 2000.

Hundley, Norris, Jr. *The Great Thirst: Californians and Water, A History.* Berkeley and Los Angeles: University of California Press, 2001.

Jackson, Helen Hunt. *Ramona.* New York: Signet Classics, 2002.

Jeffers, Robinson. *The Wild God of the World.* Stanford: Stanford University Press, 2003.

Jones, Cathrine Ann. *The Way of Story: The Craft and Soul of Writing.* Ojai, California: Prasana Press, 2004.

Leamer, Laurence. *Fantastic: The Life of Arnold Schwarzenegger.* New York: St. Martin's Press, 2005.

London, Jack. *The Call of the Wild.* New York: Macmillan, 1903.

———. *Martin Eden.* New York: Macmillan, 1909.

Lord, Rosemary. *Los Angeles Then and Now.* San Diego: Thunder Bay Press, 2002.

Manly, William Lewis. *Death Valley in '49.* Edited by Leroy and Jean Johnson. Santa Clara and Berkeley: Santa Clara University and Heyday Books, 2001.

Lord, Rosemary. *Los Angeles Then and Now.* San Diego: Thunder Bay Press, 2002.

McWilliams, Carey. *California: The Great Exception.* New York: Current Books, 1949.

———. *Southern California: An Island on the Land.* Salt Lake City: Peregrine-Smith Books, 1946.

Miller, Henry. *Big Sur and the Oranges of Hieronymus Bosch.* New York: New Directions, 1957.

Muir, John. *In His Own Words.* Compiled and edited by Peter Browning. Layfayette, California: Great West Books, 1988.

———. *The Mountains of California.* New York: Century Co., 1894.

Murphy, Edith Van Allen. *Indian Uses of Native Plants.* Glenwood, Illinois: Meyerbooks, 1958.

Nadeau, Remi. *The Water Seekers*. Santa Barbara: Crest Publishers, 1950.

Norman, Jeff, and the Big Sur Historical Society. *Big Sur: Images of America*. Charleston, S.C.: Arcadia, 2004.

Normark, Don. *Chavez Ravine, 1949: A Los Angeles Story*. San Francisco: Chronicle Books, 1999.

Norris, Frank. *The Octopus*, New York: Doubleday, 1901.

Nunn, Kem. *Tapping the Source*. New York: Four Walls Eight Windows/No Exit Press, 1984.

Olin, Spencer C., Jr. *California's Prodigal Sons: Hiram Johnson and the Progressives, 1911–1917*. Berkeley and Los Angeles: University of California Press, 1968.

Olmsted, Roger R., ed. *Scenes of Wonder and Curiosity: Hutchings' California Magazine, 1856–1861*. Berkeley: Howell-North Publishers, 1962.

Osio, Antonio Maria. *The History of Alta California: A Memoir of Mexican California*. Translated by Rose Marie Beebe and Robert M. Senkewicz. Madison: The University of Wisconsin Press, 1996.

Pavlik, Bruce M., with Pamela C. Muick, Sharon G. Johnson, and Marjorie Popper. *Oaks of California*. Oakland: Cachuma Press, 1991.

Phoenix, Charles. *Southern California in the '50s: Sun, Fun, Fantasy*. Santa Monica: Angel City Press, 2001.

Pitt, Leonard and Dale. *Los Angeles A to Z: An Enclyclopedia of the City and County*. Berkeley and Los Angeles: University of California Press, 1997.

Poole, Jean Bruce, and Tevvy Ball. *El Pueblo: The Historic Heart of Los Angeles*. Los Angeles: The Getty Conservation Institute and the J. Paul Getty Museum, 2002.

Powell, A. E. *The Solar System*, London: The Theosophical Publishing House Ltd., 1930.

Reisner, Marc. *Cadillac Desert: The American West and Its Disappearing Water*. New York: Penguin Books, 1986.

———. *A Dangerous Place: California's Unsettling Fate*. New York: Pantheon, 2003.

Rintoul, William. *Oildorado: Boom Times on the West Side*. Fresno: Valley Publishers, 1978.

Robinson, W. W., introduction. *Thompson and West's History of Los Angeles County, California, With Illustrations, 1880*. Reproduction, Berkeley: Howell-North Publishers, 1959.

Roderick, Kevin, and J. Eric Lynxwiler. *Wilshire Boulevard: Grand Concourse of Los Angeles*. Santa Monica: Angel City Press, 2005.

Roth, John K., ed. *The Philosophy of Josiah Royce.* Indianapolis: Hackett Publishing Co., 1982.

Royce, Josiah. *California: A Study of the American Character: From the Conquest in 1846 to the Second Vigilance Committee in San Francisco.* Berkeley: Heyday Books, 2002. First edition, 1886.

Schrag, Peter. *Paradise Lost: California's Experience, America's Future.* New York: The New Press, 1998.

Sinclair, Upton. *I, Candidate for Governor: And How I Got Licked.* Berkeley and Los Angeles: University of California Press, 1934

Skolnick, Arnold. *Paintings of California.* Introduction by Ilene Susan Fort. Berkeley and Los Angeles: University of California Press, 1993.

Solnit, Rebecca. *River of Shadows: Eadweard Muybridge and the Technological Wild West.* New York: Penguin Books, 2003.

Starr, Kevin. *Americans and the California Dream: 1850–1915.* New York and Oxford: Oxford University Press, 1973.

———. *Coast of Dreams: California on the Edge, 1990–2003.* New York: Alfred A. Knopf, 2004.

———. *Inventing the Dream: California Through the Progressive Era.* New York and Oxford: Oxford University Press, 1985.

Stegner, Wallace, Wright Morris, and Ivan Doig. *A Land Fair and Bright: Growing Up in the American West.* Book-of-the-Month Club, 1993.

Taylor, Bayard. *Eldorado: or Adventures in the Path of Empire—A Sophisticated Newpaperman's Report of the New Violence and Excitement of California in 1949.* Introduction by Robert Glass Cleland. New York: Alfred A. Knopf, 1949.

Thompson, Hunter. *Hell's Angels.* London: Penguin Books, 1966.

Trollope, Frances. *Domestic Manners of the Americans.* St. James, New York: Brandywine Press, 1993. First edition, 1832.

Twain, Mark. *Collected Tales, Sketches, Speeches & Essays: 1852–1890.* New York: The Library of America, 1992.

———. *Roughing It.* New York: New American Library, 1962.

Tygiel, Jules. *The Great Los Angeles Swindle: Oil, Stocks, and Scandal During the Roaring Twenties.* Berkeley and Los Angeles: University of California Press, 1994.

Ulin, David L. *The Myth of Solid Ground: Earthquakes, Prediction, and the Fault Line Between Reason and Faith.* New York: Viking, 2004.

———, ed. *Writing Los Angeles: A Literary Anthology.* New York: The Library of America, 2002.

Underhill, Paco. *The Call of the Mall.* New York: Simon & Schuster, 2004.

Waldie, D. J. *Holy Land: A Suburban Memoir.* New York: W. W. Norton, 1996.

———. *Where We Are Now: Notes from Los Angeles.* Santa Monica: Angel City Press, 2004.

Walker, Richard A. *The Conquest of Bread: 150 Years of Agribusiness in California.* New York and London: The New Press, 2004.

Ward, Elizabeth, and Alain Silver. *Raymond Chandler's Los Angeles.* Woodstock, New York: The Overlook Press, 1987.

Wartzman, Rick, and Mark Arax. *The King of California: J. G. Boswell and the Making of a Secret American Empire.* New York: Public Affairs, 2003.

Wechsler, Lawrence. *Mr. Wilson's Cabinet of Wonders: Pronged Ants, Horned Humans, Mice on Toast, and Other Marvels of Jurassic Technology.* New York: Pantheon, 1995.

Weddle, David. *Among the Mansions of Eden: Tales of Love, Lust, and Land in Beverly Hills.* New York: William Morrow, 2003.

Whipple, T. K. *Study Out the Land: Essays.* Introduction by Edmund Wilson. Berkeley: University of California Press, 1943.

Wilson, Edmund. *The Twenties: From Notebooks and Diaries of the Period.* Edited and with an introduction by Leon Edel. New York: Farrar, Straus & Giroux, 1975.

Wold, Marvin J., and Katherine Mader. *Fallen Angels: Chronicles of L.A. Crime and Mystery.* New York and London: Facts on File Publications, 1986.

Wyman, Walker D., ed. *California Emigrant Letters: The Forty-Niners Write Home.* New York: Bookman Associates, 1952.

Zack, Michele. *Altadena: Between Wilderness and City.* Altadena: Altadena Historical Society, 2004.

Index

308

Index

About the Author

Amy Wilentz grew up in New Jersey, where her family was involved in Democratic Party politics. She is the author of *The Rainy Season: Haiti Since Duvalier*, which won the 1990 Whiting Writers Award, and of *Martyrs' Crossing*, a novel about Jerusalem that received the 2002 Rosenthal Foundation Award from the American Academy of Arts and Letters. She is a former Jerusalem bureau chief for *The New Yorker*. She moved to Los Angeles in 2003, when the gubernatorial recall election was heating up, and she lives there now with her husband and three sons.